# SAMUEL BUTLER'S NOTEBOOKS

# SAMUEL BUTLER'S NOTEBOOKS

*Selections edited by*

GEOFFREY KEYNES and BRIAN HILL

JONATHAN CAPE
THIRTY BEDFORD SQUARE
LONDON

THE NOTEBOOKS OF SAMUEL BUTLER 1912
FURTHER EXTRACTS FROM THE NOTEBOOKS 1934
SAMUEL BUTLER'S NOTEBOOKS 1951
REPRINTED 1952

Dewey Classification
823.89

PRINTED IN GREAT BRITAIN IN THE CITY OF OXFORD
AT THE ALDEN PRESS
BOUND BY A. W. BAIN & CO. LTD., LONDON

# INTRODUCTION

'The literary instinct', said Samuel Butler in *The Way of All Flesh*, 'may be known by a man's keeping a small notebook in his waistcoat pocket, into which he jots down anything that strikes him, or any good thing that he hears said, or a reference he thinks will come in useful to him.'

He was describing a habit of his own. For the greater part of his life he used to carry about with him a pocket book for the very purposes he mentions. In due course the notes he made were copied into larger books (called at first commonplace books) and the contents of these were in turn revised, re-copied and indexed. At the time of his death there were six of these notebooks or commonplace books, beginning in 1874 and ending in 1902, containing some hundreds of notes. They have been described in detail by A. T. Bartholomew in his introduction to the selection of notes he edited.

Butler himself made good use of his notes. Many of them appear in his published works; sometimes the same note in different forms is to be found in several of his books. In addition, since his death in 1902, two volumes of extracts from his notebooks have been published.

In 1912, his friend and biographer, Henry Festing Jones, edited a selection entitled *The Notebooks of Samuel Butler*. This was followed in 1934 by *Further Extracts from the Notebooks of Samuel Butler*, edited by his then literary executor, A. T. Bartholomew. There was, however, a marked difference in the arrangement and editing of these two volumes. Festing Jones grouped his selection of notes under appropriate headings and edited the material very considerably. Not only did he often amalgamate several of Butler's entries on the same subject into one longer note, but he used his discretion in altering words and phrases and even on occasion added a sentence here and there. In so doing he was supported by Butler's own views on the duties of an editor. 'Granted', said Butler, 'that an editor, like a translator, should keep as religiously close to the original text as he reasonably can, and, in every alteration, should consider what the writer would have wished and done if he or she could have been consulted, yet, subject to these limitations, he should be free to alter according to his discretion or indiscretion.'

Bartholomew's selection, on the other hand, allowed the notes to speak for themselves. They were published almost entirely as Butler wrote them and in the chronological order in which they appear in the manuscript notebooks.

In making the present selection of notes from the two volumes mentioned above we are of the opinion that the method adopted by Bartholomew is the better one. As a first step, therefore, the Festing Jones selection of 1912 was collated with the manuscript notebooks and the notes restored to the form in which Butler left them. Our next step was to select from the two volumes those notes which in our opinion give the best picture of the range of Butler's mind and the diversity of his interests. We have tried to avoid emphasizing overmuch any one of the main subjects that occupied Butler at one time or another, the music of Handel, his quarrel with Charles Darwin and so forth. In any event space would preclude the inclusion of all the notes in a single volume.

Previous literary executors have made use of Butler's notes in other ways. Much of the autobiographical material was used by Festing Jones in his exhaustive two-volume *Memoir of Samuel Butler* (1912), and other autobiographical notes were included in *Butleriana* which was published by the Nonesuch Press in a limited edition in 1932. Neither of these two works is readily accessible to the ordinary reader today. We have, therefore, added to our selection a number of notes that are only to be found in one or other of these volumes.

Finally, although Bartholomew, in his introduction to *Further Extracts*, expressed the view that the manuscript notebooks had been milked dry and that no further selection from them should be attempted, we have found a few unpublished notes which seem to us to be well worthy of inclusion in the present volume. Some of these, like the notes on George Bernard Shaw, Augustine Birrell and Butler's sisters, may have been omitted from previous selections on the ground that they might cause pain to their subjects or to the relatives of those subjects. We do not feel that this objection holds good today. Mr. Shaw, in fact, authorized us to publish the note about himself.

The present selection of notes, therefore, falls into four sections:

(1) Previously unpublished notes and notes which have appeared only in the *Memoir* or *Butleriana*.

(2) A selection of the notes previously used in the compilation of *The Notebooks* and *Further Extracts*. These are now printed in chronological order and with only such editing as was necessary to amend obvious slips of Butler's pen or imperfections of punctuation.

(3) A few notes which we have been unable to trace back to their source in the manuscript notebooks, but which we did not wish to omit.

(4) A number of short passages from Butler's published works which were included in *Further Extracts*, but are not in the original notebooks.

Butler students need no introduction to the members of his family, Alfred Emery Cathie, Charles Gogin and the other people who figure in the notebooks. New readers may, however, like a brief description of some of them.

Samuel Butler was born on December 4th, 1835, at Langar Rectory in Nottinghamshire. His father was the Rev. Thomas Butler and his grandfather Samuel Butler, Headmaster of Shrewsbury School from 1798 to 1836, and afterwards Bishop of Lichfield. His mother was Fanny

Worsley. The Rev. Thomas Butler had five children. The eldest, Harriet, or 'Harrie', married George L. Bridges, brother of Robert Bridges, the Poet Laureate. Samuel was the second child. Next came Thomas, then William who died in infancy and lastly Mary, known to the family as 'May'. After Canon Butler retired in 1876, he and his two daughters (Butler's mother and Harriet's husband were both dead) went to live at Wilderhope House, near Shrewsbury.

Butler's father and mother have achieved an unenviable immortality as Theobald and Christina Pontifex in *The Way of All Flesh*. His sisters' less amiable characteristics are reflected in Charlotte Pontifex in the same book.

Of Butler's friends and acquaintances whose names recur in the notebooks, Miss Eliza Mary Ann Savage was his closest woman friend. He was in the habit of submitting everything he wrote for her criticism and approval and she encouraged him to continue at his novel. Her witty and amusing letters to him were edited by Butler before his death and were published in 1935 (*Letters Between Samuel Butler and Miss E. M. A. Savage*). Miss Savage's character, but not her physical appearance, was used by Butler for Alethea Pontifex in *The Way of All Flesh*.

Another of Butler's woman friends was Mrs. Alfred Bovill, afterwards the Hon. Mrs. Richard Grosvenor. She was the daughter of the Rev. Charles Clarke, a now-forgotten Victorian novelist.

Alfred Emery Cathie, Butler's clerk, 'servant and friend', has been sufficiently described by Butler himself in the note on page 39. His aunt, Mrs. Cathie, was Butler's laundress.

Charles Paine Pauli's friendship with Butler dated from the latter's sheep-farming days in New Zealand. Until Pauli's death in 1897 Butler jeopardized his own financial position by making Pauli a regular allowance, only to learn on his friend's death that he had been deceived over a long period of years and Pauli had been much better off financially than he had made himself out to be. A full account of this painful friendship is included, in Butler's own words, in *Butleriana*.

Charles Gogin and Thomas Ballard were artist friends whom Butler met when he was studying at Heatherley's School of Art in Newman Street. Gogin, according to Festing Jones, was one of the very few men who really understood Butler. He painted the portrait of Butler which is now in the National Portrait Gallery.

Richard Garnett, LL.D., is remembered as the author of *The Twilight of the Gods*. His duties as Superintendent of the Reading Room at the British Museum brought him into touch with Butler, who delighted in pulling his leg, as can be seen from his notes on him. Butler dedicated his *Unconscious Memory* to Garnett.

Miss Arabella Buckley, another of Butler's female acquaintances, moved in scientific circles and was the author of *The Fairyland of Science* and other works.

Henry Hoare, a member of the well-known banking family, was at Cambridge with Butler. He provided the money to pay for the original publication of *Erewhon*. Butler in turn invested the proceeds of the sale of his New Zealand sheep farm in various companies started by Hoare. Their subsequent failure was the main reason why Butler was in such financial difficulties for many years of his life.

Finally, there is Mrs. Boss. 'Ernest's landlady, Mrs. Jupp,' said Butler of *The Way of All Flesh*, 'was in real life, Mrs. Boss, who used to wait on Reginald Worsley [Butler's cousin]. But Mrs. Jupp had to be edited into a far more respectable person than ever poor old Boss was.' Mrs. Boss's collected sayings form part of *Butleriana*; we have included some of the more decorous in our selection of notes.

GEOFFREY KEYNES
BRIAN HILL

# SAMUEL BUTLER'S NOTEBOOKS

I should say, 'I was sick, and you were kind enough to leave me quite alone.'

Against this note I found Jones had written in pencil, 'It must have been a reproach, H. F. J.'

### MRS. BOSS

said that if Alice meant bringing my cousin's children to tea she supposed she should have to grease her sides (for a curtsey).

### OLD MRS. PAULI

wanted to be buried in a vault at Brighton, but did not want her husband to be buried there. 'Besides, my dear,' she continued, 'there is no room for him, the vault will only hold four, and five would crowd it inconveniently.'

### ORGIES OF VIRTUE

Consecrations, ordinations, etc.

### MRS. BOSS

She said she wished the horn would blow for her and the worms take her that very night.

### CONTRALTO VOICE

My mother used to say that my elder sister had a beautiful contralto voice. This was arrived at not through her ability to reach the low notes — which she could not do — but because she could not reach the high ones.

### MRS. BOSS

during the cold weather applied to the churchwarden for a ticket for coals. The churchwarden, who like everyone else knows her exceedingly well, told her she was not a church-goer. Mrs. Boss said she couldn't look him in the face and say she had been a *regular* churchgoer. (She had never been inside the church at all.)

### NAMES; JINKS

would be a good name for the author of a book of family prayers; Badcock or Hitchcock — Bishop Badcock, Arch-deacon Hitchcock, Canon Treadwell or Canon Grout, again, would be nice names. At Hornchurch I saw the name Grout on a tombstone. Sancton would be a good name for a curate. There is a Mr. Sancton Wood, an architect and surveyor at Putney. Tabitha Pizzey.

### OLD MRS. PRING

My Aunt Philip's aunt, Mrs. Pring, complained bitterly to my aunt of the parson of her village (of which she was squire) who had come to see her during a serious illness, 'and you know, my dear,' she said, 'he read the bible to me, just as if I had been any old woman in the village'.

Her gardener, Curtis, had consulted her as to how and where some cabbages were to be planted. Later on the gardener came again with a suggestion which was obviously an improvement. 'Curtis', said she, 'if I tell you to plant the cabbages with their leaves in the ground and their roots in the air you will be pleased to do so.' And yet, as she said to my aunt, she knew Curtis's way was much better, but she was not going to have settled questions re-opened, and she was going to be mistress in her own house.

### MRS. BOSS

She says she can't abear to see Ivens now; she's got the water nearly right up to her heart, and a polly punch on her head.

said that when young Watkins died his poor dear skin was like alablaster.

said that Mrs. Honor would drink everything she could stand upright and pay her money for.

### THAT MIGHT BE MADE VERY AMUSING

This is what my sisters say when I tell them the subject of any new book which has made a stir such as *The Revolt of Man*. What they mean in a quiet way is, 'I could make a very amusing book upon this subject, I don't happen to have done so because I have so many other things on hand, but I see perfectly well how it could be done — and you will therefore please to consider that to all intents and purposes I have done it — but I don't think you could.'

### JONES AND MY KNOWING THE MOON

The first time Jones came abroad to me, I had not seen much of him, and had had no idea of his joining me abroad. He wrote to me however in 1877 proposing to join me, and I let him come. He was to join me at Varese. I was on my best behaviour and Jones was still untainted. We had dinner at the Riposo, and then sat outside under the verandah of the house opposite to smoke our cigarette. Jones asked me if I knew much about the stars. 'No', I said, a trifle sternly — for I am like Marcus Aurelius Antoninus and am thankful to say that I have never troubled myself about the appearance of things in the heavens. Then seeing that Jones was a little frightened I said more softly, 'I know the moon', and so the matter ended. I never heeded the matter, but Jones told me of it this summer (1882) and we both laughed.

Call it somewhere the woman of the pond.


## MY SISTER AND MY PAINTING

One of my sisters' amenities is to call my painting 'drawing'. If I say I am painting such and such a picture they reply that they are glad I am 'getting on with my drawing' — they never call it painting; they know the difference very well, they don't make the mistake to Edith Hall; it is intended as a way of cheapening what I am doing. If it pleases them it does not hurt me.


## THAT WOULD BE VERY NICE

Another trick that my elder sister has is, when I play her anything on the piano, to say, 'Oh yes, yes, I can see that would be very nice' — meaning of course — 'if it was properly played, but you play it so damned badly that I can only see it would be very nice.'


## MY COUSIN AND GOTHIC

At Sheerness the other day he paused before a minute corrugated iron chapel, very small and as bald as it could possibly be. Then he said, 'How I do hate Gothic.'


## SOUNDS AND ECHOES

A man may begin as a bad sound, or even as a bad echo, but he is to be distrusted if he begins as a good echo.


## WATER CANARIES

Gold fish.


## SPIRITUALISM

'Promise me solemnly,' I said to her as she lay on what I believed to be her death bed, 'if you find in the world beyond the grave that you can communicate with me — that there is some way in which you can make me aware of your continued existence — promise me solemnly that you will never, never avail yourself of it.' She recovered and never, never forgave me.

### OPENING FOR MY BIOGRAPHY

Jones laughingly talked of writing my life. I said I would give him an opening sentence, thus:

The subject of this memoir was born of wealthy but dishonest parents, Dec. 4th, 1835. He inherited the dishonesty, but not the wealth of his family.

### METHODIST SERMON

Ballard heard a Methodist preacher as follows:

And what, I wonder, must have been Joab's feelings on receiving the letter from David telling him to put Uriah the Hittite in the front of the battle. Why he must have said to himself, 'dear, dear, dear me, whatever can my old uncle be thinking about? Such beautiful psalms as he used to write too.'

### SAILOR JIM OR MY FIRST SOUL, BY K.

I found this tract — as odious as anything could well be — in my bedroom at Wilderhope last month — doubtless put there by my sister for me to read. She might as well have put breadcrumbs in my bed.

### STEEL AND QUILL PENS

It is only during the last ten years or so that quill pens have quite gone out. I wrote *Erewhon* and *The Fair Haven* with quill pens, but no book since.

## LARGE AND SMALL PEOPLE

We do not make allowance enough for the different ways in which things strike us as children, we will say of 3 feet high, and as men of nearly 6 foot. Children think snow deeper than we do. They see things on the ground better, such as agates and shells, and one reason why things look so small to us when we revisit our childish haunts is because we are ourselves larger.

## BOSS ON MY FATHER'S ILLNESS

When she heard of it she said, 'I did want our horn to blow first. I suppose Mr. Butler will have a bird's eye view of me now.'

## IF I WERE TO CHOOSE A MEMORIAL FOR MYSELF

I should get up a good performance of 'Narcissus', and give tickets to the subscribers, who would then get something for their money. To do this by me would be running me; ordinarily the last person thought of in a memorial is the one in whose honour it is being raised. Generally it is a job to get a commission for some painter or sculptor or architect, or to found a scholarship to support men in doing something they had much better leave undone. And of all memorials those to a man who in his own lifetime has been neglected are sure to be the most vain. Because they did not see merit where they should have seen it, people, to express their regret, will go and give a lot of money to the very people who will be the first to throw stones at the next person who has anything to say and finds a difficulty in getting a hearing. These foundations of colleges and scholarships are just as bad as the foundations of monasteries and religious houses in the middle ages, and the law should interfere with its statute of mortmain as it did in old times.

What a beast a man must be too who leaves his money in this way. I wonder he is not ashamed to tell the world that he has died without having seen one person whom he has loved well enough to let him have his money when he can no longer use it himself. Look at Erasmus Wilson who has just died and left his money to the College of Surgeons — what an awful thing to do.

## MY SISTER MAY AND THE TRUTH

My sister-in-law Henrietta wrote to me that May had been sending for my nephew Hal and telling him (according to her account) 'some truths', and my sister Harriet said it had upset May very much and they had had to send for the doctor, and May had hardly got over it yet. I said that if May had been trying to speak the truth the only wonder was that it didn't kill her outright.

## EXPLAINING SOMETHING TO HIS UNBORN CHILDREN

Say of someone who looked very grave and solemn, that he looked as if he was trying to do this.

## MRS. BOSS AND MRS. WILLIE

Mrs. Boss had a friend, a certain Mrs. Willie. She said the other day, 'Willie, you have had three husbands, you ought to know the ins and outs of everything; you have tackled three men; I have no patience with you, you have been and sold your bed over in the Blackfriars road for three shillings.'

## BOSS ON SLOPER WHO IS DYING

She said, 'Mrs. Sloper don't know what to do. Sloper won't lay on his bed and die, and if anyone comes to the door there is Sloper behind her. What with the girl with St. Pancras dance, don't you call it, and Sloper, she does not know which way to turn.'

### A DAFFODIL PEDAL
My sisters invariably put in a paragraph near the end of their letters about the flowers that are coming out in the garden or greenhouse. I call it their daffodil pedal.

### BOSS
When she's pleased she says it's 'as good as a shilling off the rent'.

### MY PEOPLE AND MISS SAVAGE
Harrie had written me a letter ostentatiously telling me about things she knew I should not care for, and saying nothing about my father beyond the words 'my father seems pretty well', not one word more. She did not say whether he had been to church last Sunday, whether he had had an outing in the garden, how his cough was, not a word in fact beyond what I have said. This was *finesse*, she knew very well that I should think he had not been to church, and had not been out, if she did not say he had; I did think this, so did Jones and my cousin, but we were wrong, for I went up to Henrietta's and saw a letter from May which said my father had been to church. They want me never to know how to interpret even their silence; and they know I know this, and their letters are intended to irritate me without giving me anything which I can properly lay hold of. Of all things Harrie would like a row, and this of course I am especially anxious to avoid. I replied to this letter with one saying how much cut up I was about Miss Savage's death. I knew it was profanation writing to such women as my sisters about this, but the blame is theirs, not mine; by writing about Miss Savage, I could more easily escape saying anything to betray irritation at Harrie's letter, and if I said one word about her, it was much easier and more natural to say a little at any rate of what I thought and felt about her, than just to say, 'Miss Savage is dead and I am very sorry'.

At any rate the letter came as it came and I sent it. I asked them not to allude to the matter. Harrie replied at once.

'Just a special message of love from us all, dear Sam, and thanks for your letter. I hope you shall have some family tidings before very long. Your loving sister, Harriet F. Bridges, Wilderhope House, Feb. 25.'

'I hope you shall have some family tidings,' indeed; I suppose it rests with her whether I do or don't. Whether she means to say, 'very well, now that Miss Savage is dead, we must comfort you, so before very long I hope you shall receive some family tidings, we will tell you that there is a purple crocus coming up under the elm tree and that will set you all right'; or whether she meant, 'if I had known Miss Savage was going to die I should perhaps have told you that there was a crocus coming up under the elm tree when I wrote last', I don't know. She wishes to pose as sweet and as knowing how in a 'few simple words' to say the exact thing that ought to be said. I suppose she thinks she has succeeded in doing this. All I know is that I dislike her more than I can properly say. Then she wrote to my sister-in-law and said she was to be 'especially kind' to me 'if there is opportunity'. I wish I knew whether they think I see through them or no. I do my best to make them think I do not, but I expect they pretty well know.

### JONES AND I AT THE ROYAL INSTITUTION

We went at the beginning of this month to hear a lecture on evolution by a man named Weldon. It was very dull, we thought it would be, but I thought I rather ought to go. I sat just below James Martineau; he looked very old; I think he knew me, but I am not sure. Jones and I arrived some half an hour before the lecture began, so we brought out *The Bird o' Freedom* and *The Sporting Times*, perhaps the two most uncultured newspapers in London, and read them till the lecture began.

There is one neglected grave with a grim gaunt mould-grown headstone, looking wicked all over, on which is written:

Near this spot (AT °20.67)
[What this means I know not. S.B.]
Lies interred, aged 39
EMMA
Wife of Charles Seymour
Cut off by a mysterious accident
on the 3rd Oct. 1867.

'Have mercy upon me oh Lord, thou Son of David.'
'Behold I am alive for ever more; Amen; and have the keys
of Heaven and Hell.'

If a corpse can drink, I am sure this one does, and am also sure that if she has the keys of Heaven and Hell, she is not at all a fit person to be entrusted with them.

### PART OF A NOTE ON MRS. BRIDGES

I saw Harrie look up at the sketches which hang over my mantelpiece; she said nothing, and I said they were most of them my own. Harrie said, 'Yes, I see they ——' and then stopped. She meant to say she could see they were by me as they were so bad, but stopped before she got to the word 'are' which however she knew very well would go without saying.

### JONES AND MYSELF AT RADLEY

Jones wanted me to see Radley so we went to Oxford this Whitsuntide. We did not like Oxford. I only saw one thing I should like to paint; it was up a court a little lower down than Christ Church, but the other side of the way, it was called Littlemore Court or some such name, and is extremely beautiful, but I saw nothing else that I should greatly care to do. On Sunday we went to Radley and caught Mr. Wharton, the organist, as he was coming down from the organ after church; he looked like an Italian sacristan. He was superficially polite but really spiteful — this is why the boys call him 'Kitty'; at any rate he would not say a word to Jones about our music which Jones had sent him, and the receipt of which he had acknowledged. He took us up to show us his room which was full of bric-à-brac and a small collection of pictures, some of them good or at any rate by well-known names as Cox and Turner, etc. They were none of them very good examples. I praised them warmly and said everything that was polite, but I do not think he liked either of us. While we were there, Horse-borough (if that is the right way to spell him) of the London Institution came in, and he and I spoke, which I think rather surprised Wharton. Then we went away, refusing to stay to lunch, which I did not want to do, more especially when I saw Horseborough was there; for knowing him to be intimate with Romanes, I thought the more I kept out of his way the better.

We went down to the Inn near the station and got some bread and cheese and beer. When we got into the parlour of the Inn, I thought of how the Abbé Macé of Lisieux raved about the country between Condé le Noireau and Caen and how he kept saying to me, 'Vous avez La Suisse en petit' (as though it was not the essence of La Suisse not to be *petite*). Here we had Mr. Wharton *en petit*. There was a lithograph of Dyckman's blind beggar, a clock covered with artificial seaweed made out of oiled paper, two little china shepherds and shepherdesses, matchboxes, and nine things upon the chimney piece. There were framed senti-ments — 'Welcome friends old and new' and two more which came to much the same thing, the one saying 'Forget me not' and the other 'Remember me'; a photograph of an Oxford College and a frame with a good deal of parade about someone who wanted to bow humbly at thy cross. Over the door there was an interesting little bit of old tapestry, and on the opposite wall a real, and to some extent original painting of a goose; on a small side table was a glass shade covering a lot of stuffed birds, empty honeycomb, seeds of grass, etc., and a little black person who called himself 'Off to Cyprus'. We both felt that we would rather live with these objects of art than with Mr. Wharton's, but that we got along quite nicely without either one or the other.

### NOTES ON MY SISTER HARRIE

Hodgkinson's successor Rogers says he 'can't stand Mrs. Bridges not no how'. It seems there had been some trouble about a plate of soup which was to go up to my father, and did not go right. Harrie said to him 'don't apologize, it's no use your apologizing, you shall go', however it was patched up: so far as I can see he is a good servant and very attentive to my father. She will not let Maysie accept invitations, saying to her, 'You came here to take care of grandpapa, and you must stay at home with him'. My niece says my father hates Harrie, and at times will not speak to her. She bothered him so about his going to Kenilworth alone that he said 'whoever goes with me, you shall not, that's certain', but it was settled she might go with him to Bangor after he had done Kenilworth and Southport. She went on plaguing him, so he said she should not go with him anywhere; then she burst into tears and left the room; the next day he left home and according to present arrangements Maysie is to be with him the whole time. Then Harrie sent for May to come back, I suppose to talk over the situation, my father having broken out into open rebellion, and taken

24

sanctuary, as it were, with Maysie, which will of course make Harrie and May furious. My father will know that May is come back and will also know why, for he is as sharp as a needle about all matters of that sort, and he won't like it. I don't know whether he will go home at once or stop away to make them feel that he is independent of them, which, by the way, he by no means is.

She gave Maysie a very good dress about 10 days ago, and Maysie was to make it up herself; of course there must be some improving proviso of this sort. The dress was of a check pattern and tried Maysie's eyes, so she said she would get Lizzie, my younger sister's maid, to help her. Harrie said she could not have Lizzie, as she herself wanted her to do some work for her. On this Maysie sent the dress to a dressmaker. Harrie was furious and said, 'I never would have given you the dress if I had known what you would do' adding that she was sorry she had given it. 'Besides', she said, 'you might have got Lizzie to help you'. Maysie reminded her of what she had said about this, to which she answered that she had only said what she did because Maysie had said, 'I will get Lizzie to help me', whereas she ought to have said 'May I have Lizzie to help me?' Maysie is now 25 years old. And now here is Maysie gone off with grandpapa, and Harrie left to sulk at Wilderhope. There must be a row soon.

THERE WAS A MAN NAMED ROSS
who is just dead — a friend of Gogin's and I should think a good fellow. He was an engineer and was making a railway somewhere in Central America with about 500 black men, only half civilized, under him and no one but himself in command. One day one of his men said he was going to marry the cook, who was one of the few women in the camp; there was no parson nor in fact authority of any kind, and

25

Ross thought it would tend better to preserve decency and order if the union were not allowed to take place without ceremony of some kind. He had only one book and that was *Tristram Shandy*, but as the people spoke nothing but Spanish it did not much matter. At any rate he determined to marry them out of *Tristram Shandy*, and on the first Sunday after the wedding had been fixed on he proclaimed it a high holiday, put on an old but clean night shirt over all his clothes, looked exceedingly solemn and read the assembled people and the bride and bridegroom in particular about a page and a half out of *Tristram Shandy*.

All were much affected and the bride wept with emotion, but it went off very nicely, and the pair were declared not only married but very much married.

### CIRCE

We generally think of her as living in the depths of some gloomy forest, far from the haunts of men; but Jones has been looking up Charles Lamb's prose version of *The Odyssey* with a view to *Ulysses*, and he assures me that Circe lived in a large white house by the side of the road, probably with green venetian blinds and a verandah. (1887) (How little did I then guess what a dance Circe and Ulysses were about to lead me. (1898))

### MYSELF AND MY FATHER

I said once when I wanted to be exceedingly proper without going beyond the truth, that I was sure no one could feel his father's death more than I did.

### JONES ON SHOPS

Jones said one day that pretty things looked so much nicer in the shop windows than anywhere else. That, he said, was the proper place for them; there they were at home growing in a state of nature, or at any rate as flowers in a garden; whereas if they were gathered and brought home half their charm was gone.

### JONES, MYSELF AND MISS HOLLAND

We went to see her by the advice of Mr. Barclay Squire of the British Museum, who had told her about *Narcissus* and us, that she would be glad to know more about the work. We found her a large-framed person with a big nose, and had not been with her ten minutes before she told us she was Sydney Smith's granddaughter. She said we were to be sure and cut out all our favourite passages; her grandfather used to say that authors always ought to cut out their favourite passages, and it was just the same with music; she liked what we played her very fairly well, but it would all gain immensely by being cut down, and if she did it she should cut it about to suit her own views — which appeared to be that whenever the same harmony could be found with the same treble note as in an earlier bar, all the intervening bars should be invariably cut out. She played a little to us herself, and put in trills and turns, just as she thought proper — and this was very often. I had seen that the second Duke of Wellington did not like Sydney Smith and found him a loud over-bearing talker, who would not let anyone be listened to except himself. After having seen Miss Holland, we thought we could understand Sydney Smith better. It was July 26 or 27, 1887, that we went.

### JEREMIAH

In private life he was very likely a person of the most playful humour, brimful of fun and merriment.

### MRS. JONES

H. F. Jones's mother — I said of her once that to have known her is an illiberal education.

Mrs. W. M. Rossetti (*née* Maddox? Madox? Brown — whom, by the way, I hardly know) sent me a note a few weeks back desiring me to come and sign a memorial in order to get a pension for her sister (Dr. Hueffer's widow). Dr. Hueffer was musical critic for the *Times* and ought to have insured his life, but it seems he had not done so, and Mrs. Hueffer must therefore have a pension. I did not like signing. I knew nothing of Dr. Hueffer, except that he would have snarled at my music if he had ever taken any notice of it — which he assuredly did not. I shall never get any public money myself, and am therefore naturally jealous of seeing others get it. The people who get pensions are invariably those who are most bitter and contemptuous towards myself; nevertheless I thought that to sign would be, as Jones expressed it, 'the smoothest progression open to me', so I said I would call and sign, which at the appointed hour I did.

She, of course, was on her good behaviour; so was I, for there is no use doing things by halves. We deplored the rapid flight of time, and Mrs. Rossetti said she felt as though her life had flown by and she had nothing to show for it. I said that was exactly how I felt myself.

'Oh, no,' she exclaimed immediately, 'you have really *almost* something to show for your life.'

I had hard work to prevent laughing, but turned it off and I don't think she noticed it.


EXTRACTS FROM SOME NOTES WRITTEN AT THE TIME OF MY FATHER'S DANGEROUS ILLNESS IN DECEMBER, 1883

I was sent for by telegraph about 6 o'clock in the evening early in December, and reaching Wilderhope about midnight, found my father, as was then supposed, *in extremis*.

For the first few days there seemed no hope whatever,

and my sisters were very civil, but as he gradually recovered they became ruder and ruder. It was in a high degree comic to see how when my father relapsed they became civil, and when he rallied, rude.

I only keep the following from the notes made at the time.

At 4 p.m. Harrie was making a fuss with Henry Bather about how they were to get money for the household expenses. She would not consult me. Of course the thing was perfectly simple, and when I came in to the work room and caught her worrying about it, Henry Bather said, 'Well there's Sam here, why don't you ask him?' Harrie did not like this, and dropped the matter at once.

I walked with Henry Bather to Meole and had a cup of tea with Rhoda and Bessie Bather. Rhoda did her best to scratch me about my painting and my books, but I was impervious.

Wed. Dec. 19th. May supposed to be unwell and did not show. My father much better. Harrie made a great parade about getting the cheque book, and running the cheque for the household expenses. When Dr. Burd came he gave me a hint that I had better go, so I decided to do so at once by the 1.25 train. He said my father was so much better that if he was a younger man he should have no doubt about his recovery, but I could not make him say he thought he would recover though I tried my best to do so.

Dr. Burd got my father to sign the cheque, and I was to take it to the bank and bring £85 in notes and £15 in gold and silver. I did so and handed Harrie the 17 notes. She tried to count them and said, 'No, Sam, there's only £80 here.' I was a little alarmed and took them and counted them again, there were 17 £5 notes. I handed them back and said they were all right. Harrie was in one of her tantrums because my father was better and counted again very ungraciously. Again she said there were only 16 notes. I was cross at this, for she said it so rudely, and I demurred to being troubled further. 'But, Sam,' said she, 'it is only right that I should satisfy myself that you have given me the right sum. I only find £80'. She made sure that I had put a £5 note in my pocket. Nothing that I can say can give any adequate idea of her tone and manner; I was angry — for the first time during my visit I was in danger of losing my temper — then taking the notes, I laid them out in fours on the table, and showed her that there were 17. This she unwillingly admitted proved that there were what I said there were, but she never made the least apology, and I believe still thinks I took one and put it back when she found me out.

I had come from town with hardly any money in my pocket, for the banks were shut when their telegram reached me and I came away with hardly more than enough money to pay my fare, so I borrowed a couple of pounds of May. I had spent almost all this either on my sister's account or my own, and had not enough to take me back so I suggested that May should cash my cheque for £5. Pauli had sent me a few blank cheques, and this seemed the simplest way of doing it. Harrie said she would do it herself. I said it did not matter who did it, so it was settled that she was to do it, and I wrote out a cheque for £5. Harrie eyed it suspiciously and said, 'very well then, I will give you five pounds if this (the cheque) is all right'. I did not notice or rather pretended not to notice her implied doubt as to whether it was possible that a cheque drawn by me for so large an amount could be all right, but took the money and left her the cheque. I saw afterwards by my pass book that she prudently sent it to London that very afternoon. There was no reason why she should not.

I then went up to see my father. I found him, as I thought, very feeble. He took my going as he had taken my coming — as a matter of course. I said I was very glad he was so much better and hoped that he would now soon be well. He said with some difficulty, 'Yes, I'm better. Next time you come I hope you will have better weather.' I said, 'I should not have come if Dr. Burd had not sent for me.' He said more quickly, 'Did Dr. Burd send for you?' I said, 'Yes, and now he says I may go'. Then I said good-bye. He said good-bye and I left. I cannot say that I had a very pleasant journey home.

All the time I was down my father was perfectly civil to me. He never even pretended to care two straws about me. He never said anything to me except the merest common-places; he does not care about my sisters; I think he likes me quite as well as he likes them, but he does not really like anybody or anything. He likes Dr. Burd, Hodgkinson and the Nurse better than anyone else, but he likes nobody more than skin deep. When he felt better what he turned to instinctively was shaving water and the *Daily Telegraph*. He gave a few directions such as that Maggie Goodwin was to have a Christmas Card, and that Mrs. Snow was to have her Christmas Hamper, and he asked how Mrs. Fletcher's eye was, and inquired what accounts had come from Etta about Charlie who has scarlet fever. Sometimes he asked me what France was doing about China, and twice he spoke about business, once dictating a letter to Woodcock and once talking to me about a fence, but on these two occasions he was, I am confident, mainly actuated by a desire to make us think him better. He has made up his mind to get well, that is clear, and I should think will probably do so. He has shown no apprehension of death, but at the same time I think he has really feared it a good deal, as I daresay I shall do myself, if I have a like illness, though at the present moment I hardly feel as if I should do so.

He has not suffered at all, and of course all that incessant care could do for him was done.

(He never fully recovered his former strength; but he had another three years of very fair health and activity. Dec. 19, 1899.)

To the Rembrandt and Burne Jones exhibitions. What a contrast! No words can express my dislike for Burne Jones.

### MYSELF AND DISTRUST OF MEN OF SCIENCE

I do not know whether my distrust of men of science is congenital or acquired, but I think I should have transmitted it to descendants.

### MY FATHER AND MYSELF

Dr. Burd soon after my father died was holding forth and suggesting things for me to mention in the obituary notice I had to write for the Shrewsbury papers. I said, to tease him, 'you see, Dr. Burd, one of the greatest feathers in my father's cap was one that I cannot refer to'. Dr. Burd was surprised and asked my meaning. 'I mean,' said I somewhat freezingly, 'that he was *my* father'. Dr. B. did not like this and said he had not looked at the matter in that light hitherto. Whether he knew that I was only wanting to tease him or no I neither know nor care.

### MRS. HOBSON'S PARROTS AND MEN OF SCIENCE

Mrs. Hobson's parrots would not allow any reading aloud in their presence unless their own names were frequently introduced. If they heard these interspersed among the reading they would be quiet, for they believed it was all about themselves; they did not understand it, but no matter what it was, it must be all right if it was about them. Modern men of science are like Mrs. Hobson's parrots. If they see their own names frequently introduced with praise into an author's work, it does not matter what he says in other respects, they will allow the writer a hearing; failing this, they will scream so that he cannot be heard till he has chased them out of the room; and this may give him some little trouble if they are loose.

in my mother, or one of the first, was at Bonn in the summer of 1843 (or 1842, I must find out). My mother, Miss Ward, the governess, and the rest of us except my father had been at the *table d'hôte* and a dispute began afterwards between my mother and Miss Ward as to whether a man at the table was a gentleman or not. Womenlike they were talking the men over. My mother said the man was a gentleman — Miss Ward said he was not. Pressed for her reasons, she said, 'because he had dirty nails.'

I thought this so convincing that it seemed to me that my mother had got the worst of it, and been worsted too by her own governess. It began therefore to dawn upon me that she might be mistaken, and did not know so much as I had supposed.


## MY LECTURE ON THE HUMOUR OF HOMER

This came off on Saturday night at the Working Men's College, and I should say went off very well. The room was full and Garnett tells me that several had to stand, but I was too much occupied with the lecture to see.

I called on Garnett this morning, and should say he had been a good deal frightened and shocked. I could not get a word out of him but the merest common form remarks; the most definite thing he said was that my suggestion about Mrs. Homer had a great many potentialities — as for my letter in Friday's *Athenaeum* about Trapani, he said it was a very ingenious plausible suggestion, but that he did not know enough about the subject to be able to form an opinion. Garnett is an excellent donometer, and what he said shows me what dons at Oxford and Cambridge will say generally — which was what I wanted to be sure about.

The wonder is that one so cautious and Academic as he is should be, as he not less certainly is, one of the most brilliantly humorous and in all respects fascinating writers of the time, if not the very best we have, for I know not who to place above him.

I told Fortescue laughingly of Garnett's attitude, and he laughed and said, 'Garnett hates anything downright and outspoken. There came here once a Siamese prince, a very intelligent fellow, who, among other things, was president of the library and educational department in Siam. Garnett and I went round with him, and showed him among other things the way in which the place was heated. "And does it answer?" said the prince. "Infernally badly," answered I, and I could see Garnett writhed with agony. He shuddered and gasped for breath.'

### THE CLERGYMAN A HUMAN SUNDAY

I said in my novel that the clergyman is a kind of human Sunday. Jones and I settled that my sister May was a kind of human Good Friday and Mrs. Bovill an Easter Monday or some other Bank Holiday.

### PAULI AND SIR JOHN LUBBOCK

Their birthdays are on the same day, and Pauli was once dining at the house of some cousin or distant relation of Sir John's and was made after much protest to write his name in her birthday book. Sir John Lubbock's name was down already and beneath it he had written 'The greatest happiness of the greatest number.' So Pauli wickedly wrote under his own name 'Every man for himself and may the devil take the hindmost.'

### ALFRED AND THE STARS

A few nights ago there were two large bright stars quite near a new moon where no other stars had yet come out. Alfred did not like it and said, 'Do you think, sir, that that is quite right?' I said I thought it was and the matter dropped. Next night he said about the same time, 'There, sir, you see those stars are not near the moon now.' I said the moon rose an hour or so later every night and therefore it could not be near those stars for another hour. This was becoming a little difficult, so he said, 'Very well, sir, I forgive you this time, but never allude to the subject in my presence again.'

### ALFRED AND 'FOR THE FUTURE'

Mrs. Bovill and Miss Hickman were to come to tea at Jones's and I and Alfred were to go too. Through a combination of accidents I forgot, and they expected us at Jones's without our coming. Alfred was very much put out and, after blowing me up sufficiently, said, 'And now, for the future, let it be understood — and Mr. Jones — that if I am told, nothing will ever go wrong.' Which indeed is neither more nor less than the truth. Why does not God have an Alfred and tell him everything?

### MYSELF AND JOWETT AT MR. MOSS'S

Jowett came down to the Shrewsbury speeches last week, and I was asked to meet him at dinner at Moss's house. I heard the speech he made — it was a sermon, not a speech — on the duties of a master and on those of a schoolboy. He read it badly and it bored everyone. Seeing, therefore, how old, feeble and dull he was, I determined to keep out of his way and not to try and draw him about the *Odyssey*. I was put to sit pretty near him at dinner, but we did not speak — we hardly could. Nor did we speak after dinner. In the drawing room I kept near the door right at the other end of the room, while he seemed well occupied with those who were round him.

Presently, however, he rose, toddled across the room and came up to me.

'I think I have had the pleasure of meeting you here before, Mr. Butler.'

'Yes, sir, but I did not think you would remember me.'

'Oh, I remember you very well — you know how heartily we all laughed over your *Erewhon* — and moreover there was a great deal of truth in that book.'

'It was like everything else, sir, true and not true.'

'Well, yes, I suppose that is it.'

'And then *Erewhon* was published more than twenty years ago and I have never succeeded in making you all laugh again.'

'But have you ever tried?'

'Oh yes, I have written a good many books since *Erewhon*.'

'How is it then that I have never heard of any of them?'

'I suppose, sir,' I said laughing, 'because they failed to attract attention — but a year ago I did myself the honour to send you a pamphlet on the *Humour of Homer* and another this spring on the Sicilian *provenance* of the Odyssey.'

'Ah, to be sure, I remember there was something of the kind, but I have so many of these things sent me that — well, to speak frankly, I never read either of them.'

'Why should you, sir? It was proper of me to send them as a mark of respect which I should have been sorry to omit, but I had very little idea that you would read them.'

I kept smiling all the time, but was particularly careful not to try to draw him or tell him anything. He then turned the subject on to Dr. Butler and assured me that everyone interested in the classics would read my book, etc., etc., whereon we talked for another five minutes or so and parted very amicably.

The conversation however confirmed me in the opinion I had formed already that very few people know any of my books except *Erewhon*, which hangs rather as a millstone about my neck.

ALFRED

Just before I went for my holiday he said to me, 'You know, sir, I did not intend that you should get away till you had done the accounts.'

36

*Mond. Sept.* 30. 1901

Miss Sichel had several times got me down to her house on the plea that I was to meet Augustine Birrell, but on each occasion Birrell, though I had been told much about his great anxiety to meet me, failed to come. A good many months ago, however, the meeting came off. Now Birrell was a man whom I regarded as a self-advertising poseur, and whom I did not want to meet, feeling sure that, as in the case of several other lights of literature who at various times have made advances to me, he only wanted me to become one of his admirers and to tell him how clever he was. I never read, nor even saw his *Obiter Dicta*, but the reports of some of his lectures and speeches that I had seen in various papers had left me with no very favourable idea of him; besides a year or two ago Fisher Unwin, whom I dislike, had called on me and tried to drag me off with him to hear Birrell lecture on Johnson, and I resented this, moreover he is a dissenter and a radical, and is review-puffed and in favour with the *Times*, and has married the late Lord Tennyson's daughter-in-law. I knew I should get nothing by meeting him and should be certainly bored and possibly mauled, for we are as oil and vinegar to one another; but Miss Sichel was obdurate and I had to go.

*Sat. Oct.* 5. 1901

It is now many months since the meeting took place and I forget how the conversation opened. Jones was there when I reached the house; there was nothing very noticeable one way or another in Birrell's appearance — he looked just a shade like the nonconformist which he either is or professes to be, but there was nothing to complain of. After a few minutes he set himself to be interesting, and gave us a long account of his having gone by invitation of some society at Sheffield to lecture upon English literature. It seems he had been met at the station by some Sheffield magnate whose name — let me continue in the first person —

'to this day I do not know. I was driven to his house and we sat down, a large party, to a capital dinner before my lecture. Oh, how we did laugh! I forget what it was all about, but I do not believe I ever talked so much nonsense in my life, we were splitting with laughter the whole time. I could never have done it, my dear' (to his wife), 'if you had been there. I should have been ashamed to let you hear me rattle off such nonsense, but we were laughing incessantly, and the funny part of it all was that I did not know the name of the man at whose house I was staying. When it was time to go to the lecture the young men of the house very sensibly excused themselves — there was a circus or a menagerie or a hippodrome or something of the kind on, and they showed their good sense by preferring it to my lecture, for as it would happen I did not hit off the taste of the audience as happily as I have sometimes been able to do. I did not find this out at the time but I suppose it must have been so, for the Sheffield papers were frigid in their remarks upon the lecture. Next morning I was again driven down to the station, but still, though you would hardly believe it possible, I do not know my host's name. Everything was in the most sumptuous style — he must be enormously rich. I shall never forget the way in which we laughed — and yet — to think that I should still not know the man's name.'

It was just like Pandarus talking to Cressida (*Troilus and Cressida*, Act I, Sc. 2).

PAN.  But there was such laughing. Queen Hecuba laughed that her eyes ran o'er . . . and Cassandra laughed . . . and Hector laughed.

CRESS.  At what was all this laughing?

PAN.  Marry, at the white hair that Helen spied on Troilus' chin . . . But there was such laughing and Helen so blushed and Paris so chafed, and all the rest so laughed that it passed.

CRESS.  So let it now; for it has been a great while going by.

So indeed was Mr. Birrell's story.

I believe I laughed at the proper places and behaved myself in all respects as I should, but I suppose Birrell, who must have known that he was lying and trying to show off, felt that he had not been successful in making me an admirer — at any rate when Jones and his sister called on Miss Sichel a few weeks later, she made no secret of her perception that the meeting between me and Birrell had been a failure — and admitted that it had been Birrell's fault, not mine — but she has not forgiven me. I had been asked to fall down and worship one of her idols and I had not done so.

QUILTER'S ENTRY IN 'WHAT'S WHAT'

He professes to give an article on 'Samuel Butler and his work.' I glanced at it and saw that I need not read unless I wished to be annoyed. He concludes his article:

> He lived when we first knew him, and probably does still, the queerest hermit-like life in an old Inn of Court attended only by a boy called Alfred, who was at once servant, friend and a butt for his master's good-humoured pleasantries. Butler used to tell with great delight the story of having left this youth to catalogue some photographs taken by his master on a foreign trip, and how he gave to each in which he had been introduced as a foreground figure, his own name, followed by that of the famous place — 'Alfred on the Field of Waterloo,' 'Alfred at the Falls of the Rhine'.

It is true that I have lived at 15 Clifford's Inn ever since August 1864, but it is not true that I have lived a 'hermit-like life.' I avoided the Quilters as far as I could because I disliked them. I have always avoided people whom I disliked, but never those whom I liked.

As for Alfred, he had been brought up from childhood by the woman who was my laundress. His mother and father had both died when he was only 2 or 3 years old; my laundress, a sister of his mother, had taken to him and his sister — and right well had she done for them. My old servant Robert had died in August 1886, aged 70, and I was then too poor to get a substitute. When my father died at the end of December 1886, times were changed, and I wanted someone whom I could trust, who should be half clerk and accountant, half private secretary, and also generally useful. My laundress asked if Alfred would do. He was just then out of a situation, and was about 23 or 24 years. He came to me January 18, 1887, and has remained with me to to the present time, as I trust he will continue to do till I die. He was about 26 or 27 when Quilter first saw him, I suppose in 1890.

So much for my being attended only by a boy. It is quite true that Alfred was almost from the very day he came to me at once servant and friend; that he was ever a butt for any pleasantries on my part I utterly deny. I began to feel almost immediately that I was like a basket that had been entrusted to a dog. I had Alfred and myself in view when I used this simile in *Erewhon Revisited*. He liked to have someone who appreciated him, and whom he could run and keep straight. I was so much older, that to him I was a poor old thing with one foot in the grave, who but for his watchful eye and sustaining hand might tumble into it at any moment.

Did I want a new hat? Alfred knew very well that I should rub on with the old one unless I was kept up to getting a new one.

> 'Here, Sir, is a reminder for you. You must keep it in your waistcoat pocket and keep on repeating it to yourself'

— and the reminder was slipped by him into my waistcoat pocket. It ran:

I am to buy a new hat, and a new pair of boots.

On another like occasion I received the following:

This is the last notice from Alfred to the effect that Samuel Butler Esqr. is to buy himself a new Hat on Wednesday morning the 8th November, 1893. Failing to do so there will be an awful scene on his return to Clifford's Inn — Alfred.

Here are others:

You are to work here to-morrow (Tuesday) until 12 o'clock, then you are to go to Peele's or Wilkinson's and get your dinner. Then reach Drury Lane by 5 to 1 (not later). Pit early door 2s. 6d. When you are inside and cannot get a seat in the middle, go to the left hand side and you will see better — Feb. 8, 1892.

March 15, 1893. I have taken a great fancy to the plant we bought at Peckham on Tuesday and should be very pleased and gratified if you gave it to me, and get yourself a geranium when next we go down there. — Alfred.

Dec. 20, 1894. Please you are to change your flannels and socks to-morrow morning. — Alfred.

In 1895 I spent several mornings in the Manuscript Room of the British Museum, rubbing out pencil marks I had made on many of Dr. Butler's letters, while I was writing my *Life of Dr. Butler*. Before giving the letters to the Museum I wanted these marks rubbed out, and the letters being already in the keeping of the Museum (though not yet their property), it was arranged that Alfred and I should have a quiet corner in the Manuscript Room and rub out marks till we had cleaned up the letters. Alfred and I sat side by side and presently I found the following scrap thrust under my notice:

You cannot rub out half so nice as Alfred can.

Friday 3.15 p.m. Dear Sir. Do not forget to give Mr. Gogin the things I have put in the arm chair, if you do there is no excuse for you. The brown paper is to wrap up what he wants of them. — Alfred.

Nov. 13, 1901 (to quote the latest) My dear Sir. You are requested by Alfred to leave off your music composing at 8 o'clock sharp, and to go for a walk on the Embankment (weather permitting). Please don't forget, for there will be no excuse for you.

Here is one to Jones:

Nov. 28/92. Dear Sir. When you are booking seats at the Prince's for yourself and Mr. Rockstro, kindly book one for the Governor as I consider it necessary that he should see 'In Town', as it would then give him an idea of what kind of music the public have a taste for. Am sorry you have to leave Barnard's Inn. I will keep a lookout for chambers for you. With love from yours very truly, Alfred.'

I am prouder of having received and treasured these scraps of Alfred's than I am of all my books put together.

Almost immediately after he had been well established as my clerk (hours from 9.30 to 12.45, and from 2 — 5.30) he wanted to be married. I was then only giving him 25s. a week, and he had nothing behind him, so I said that if he married now, he had better stay with me till he could find some better place, and then take it. The lady, finding that Alfred could not marry at once, married someone else, and I am not sure that Alfred was altogether displeased.

We immediately began putting by a fund at the Savings Bank, and by the time he was 30 he and I between us had got it up to £150. He then broached the subject of marriage again, and there being no reason why he sould not marry, I raised no objection. He has three very engaging children, the eldest of whom is now about 8 years old. He has been with me just 15 years; his savings — I believe I may say chiefly my doing — save that if I give him the money he saves it — are about £230. He has from me about (includ-

42

ing a holiday of 4 weeks at the sea-side for himself and family), £150 a year, but I know that this will have to be increased as the children get bigger.

I do not believe that two men were ever thrown together more exactly suited to one another. My place is exactly the one for which he is most adapted, and he is absolutely the sort of man I like to have about me. There is, in fact, 'a semblable coherence between his spirits and mine,' than which I can imagine nothing more enviable nor more likely to be enduring.

To return to Quilter — when he first heard of Alfred, he (Alfred) was, as I have said, about 26 or 27 and I leave the reader to imagine the deep indignation and disgust with which I read what Quilter had written. I do not believe that poor dear Alfred himself even suspected the impression that many a reader would derive from it, and he was rather proud at finding himself mentioned in a work that would be so widely read; I therefore gave him the book and bade him take it out of my sight.

Angry as I was, I said nothing, but on January 1st Quilter wrote me a letter asking me to write him what was tantamount to a puff of *What's What* like some that he enclosed from Thomas Hardy, Dr. Garnett, and the head-master of Charterhouse. He continued, 'you never told me whether you liked what I wrote concerning you in *What's What*, I should be glad to know whether you considered it pleasant or the reverse.'

To this I wrote a few lines, I suppose angrily, for Streatfeild (whose word is law to me) wished me not to send them. I destroyed them, and wrote a very quiet, but straightforward answer saying that the article in *What's What* had pained me very much, but that as I knew he (Quilter) had not intended it to do so, I could take no offence, and wished him every success with his book, though I was not able to write anything about it that would be of service to him.

He wrote back what I consider a grossly impertinent

letter to which I did not reply. He charged me with not having answered a letter written to me by Mrs. Quilter about two years ago. The fact was I had disliked both Mr. and Mrs. Quilter so cordially that I was only too thankful when they dropped me. For eight years I never saw or heard of either of them and then, as thunder from a clear sky, came a letter from Mrs. Q. saying how much they should like to see me; loss of health and loss of money had told heavily upon them, and unless I called soon she should begin to think I had forgotten the little girl whose wedding feast I had attended — 'years ago'. (I quote from memory but the letter is among my correspondence.)

I never attended her 'wedding feast' by invitation. I blurted into the office of the *Universal Review* with copy for the press, and to my surprise found a small wedding breakfast in progress. I had a glass of champagne and went away.

I therefore considered Mrs. Quilter's letter as an impudent attempt to make out that I had been much more intimate with her husband and herself than I had ever been, and to catch on to me now that they were on their beam ends. To call, or to write civilly, was to walk straight into her trap. To write anything like what I thought was impossible, I therefore neither called nor wrote, and I am very glad that I did neither.

Returning for a moment to Alfred, readers of *Erewhon Revisited* will find him described with his name in full, as solicitor to the Higgs family. This was done in answer to a complaint from Alfred that I had never put him in any of my books:

> You know, Sir, you have put Mr. Pauli in and Mr. Jones and Mr. Gogin in, and I think you ought to put me in too.

So I put him in, and I believe he is now quite contented (1901-2).

It is a mercy that the dead cannot come back and haunt us while we are alive — not but what a good many dead people as W. S. Moorhouse and Miss Savage, not to mention others, haunt me every day of my life. I do not suppose a day ever passes but it comes up to me with a stab that these people were kinder and better friends to me than I to them — however, let that be. Thank Heaven the dead cannot haunt us visibly. What a mercy also that when we are dead the living whom our wills have disappointed cannot visit us in the grave and haunt us.

And yet in a way they can. For they can abuse us and thus prejudice the life that we live beyond the grave — the life we live in others, which is our truest life.

### HUSBAND AND WIFE

The following dialogue between a recently married couple was overheard not many weeks since by Gogin: 'My dear, what do you want? Do you want to have the baby by me, or am I to have it by you?'

### VERY USELESS THINGS

we neglect, till they become old and useless enough to be put in Museums: and so very important things we study till, when they become important enough, we ignore them — and rightly.

### G. BERNARD SHAW

I have long been repelled by this man though at the same time attracted by his coruscating power. Emery Walker once brought him up to see me, on the score that he was a great lover of Handel. He did nothing but cry down Handel and cry up Wagner. I did not like him and am sure that neither did he like me.

Still at the Fabian Society when I had delivered my

lecture — 'Was the *Odyssey* written by a woman?' — (not, heaven forbid, that I belong to or have any sympathy with the Fabian Society) he got up at once and said that when he had heard of my title first he supposed it was some mere fad or fancy of mine, but that on turning to the *Odyssey* to see what had induced me to take it up, he had not read a hundred lines before he found himself saying, 'Why, of course it is a woman.' He spoke so strongly that people who had only laughed with me all through my lecture began to think there might be something in it after all. Still, there is something uncomfortable about the man which makes him uncongenial to me.

The dislike — no this is too strong a word — the dissatisfaction with which he impressed me has been increased by his articles in the *Saturday Review* since it has been under Frank Harris's management — brilliant, amusing, and often sound though many of them have been. His cult of Ibsen disgusts me, and my displeasure has been roused to such a pitch as to have led me to this note, by his article 'Better than Shakespeare' in this morning's *Saturday Review*. Of course Bunyan is better than Shakespeare in some respects, so is Bernard Shaw himself, so am I, so is everybody. Of course also Bunyan is one of our very foremost classics — but I cannot forgive Bernard Shaw for sneering at Shakespeare as he has done this morning. If he means it, there is no trusting his judgement — if he does not mean it I have no time to waste on such trifling. If Shaw embeds his plums in such a cake as this, they must stay there. I cannot trouble to pick them out.

MYSELF AND ITALY

When I first knew it in 1843 there was no railway but the one between Naples and Castellamare. We seemed to pass through a fresh Custom House every day, but by tipping the searchers we generally got through without inconvenience. Napoleon Bonaparte's widow was still reigning at Parma. Beggars would run after my Father's carriage all day long, and when they found they got nothing they often took to crying 'Eretici' after us. At Rome I saw the Cardinals, or some of them, or some Bishops, or at any rate some important ecclesiastics, kiss Pope Gregory XVI's toe in the Sistine Chapel, and in the Corso I saw a monk come rolling down a staircase like a sack of potatoes, bundled into the street by a man and his wife — all in broad daylight.

The bread was sour (leavened) all the way from Boulogne to Naples, and the butter in Italy (when we got it at all) was rank and cheesy — often quite uneatable.

### MORAL FORCE AND IMMORAL FORCE

We make moral force so like physical force, and it suggests physical force so strongly that it acts as though it were physical force and produces exactly the same mechanical, chemical and physiological (I am never quite certain about the meaning of this word) effects as though it were physical force. But if there be no physical force ultimately behind it, it is immoral force, not moral. It is like a forged bank note, or a note of a bank that is insolvent. It may pass for some time, but it will be found out in the end. Physical force is to moral force as gold to paper money.

### MY AUNT BATHER AND BUTTER AND HONEY

She was a good old soul, and I had great pleasure in giving her memory what tribute I could in my *Life of Dr. Butler*, but she used (as all elderly aunts will do) to preach to me a good deal. One day she saw me eating bread and butter and honey; brought up as she was during the early days of Dr. Butler's married life, while he was still poor, no doubt she had been allowed either bread and honey, or bread and butter, but not bread and butter and honey; such extravagance alarmed her, and she said that it was not heard of in her youth, neither among the young people whom she knew, nor yet as far as she could gather in any class of society. 'Why, my dear' she said, 'don't you remember "The queen was in the parlour[1] eating bread and honey"'? To which I replied, being I suppose then about 14 or 15, that the Bible expressly enjoined us to eat butter with our honey. 'Butter and honey', it said, '*shalt* thou eat.' Whereon she dropped the subject.

### ONERY TWOERY

A good old servant who had been nurse in my Grandmother Worsley's family used to come to Langar sometimes when we were little children, and we were very fond of her. Her name was Mary Clow, or that was how she was commonly called, though her name was probably spelt Clough. When we had to take physic she would say:

'Onery Twoery Ziggory Zan
Pops and periwig, little old man.
Little old man and I fell out
Out, out with a great long snout.'

When she said 'snout' we were to gulp the medicine down.

### JOWETT AND 'EVERYTHING'

A parent of a man who had been ploughed for matriculation (?) came from the North of Scotland to argue with the tutor or whoever it was that had examined his son. The tutor would give him no information — it was against rules, etc., etc., so the angry Father went to Jowett and told him what the tutor had said. Jowett in his blandest manner said that the tutor was quite right. 'It certainly is', he said,

---

[1] Butler has 'garden' here and the word has been crossed out in pencil and 'Larder' written in.

'contrary to our regulations to say in what men have failed when we are satisfied that they ought not to pass. But I think we may set the rule aside in your son's case. He failed in *everything*.'


ROBERT BRIDGES AND MY BOOK ON SHAKESPEARE'S SONNETS

Bridges objects (1) that the mean personality which I assign to W.H. 'disagrees with the hints that other poets wrote of and to him, and that books were dedicated to him.'

I reply that I have not attributed a mean personality to W.H. All I contend for is that there is strong ground for thinking that he was not a peer, or indeed in any way of higher social status than Shakespeare's own. That he was well known is obvious, but he might be this in twenty ways without being a peer, and we have no reason for thinking that he was well known in any higher circle than that in which Shakespeare himself moved. I know of no books having been dedicated to him — I can find no ground for the supposition that there were any. Certainly more than one poet wrote occasional verses to him, but there is only one of whom Shakespeare is really jealous.

(2) Bridges says that my view of the worthlessness of W.H.'s character and conduct 'disagrees with the very frequent assertion of his reciprocal affection, which is so beautifully and passionately told.'

I need not quote passages which show that public opinion condemned Mr. W.H.'s character within a very few months of Shakespeare's beginning to write to him. They abound. As for Shakespeare's word that W.H.'s affection for him was reciprocal, I want Mr. W.H.'s word for this, not Shakespeare's. No man keeps on telling another person, either man or woman, that he or she is so very fond of him, unless he has a strong misgiving that his wish is father to his thought. I desire no more convincing proof that pretty

Mr. smooth-faced W.H. never cared two straws for Shakespeare than Shakespeare's reiterated assertion that the affection between them was reciprocal.

(3) Bridges says that it is not believable that Shakespeare 'would have disliked the publication of his Sonnets in the face of his plain statement that they would immortalize the recipient.'

I have no doubt that when Shakespeare began to discover his own power, the exuberance of his delight would make him recite them very freely, and contemplate with satisfaction the idea that they should be read by others; but I cannot think that this would apply to all the sonnets. Because he evidently contemplated eventual publication when he wrote in Sonnet 18:

> So long as breath can breathe or eyes can see
> So long lives this, and this gives life to thee

it does not follow that he wrote Sonnet 23 with a view to publication. If the poor fellow could not bring his tongue to utter his own meaning, can we think that he would want the whole world to know what that meaning was? But even granting this impossible supposition, and supposing that in the recklessness of extreme youth and the delirium of finding that dreams concerning his own powers, which no doubt had many a time flitted across his mind, were really true — granting that he would have published anything and everything, if he had the money to do it with, or if a publisher had made him an offer — granted that while the fire was blazing hot and furious he might have wished the world to note it, it is inconceivable that he would have wished to do so twenty years after the ashes had been raked out and thrown upon the dust heap. When a man has long recovered from a fit of extreme folly, he does not find his sayings and doings pleasant reading, however infatuated he may have been with them while the fit was still upon him. This paragraph covers Bridges' 4th objection also.

He objects to my 'assumption that the Sonnets not addressed to W.H. should be put with those addressed to him.' A man who is trying to arrange documents in chronological order can have no regard for any other than chronological considerations. Bridges however does not 'object to the idea that they may have been contemporary and even have relation to the events touched on in the W.H. series.' Then he who would understand what those events were must put documents that relate to them in their proper order of date.

When he speaks of these Sonnets as not being intended to form part of the 'immortal' poem, and repeatedly in his letter speaks of the Sonnets as 'a poem', I see that our fundamental ideas concerning the Sonnets differ so widely as to make agreement impossible. I see them as a series of letters — as units. He sees them as a single composition — as an organic whole. To this conception he has adhered in a later letter. I will therefore follow him no further.

### WRIGHT AND MOORHOUSE

Wright, that clever fellow who wrote the epigram[1] which I am sure I have given in earlier vol. of these notes — I mean 'He was leaving the settlement half broken-hearted', etc. — was obviously dying, and Moorhouse went over to Port Lyttelton to see him. After Moorhouse had stayed a little while Wright said to him quite naturally, 'Be pleased to leave the room. I want to die.' Moorhouse did as he was told, and in a few minutes all was over. Moorhouse told me this.

---

[1]
> He was leaving the Settlement, half broken-hearted,
> For his friends to his going would hardly consent;
> But he came to a settlement ere he departed,
> And the last tie which bound the poor pilgrim was — rent.'

The epigram was apropos of a settler who was involved in a dispute over the rent of the house he had occupied in the Canterbury Settlement.

### SPOILED TARTS

Mrs. Brown at Shrewsbury used to keep a tray of spoiled tarts which she sold cheaper. They most of them looked pretty right till you handled them. We are all spoiled tarts.


### MYSELF AT DOCTORS' COMMONS

A woman once stopped me at the entrance to Doctors' Commons and said:

'If you please, sir, can you tell me — is this the place that I came to before?'

Not knowing where she had been before I could not tell her.


### THE FLYING BALANCE

The ghost of an old cashier haunts a ledger, so that the books always refuse to balance by the sum of, say, £1.15.11. No matter how many accountants are called in, year after year the same error always turns up; sometimes they think they have it right and it turns out there was a mistake, so the old error reappears. At last a son and heir is born, and at some festivities the old cashier's name is mentioned with honour. This lays his ghost. Next morning the books are found correct and remain so.


### FAMILIAR MISQUOTATION

There is more truth in honest lies,
Believe me, than in half the truths.


### MY THOUGHTS

They are like persons met upon a journey — I think them very agreeable at first, but soon find, as a rule, that I am tired of them.

may not be particularly wise — still we know of nothing wiser.

## MAN

is the only animal that can remain on friendly terms with the victims he intends to eat until he eats them.

### A MAN ON HIMSELF

He may make as it were cash entries of himself in a day-book, but the entries in the ledger and the balancing of the accounts should be done by others.

### CONSERVATORIES

One of the main objects of a conservatory is to make believe that there is no such thing as death and decay. The man who attends to it should never be seen at work there. But he may be seen at work in the kitchen garden.

### GERM CELLS

will not be humbugged and they will tell the truth as near as they can.

Thus if a painter has not tried hard to paint well, and has tried hard to hoodwink the public, his offspring is not likely to show hereditary aptitude for painting, but is likely to have an improved power of hoodwinking the public. The germ cells know what the parent meant perfectly well and will be a good deal more sincere than himself. So it is with music, literature, science or anything else. The only thing the public can do against this is to try very hard to develop a hereditary power of not being hoodwinked. From the small success it has met with hitherto we may think that the effort on its part can neither have been severe nor long sustained.

Indeed, all ages seem to have held that 'the pleasure is as great of being cheated as to cheat.' (*Hudibras*.)

### DEATH AND THE RESURRECTION

There are savages who have not yet come to believe in death. There are very able people who have not yet left off believing in the resurrection from the dead. Others again have got beyond believing in either death or resurrection.

### RIGHT AND WRONG

It is wrong to be too right. To be too good is as bad — or nearly so — as to be too wicked.

### PART OF A NOTE HEADED SHAKESPEARIAN FRAGMENTS

It came out in evidence at a trial in New Zealand about 1863 or 1864 of some very atrocious murderers that a poor old man on the point of being murdered said:

'If you murder me, I shall be foully murdered.'

And they murdered him.

In regard to this last note. Suppose this subject given out as an exercise for an imaginary dying speech — how few of those who tried to do it would hit upon anything like the real thing — and how the verisimilitude of nature would strike them at once when what had been really said was read to them.

### CHRISTIANITY

People say you must not try to do away with Christianity till you have something better to put in its place. They might as well say that we must not take away turnpikes and corn laws till we have some other hindrance to put in its place. Besides no one wants to do away with Christianity — all we want is not to be snubbed and bullied if we reject the miraculous part of it for ourselves.

At present I am obliged, for example, to keep out of English-frequented hotels in Switzerland and Italy because I find that if I do not go to service on Sunday I am made uncomfortable. It is this bullying that I want to do away with. As regards Christianity I should hope and think that I am more Christian than not.

### HOGARTH'S 'IDLE AND VIRTUOUS APPRENTICE'

is an immoral work for it represents virtue and its consequences in a light nearly as odious as vice. Those are best who are neither virtuous nor idle.

### FAITH

What is faith but a kind of betting or speculation after all? It should be, 'I bet that my Redeemer liveth.'

### HEALTH BEFORE HONESTY

It is not the interest of honesty or talent or virtue, but that of health and happiness that should take the highest place. Honesty is made for happiness, not happiness for honesty.

### HEAVEN

is the work of the best and kindest men and women. Hell is the work of prigs, pedants and professional truth-tellers. The world is an attempt to make the best of Heaven and Hell.

### MORALITY

is the custom of one's country and the current feeling of one's peers. Cannibalism is moral in a cannibal country.

are infectious. It depresses us to be much with those who have suffered long and are still suffering; it refreshes us to be with those who have suffered little and are enjoying themselves. But it is good for us to be depressed now and then.

## JUSTICE

is my being allowed to do whatever I like. Injustice is whatever prevents my doing so.

## CHRISTIANITY

is true in so far as it has fostered beauty and false in so far as it has fostered ugliness. It is therefore both very true and very false.

## THE DIVORCE NOVELETTE

The hero and heroine are engaged against their wishes. They like each other very well but are each in love with some one else; nevertheless under an uncle's will they forfeit large property unless they marry, so they get married, making no secret to one another that they dislike it very much.

On the evening of their wedding day they broach to one another the subject that has long been nearest to the heart of each — the possibility of their being divorced.

They discuss the subject tearfully, but the obstacles to their divorce seem insuperable. Nevertheless they agree that faint heart never yet got rid of fair lady. 'None but the brave,' they exclaim, 'deserve to lose the fair,' and they plight each other their most solemn vows that they will henceforth live but for the object of getting divorced from one another.

But the course of true divorce never did run smooth, and

the plot turns upon the difficulties that meet them and how they try to overcome them. At one time they seem almost certain of success, but the cup is dashed from their lips and is farther off than ever.

At last an opportunity occurs in an unlooked-for manner. They are divorced, and live happily apart ever afterwards.

### NATURE'S GREAT LIE

That one great lie she told about the earth being flat, when it was round all the time — and again how she stuck to it that the sun went round us when it was we who are going round her — this double falsehood has irretrievably ruined my confidence in her. There is no lie which she will not tell and stick to like a Gladstonian. How plausibly she told her tale, and how many ages was it before she was so much as suspected. And then when things did begin to look bad for her, how she brazened it out and what a desperate business it was to bring her shifts and prevarications to book.

### EXPRESSION

I have seen thoughts and fancies playing upon people's faces like the wind upon young heather.

### SUNDAY

The great and terrible day of the Lord.

### THE RESURRECTION

When I die at any rate I shall do so in the full and certain hope that there will be no resurrection, but that death will give me quittance in full.

If he were to apply for a divorce on the grounds of cruelty, adultery and desertion, he would probably get one.

## THE SEXUAL QUESTION
As regards the greater freedom which those who think as I do would allow the young of both sexes, with such precautions as the faculty may approve, we are met with pictures of the universal debauchery that would follow. This might perhaps have been true once, but the world is grown older and can be better trusted.

## HANDEL
I only ever met one American who seemed to like and understand Handel. How far he did so in reality I do not know, but *inter alia* he said that Handel 'struck ile' with the *Messiah* — and that 'it panned out well, the *Messiah* did.'

## A LAWYER'S DREAM OF HEAVEN
Every man reclaimed his own property at the resurrection, and each tried to recover it from all his forefathers.

## WORDS GET LICHEN-GROWN AND
crumble like stones in an old wall, but it does not do to build a new wall with old stones to make it look like an old one. Let the new work age if it will and gather picturesqueness in its own good time.

## 'GOD IS LOVE'
I like 'Love is God' better.

People ask complainingly what swells have done or do for society that they should be able to live without working. The good swell is the creature towards which all nature has been groaning and travailing together until now. He is an ideal. He shows what may be done in the way of good breeding, health, looks, temper and fortune. He realizes men's dreams of themselves at any rate vicariously. He preaches the gospel of grace. The world is like a spoilt child, it has this good thing given it at great expense, and then says it is useless!

## BEETROOT AND MODESTY

The beetroot is a better emblem of modesty than the rose. The colour is as fine; it conceals itself from the view more completely; moreover it is good to eat, and will make excellent sugar.

## CAMBRIDGE COOKING

There is a higher average of good cooking at Oxford and Cambridge than elsewhere. The dinners are better than the curriculum. But there is no chair of cookery; it is taught by apprenticeship in the kitchens.

## THE NATURE OF THINGS IN THEMSELVES

A thing 'is' whatever it gives us least trouble to think it is. There is no other 'is' than this.

## REPUTATIONS FOR ABILITY

I would rather lose twenty, than be at pains to keep one of them. Reputation is like a man's soul, which he may find in losing, or lose in finding. It is like money, more easily made than kept.

## A MAN IS SHORN OF HIS STRENGTH

if he belongs to one set or to one woman.

## OUR IDEAS

are for the most part like bad sixpences, and we spend our lives in trying to pass them on one another.

## OUR CONCEIT

He is a poor creature who does not believe himself to be better than the whole world else. No matter how ill we may be, nor how low we may have fallen, we would not change identity with any other person. Hence our self-conceit sustains and always must sustain us till death takes us and our conceit together so that we need no more sustaining.

## WALKING UPRIGHT

Walking upright was perhaps once as difficult as the feats of Blondin and Leotard appear to ourselves. Perhaps it was thought wicked, perhaps it was only an imitation of a deformity, in flattery of some semi-simian chief who had lost his arms, and could neither climb trees nor go on all fours. Perhaps it was developed by some vice, or perhaps it began as a mere piece of affectation. Anyhow until we take to flying we shall probably continue to walk as uprightly as we can if only to a cab or train.

## ALL MEN EQUAL BEFORE GOD

Men are no more all equal before God than they are so before man. The sole element of truth in the contention lies in the fact that our bodies, not to say our minds, are built all upon one general plan.

## STEALING WISELY

It is only great proprietors who can steal well and wisely. A good stealer, a good user of what he takes, is *ipso facto* a good inventor. Two men can invent after a fashion to one who knows how to make the best use of what has been done already.

## THE ONE SERIOUS CONVICTION

that a man should have is that nothing is to be taken too seriously.

## INTELLECTUAL SELF-INDULGENCE

Intellectual over-indulgence is the most gratuitous and disgraceful form which excess can take, nor is there any the consequences of which are more disastrous.

## SUBJECT

Fifteen mistresses applied for three cooks. Turn this into a little fairy story in which the mistress who thought herself nobody was chosen by the beautiful cook, etc.

## NO DRAGONS

People say that there are no dragons to be killed, nor distressed maidens to be rescued nowadays. I do not know but I think I have dropped across one or two, nor do I feel sure whether it is I or they who have inflicted the most mortal wound.

## ENTERTAINING ANGELS

I doubt whether any angel would find me very entertaining. As for myself if ever I do entertain one it will have to be unawares. When people entertain others without an introduction, they generally turn out more like devils than angels.

as now generally conceived of is only the last witch.

## MEMNON

I saw the driver of the Hampstead bus once, near St. Giles's Church. An old, fat, red-faced man sitting bolt upright on the top of his bus, in a driving storm of snow, fast asleep with a huge waterproof over his great-coat that descended with sweeping lines on to a tarpaulin. All this rose out of a cloud of steam from the horses. He had a short clay pipe in his mouth but for a moment he looked just like Memnon.

## EATING GRAPES DOWNWARDS

Always eat the best first. For so every grape will be good. This is why spring seems longer and drearier than autumn: in autumn we are eating the days downwards, in spring each one is 'still very bad.'

## THE PARABLES

The people do not act reasonably in a single instance. The sower was a bad sower; the shepherd who left his ninety-nine sheep in the wilderness was a foolish shepherd; the husbandman who would not have his corn weeded was no farmer, etc, etc. None of them go nearly on all fours, but halt so much as to have neither literary nor moral value to any but slipshod thinkers.

Granted, but are we not all slipshod thinkers?

## A GOOD TITLE

should aim at making what follows as far as possible superfluous to those who know anything of the subject.

is to have good health, good looks, good sense, experience, a kindly nature and a fair balance of cash in hand. We know that all things work together for good to them that love God. To be loved by God is the same as to love him. We love him because he first loved us.

### 'WE ARE HIS PEOPLE AND THE SHEEP OF HIS PASTURE'

*Blake*

We profess to accept with thankfulness the position of being God's sheep, yet few lambs are allowed to become full grown and it is not intended that any should die a natural death. A sheep's *raison d'être* is to be fleeced as often as possible, and then to have its throat cut.

Uriah the Hittite, if his own life had been spared, would no doubt have sat down to the little ewe lamb which he carried so tenderly in his bosom, and dined off it with much satisfaction; and when, again, we see pictures of our Saviour with sheep behind him, and a lamb in his bosom, we should remember that the matter will not end here. If a shepherd caressing a lamb is a fair statement of the case, a cat playing with a mouse should be hardly less so. We may be asked to bless the grass, the sunshine, and our fellow sheep, but can we reasonably be expected to bless the butcher? Is it not time to drop that metaphor?

### THE SELFISHNESS OF WOMEN

They say it is so selfish of men not to marry: perhaps it is; but is it not selfish of women to insist on men marrying them?

### MY UNCLE PHILIP'S CONSCIENCE, PRANKS OF

He became a partner in Whitbread's brewery, but on conscientious grounds refused a partnership in a distillery.

He drew the line at gin. What odd lines conscience does sometimes draw, to be sure!


### MARRIAGE AND HEAVEN

Marriage is distinctly and repeatedly excluded from heaven. Is this because it is thought likely to mar the general felicity?


### HANDEL AND BACH

If you tie Handel's hands by debarring him from the rendering of human emotion, and if you set Bach's free by giving him no human emotion to render — if in fact you rob Handel of his opportunities and Bach of his difficulties — the two men can fight after a fashion, but Handel will even so come off victorious. Otherwise it is absurd to let Bach compete at all. Nevertheless the cultured vulgar have at all times preferred gymnastics and display to reticence, and the healthy, graceful, normal movements of a man of birth and education and Bach is esteemed a more profound musician than Handel in virtue of his more frequent and more involved complexity of construction. In reality Handel was profound enough to eschew such wildernesses of counterpoint as Bach instinctively resorted to, but he knew also that public opinion would be sure to place Bach on a level with himself, if not above him, and probably this made him look askance at Bach. At any rate he twice went to Germany without being at any pains to meet him, and once, if not twice, refused Bach's invitation.


### EXAMPLE

is not only the best way of propagating an opinion, but it is the only way worth taking into account.

He who would propagate an opinion must begin by making sure of his ground, and holding it firmly. There is no more use in trying to breed from weak opinion than from other weak stock, animal or vegetable.

The more securely a man holds an opinion the more temperate he can afford to be, and the more temperate he is the more weight he will carry with those who are in the long run weightiest.

Ideas and opinions, like living organisms, have a normal rate of growth which cannot be either checked or forced beyond a certain point.

They can be held in check more safely than they can be hurried. They can also be killed; and one of the surest ways to kill them is to try and hurry them.

The more unpopular an opinion is the more necessary is it that the holder should be somewhat punctilious in his observance of conventionalities generally, and that, if possible, he should get the reputation of being well-to-do in the world.

Arguments are not so good as assertion. Arguments are like fire-arms which a man may keep at home but should not carry about with him.

Indirect assertion, leaving the hearer to point the inference, is generally to be preferred.

The one great argument with most people is that another should think this or that. The reasons of the belief are a detail that in nine cases out of ten are best omitted as confusing and weakening the general impression.

Many, if not most, good ideas die young — mainly from neglect on the part of the parents, but sometimes from over-fondness.

Once well started, an opinion had better be left to shift for itself.

Insist as far as possible on the insignificance of the points of difference as compared with the resemblances to those generally accepted.

When people ask what faith we would substitute for that which we would destroy, we answer that we destroy no faith and need substitute none. We hold the glory of God to be the *summum bonum* and so do Christians generally. It is a question of what is the glory of God. It is here that we join issue. We say it varies with the varying phases of God as made manifest in his works, but that so far as we are ourselves concerned the glory of God is best advanced by advancing that of man. If asked what is the glory of man, we answer 'Good breeding' — using the words in their double sense, and meaning both the continuance of the race and that grace of manner which the words are more commonly taken to signify.

The double sense of the words is all the more significant for the unconsciousness with which it is passed over.

## HANDEL

is so great and so simple that it takes a professional musician to be unable to understand him. Jones and I hammered this out between us.

## DIFFUSENESS

sometimes helps, when the subject is hard; words that may be strictly speaking unnecessary still may make things easier for the reader by giving him more time to master the thought while his eye is running over the verbiage. So a little water may prevent a strong drink from burning throat and stomach. A style that is too terse is as fatiguing as one that is too diffuse. But when a passage is written a little long with consciousness and compunction, but still deliberately, as what will probably be most easy for the reader it can hardly be called diffuse.

The case of a woman now stands thus. Every one of her ancestors for millions and millions of generations has been endowed with sexual instinct, and has effectually gratified it. For a longer time than our imagination can realize there has been no link broken, and hence no exception. The instinct has been approved, confirmed, and made stronger in each successive generation. Surely those in whom it has been thus sanctioned may claim the right to gratify it, should occasion serve.

'No', says Society to the unmarried woman very sternly; 'break the link, in your own person; stem the current of that passion to which both we and you owe our very being; run counter to the course of things that has led up to you; be indifferent to that which has ranked next to life itself in the heart of every mother from whom you are descended. If you even attempt this more than Herculean task seriously, we will not honour you, but will laugh at you for an old maid; if, on the other hand, you are disobedient, we will chase you out into the streets and call you infamous.'

And then we are surprised that women are not at all times exactly what we could wish.

### ART NOTE — INARTICULATE TOUCHES

An artist's touches are sometimes no more articulate than the barking of a dog who would call attention to something without exactly knowing what. He is a great artist who can be depended on not to bark at nothing.

### ART NOTE — GIOTTO

There are few modern painters who are not greater technically than Giotto, but I cannot call to mind a single one whose work impresses me as profoundly as his does.

How is it that our so greatly better should be so greatly worse — that the farther we go beyond him the higher he stands above us? Age no doubt has much to do with it, for great as Giotto was, there are painters of today not less so, if they only dare express themselves as frankly and unaffectedly as he did.

## ART NOTE — RELATIVE IMPORTANCES

It is the painter's business to help memory and imagination, not to supersede them. He cannot put the whole before the spectator; nothing can do this short of the thing itself; he should not therefore try to realize, and the less he looks as if he were trying to do so the more signs of judgment he will show. His business is to supply those details which will most readily bring the whole before the mind along with them. He must not give too few but it is still more imperative on him not to give too many.

Seeing, thought and expression are rendered possible only by the fact that our minds are always ready to compromise, and to take the part for the whole. We associate a number of ideas with any given object, and if a few of the most characteristic of these are put before us we take the rest as read, jump to a conclusion and realize the whole. If we did not conduct our thought on this principle i.e. simplifying by suppression of detail and breadth of treatment — it would take us a twelvemonth to say that it was a fine morning, and another for the hearer to apprehend our statement. Any other principle reduces thought to an absurdity.

He therefore tells best in painting, as in literature, who has best estimated the relative values or importances of the more special features characterizing his subject: that is to say, who appreciates most accurately how much and how fast each one of them will carry, and is at most pains to give those only that will say most in the fewest words, or touches,

It is here that the most difficult, important, and generally neglected part of an artist's business will be found to lie.

The difficulties of doing are serious enough but we can most of us overcome them with ordinary perseverance; these however are small as compared with those of knowing what not to do — with learning to disregard the incessant importunity of small nobody details that persist in trying to thrust themselves above their betters. It is less trouble to give in to these than to snub them duly and keep them in their proper places, yet it is precisely here that strength or weakness will be found to lie. It is success or failure in this respect that constitutes the difference between the artist who may claim to rank as a statesman and one who can rise no higher than a village vestryman.

It is here, moreover, that effort is most remunerative. For when we feel that a painter has made simplicity and subordination of importances his first aim, it is surprising how much shortcoming we will condone as regards actual execution. Whereas let the execution be perfect if the details given be ill-chosen in respect of relative importance the whole effect is lost; it becomes top-heavy, as it were, and collapses. As for the number of details given, this does not matter: a man may give as few or as many as he chooses; he may stop at outline, or he may go on to Jan Van Eyck; what is essential is that no matter how far or how small a distance he may go, he should have begun with the most important point, and added each subsequent feature in due order of importance, so that if he stopped at any moment there should be no detail ungiven more important than another which has been insisted on.

Supposing, by way of illustration, that the details are as grapes in a bunch; they should be eaten from the best grape to the next best, and so on down never eating a worse grape while a better remains uneaten.

Personally, I think that, as the painter cannot go the whole way, the sooner he makes it clear that he has no intention of trying to do so the better. When we look at a very highly finished picture (so called) unless we are in the hands of one who has attended successfully to the considerations insisted on above, we feel as though we were with a troublesome cicerone who will not let us look at things with our own eyes, but keeps intruding himself at every touch and turn, and trying to exercise that undue influence upon us which generally proves to have been the accompaniment of concealment and fraud. This is exactly what we feel in regard to Van Mieris and, though in a less degree, with Gerard Dow — whereas with Jan Van Eyck and Metsu, no matter how far they may have gone, we find them essentially as impressionist as Rembrandt or Velasquez.

For impressionism only means that due attention has been paid to the relative importances of the impressions made by the various characteristics of a given subject, and that they have been presented to us in order of precedence.

## ART NOTE — SINCERITY

It is not enough that the painter should make the spectator feel what he meant him to feel; he must also make him feel that this feeling was shared by the painter himself *bona fide* and without affectation. Of all the lies a painter can tell the worst is saying that he likes what he does not like. But the poor wretch seldom knows himself; for the art of knowing what gives him pleasure has been so neglected that it has been lost to all but a very few. The old Italians knew well enough what they liked and were as children in saying it.

## PROSELYTIZING

We can only proselytize fresh meat, putrid meat begins to have strong convictions of its own.

A man begins to do this about nine months before he is born. He then begins worrying his father to let him have a separate establishment, till the father finds him a nuisance and lets him have his own way.

### LIFE AND SPONTANEOUS GENERATION

Unless we begin with life of some kind omnipresent for ever throughout matter we must have spontaneous generation, i.e. transition from absolutely non-living to absolutely living somewhere. Yet the very men who are loudest in insisting on the impossibility of this insist at the same time on that which must either come to this in the end as regards the original form or forms of life, or rest on the omnipresence of low or potential life through matter.

So those who most deny the possibility of *a priori* knowledge most insist on its existence, in instinct. See *Westminster Rev.* April(?) 1880.

Change is only spontaneous generation made easy — it is hidden spontaneous generation like hidden fifths in music. It seems to me that you must not begin with life or potential life everywhere, alone, nor with a single (or more) spontaneous generation alone, but you must carry your spontaneous generation or denial of the continuity of life down *ad infinitum*, just as you must carry your continuity of life, or denial of spontaneous generation, down *ad infinitum* and compatible or incompatible you must write a scientific Athanasian creed to comprehend these two incomprehensibles.

If, then, it is only an escape from one incomprehensible position to another — *cui bono* to make a change? Why not stay quietly in the Athanasian creed as we are? I can give no answer to this as regards the unintelligible clauses, for what we come to in the end is just as abhorrent to reason and inconceivable by it as what they offer us; but as regards the intelligible parts — that Christ was born of a virgin, died, rose from the dead — we say that if it was not for the prestige that belief in these alleged facts has obtained we should refuse attention to them. As it is, out of respect to the mass of opinion that accepts them, we have looked into the matter with care, and find the evidence break down.

## MONEY

is the last enemy that shall never be subdued. While there is flesh there is money — or the want of money, but money is always on the brain so long as there is a brain in reasonable order.

## SUDDEN DEATH

Those who die suddenly and without warning not only never die (in the sense in which no man ever dies to himself), but never even think they are going to die soon. A man knocked to pieces by a passing train while greasing wheel-boxes does not even leave off greasing wheel-boxes so far as he is himself concerned, but goes on greasing them for ever and ever for such an infinity of time as is practically no time at all. Or how about one who eats a good dinner and goes to sleep after it too near a charcoal fire of which he knew nothing?

## ON BEING A SWELL ALL ROUND

I have never in my life succeeded in being this. Sometimes I get new clothes and am tidy for a while in part, meanwhile the hat, tie, boots, gloves and underclothing all clamour for attention and, before I have got them all well in hand, the clothes have lost their freshness. Still, if ever I do get any money, I will try and make myself really spruce all round for about a week till I have found out, as I probably shall, that if I give my clothes an inch they will take an ell.

Its base must be looked for not in the desire of the parents to reproduce but in the discontent of the germs with their surroundings inside those parents, and a desire on their part to have a separate maintenance. (1880.)

## HANDEL AND DICKENS

They buried Dickens in the very next grave cheek by jowl with Handel. It does not matter, but it pained me to think that people who could do this could become Deans of Westminster.

## THE FAMILY

I believe more unhappiness comes from this source than from any other — I mean from the attempt to prolong family connection unduly, and to make people hang together artificially who would never naturally do so. The mischief among the lower classes is not so great, but among the middle and upper it is killing a large number daily. And the old people do not really like it much better than the young.

## GLADSTONE AS A FINANCIER

I said to my tobacconist that Gladstone was not a financier because he bought a lot of china at high prices and it fetched very little when it was sold at Christie's.

'Did he give high prices?' said the tobacconist.

'Enormous prices,' said I emphatically.

Now, as a matter of fact, I did not know whether Mr. Gladstone had ever bought the china at all, much less what he gave for it, if he did; he may have had it all left him for aught I knew, but I was going to appeal to my tobacconist by arguments that he could understand, and I could see he was much impressed.

As people looked at glaciers for thousands of years before they found out that ice was a fluid, so it has taken them and will continue to take them not less before they see that the inorganic is not wholly inorganic.

## ADAM AND EVE

A little boy and a little girl were looking at a picture of Adam and Eve.

'Which is Adam and which Eve?' said one.

'I do not know,' said the other, 'but I should know if they had their clothes on.'

## ISAAC OFFERING UP ABRAHAM

This, I imagine, would have been very wrong, no matter how plainly God told Isaac to do it. Fancy Abraham letting Isaac get him on to the mountain on such a ridiculous pretence as this!

## A WOMAN CAME FROM NORTHUMBERLAND

to London to see her daughter who lived in some little back street in Whitechapel. She went out, lost her way, forgot the name of the street, and had to go back all the way to Northumberland before she could hitch on to her connections again!

## MY BACON FOR BREAKFAST

Written November 1890. Rewritten Sat. Dec. 2, 1893.

Now, when I am abroad, being older and taking less exercise I do not want any breakfast beyond coffee and bread and butter, but when this note was written I liked a modest rasher of bacon as well, and have often noticed the jealous indignation with which heads of families who enjoyed the privilege of Cephas and the brethren of our Lord regarded it. There were they with three or four elderly unmarried daughters as well as old mamma. How could they afford bacon? And there was I, a selfish bachelor — . The appetizing savoury smell of my rasher seemed to drive them mad. I used to feel very uncomfortable, very small, and quite aware how low it was of me to have bacon for breakfast and no daughters, instead of daughters and no bacon, but when I consulted the oracles of heaven about it I was always told to stick to my bacon and not to make a fool of myself. I despise myself, but have not withered under my own contempt so completely as I ought to have done.

### CROESUS'S KITCHEN MAID

She was part of him, bone of his bone and flesh of his flesh, for she eats what comes down from his table and, being fed of one flesh, are they not brothers and sisters to one another in virtue of community of nutriment which is but a thinly veiled travesty of descent? When she eats peas with her knife he does so; there is not a mouthful of bread and butter she eats, nor lump of sugar she drops into her tea, but he knows it altogether though he knows nothing whatever about it. She is en-Croesus-ed and he en-scullery-maided so long as she remains linked to him by the golden chain that passes from his pocket, and which is greatest of all unifiers.

True, neither party is aware of the connection at all as long as things go smoothly. Croesus no more knows the name of, or feels the existence of, his kitchen-maid than a peasant in health knows about his liver; still he is awakened to a dim sense of an undefined something when he pays his grocer or his baker. She is more definitely aware of him than he of her, but it is by way of an overshadowing presence rather than a clear and intelligent comprehension. And though Croesus does not eat his kitchen-maid's meals other-

75

wise than vicariously, still to eat vicariously is to eat: the meals so eaten by his kitchen-maid nourish the better ordering of the dinner which nourishes and engenders the better ordering of Croesus himself. He is fed therefore by the feeding of his kitchen-maid.

And so with sleep. When she goes to bed he in part does so. When she gets up and lays the fire in the back-kitchen he in part does so. He lays it through her and in her though knowing no more about his action than we do when we wink or digest, but still doing it as by what we call a reflex action. *Qui facit per alium facit per se*; and when the back-kitchen fire is lighted on Croesus's behalf, it is Croesus who lights it, though he is all the time fast asleep in bed.

If he discharges his kitchen-maid and gets another, it is as though he cut out a small piece of his finger and replaced it in due course by growth. But even the slightest cut may lead to blood poisoning, and so even the dismissal of a kitchen-maid may be big with the fate of empires. Thus the cook, a valued servant, may take the kitchen-maid's part and go too. The next cook may spoil the dinner and upset Croesus's temper, and from this all manner of consequences may be evolved even to the dethronement and death of the king himself. Nevertheless as a general rule an injury to such a low part of a great monarch's organism as a kitchen-maid has no serious results. It is only when we are attacked in such more vital organs as the solicitor or the banker that we need be seriously uneasy.

It is certain as we have seen that when the kitchen-maid lights the fire it is really Croesus who is lighting it, but it is less obvious that when Croesus goes to a ball the scullery-maid goes also. Still this should be held in the same way as it should be also held that she eats vicariously when Croesus does so. For what he eats comes out in his requiring to keep a large establishment whereby the scullery-maid keeps her place as part of Croesus's organism and is nourished also.

On the other hand, when Croesus dies it does not follow that the scullery-maid should die at the same time. She may grow a new Croesus, as Croesus, if the maid dies, will probably grow a new kitchen-maid; Croesus's son or successor may take over the kingdom and palace, and the kitchen-maid, beyond having to wash up a few extra plates and dishes at Coronation time, will know nothing about the change; it is as though the establishment had had its hair cut and its beard trimmed; it is smartened up a little, but there is no other change. If on the other hand he goes bankrupt, or his kingdom is taken from him and his whole establishment is broken up and dissipated at the auction mart, then even though not one of its component cells actually dies the organism as a whole does so, and it is interesting to see that the lowest, least specialized, and least highly differentiated parts of the organism such as the scullery-maids and the stable-boys most readily find an entry into the life of some new system, while the more specialized and highly differentiated parts such as the steward, the old housekeeper, or still more so the librarian or the chaplain may never be able to attach themselves to any new combination, and may die in consequence. I heard once of a large builder who retired somewhat unexpectedly from business and broke up his establishment to the actual death of several of his older employés.

So a bit of flesh or even a finger may be taken from one body and grafted on to another, but a leg cannot be grafted. If a leg is cut off it must die. It may however be maintained the owner dies too, even though he recovers for a man who has lost a leg is not the man he was.

JONES AND I ABOUT BLAKE, DANTE, TENNYSON AND VIRGIL

We said we knew Blake was no good because he learnt Italian at 60 in order to study Dante, and we knew Dante was no good because he ran Virgil, and we knew Virgil was

no good because Tennyson ran him, and as for Tennyson —
well, he went without saying.

### THE BIBLE

may be the truth, but it is not the whole truth and nothing
but the truth.

### WHAT IS BEING ALIVE?

If a man's body be photoed and his voice phonoed, in
such quick succession of instants and for so long that you
may watch his minutest changes of tone and expression for
half an hour, and if so many of the other phenomena of life
and consciousness be given that the others go without either
saying or being in virtue of the fact that association accepts
the part for the whole and jumps ever kangaroo-like to its
conclusions — if, moreover, what he says is something which
men are continually forgetting, and which may be repeated
*ad infinitum* so that it be well put — moreover, if this man's
other work is well known, and he is a power among men, as,
we will say Shakespeare, so that as we look upon him during
the half hour that we can watch him and hear him we are
wrapt up in him and hang upon his lips — is the man dead
though he have been in his grave this twenty years? What
is being alive but the presenting so many of the phenomena
of life that the rest are taken for granted? And are not
enough phenomena presented in this case to fulfil the con-
ditions necessary for our thinking him alive? Surely, at any
rate, the man is more alive than dead, for there is neither
sun nor moon, nor life nor death, any more than good or ill,
but thinking makes it so.

### FIRE

I was at one the other night and heard a man say: 'That
corner stack is alight now quite nicely.' People's sympathies

seem generally to be with the fire so long as no one is in danger of being burned.

### WHAT IS BEING IN A PLACE?
Am I more in the Sistine Chapel when I have first-rate photographs before me of the frescoes it contains, and can study them at my leisure (not that I have the smallest wish to do so) or when I am in the Sistine Chapel itself on a dull winter's day and pressed for time? The Sistine Chapel is more in the Autotype Gallery in Rathbone Place than it is at Rome.

So again he that is examining the moon through some great telescope is more in the moon than he is on earth.

### THE IMPORTANCE OF LITTLE THINGS
This is all very true but so also is the unimportance even of great things — sooner or later.

### HABITUAL TEETOTALLERS
There should be asylums for such people. But they would probably relapse into teetotalism as soon as they came out.

### THE RIGHTEOUS
The Psalmist says (Ps. xxxiv) that the righteous man shall not lack for anything that is good. Should it not rather be that those who do not lack anything that is good find it easy to be fairly righteous? Or that those who do not lack, etc., are generally taken as righteous?

### J. A. COOPER'S FUNERAL
Jones telling me about this said, 'And then a gentleman in a white surplice met us at the gate and announced himself

as the Resurrection and the Life. A man looked down into the grave when the body was lowered, and said cheerfully "It seems to be a nice gravelly soil," and then they all went away.'

We being all members of God, it is he that eats his dinner in us, as much as we that eat it in him. And when we say grace, it is really God in us thanking us for having eaten his dinner for him. Seeing then that we have to thank him for having been so kind as to select us as the vehicles of his dinner, and that he has to thank us back again for having conveyed it to him, there is a debtor and creditor account between him and us the entries in which so nearly balance that except as a matter of politeness one hardly sees much use in entering either. God is not so punctilious as some people would make him out, and provided he gets his dinner fairly good and fairly punctual and fairly cheap, he will not make a fuss about want of napkins. Highly cultured people, being further removed from the sources of God's grace, find it necessary to use more ceremony, but those who know God better understand that the only thing about which he is at all stiff is about having his dinner through you, and not through anyone else. If you wish to get the credit of having eaten it for him, when all the time it was really somebody else that did so, there is no one who is less likely to be imposed upon, or more certain to mark his displeasure in ways about which there will be no mistake. The most sensible grace, if any, should be something like this: 'I hope, O Lord, that you are going to have a good dinner, and that it will agree with me for you. Remember, O God, that at all times and in all places, whenever you have anything extra special which you would like to eat, I shall always be delighted to eat it for you'; and then after dinner there might be an alternative grace congratulatory or otherwise according as the dinner had been punctual, well-cooked, etc., or no.

### SCHUMANN'S MUSIC

I should like to like it better than I do; I dare say I could make myself like it better if I tried; but I do not like having to try to make myself like things; I like things that make me like them at once and no trying at all.

### WILD HOT WATER

A young student at Heatherley's once asked me if New Zealand was not the place where the hot water grows wild.

### IDIOTS

An idiot is a person who thinks for himself instead of letting other people think for him. He takes his own view of things and therefore not infrequently differs from his neighbours. Any person who differs considerably from his neighbours is an idiot *ipso facto*.

### A MAN

is a passing mood or thought coming and going in the mind of his country; he is the twitching of a nerve, a smile, a frown, a thought of shame or honour, as it may happen.

### GENTLEMAN

If we are asked what is the most essential characteristic that underlies this word, the word itself will guide us to gentleness, absence of browbeating or overbearing manners, absence of fuss, and generally consideration for other people.

## GOD

A writer in the *Pall Mall Gazette* — I think in 1874 or 1875, and in the autumn months but I cannot now remember — summed up Homer's conception of a God as that of a 'superlatively strong, amorous, beautiful, brave and cunning man.'

This is pretty much what a good working God ought to be, but he should also be kind and have a strong sense of humour. After having said the above the writer goes on, 'An impartial critic can judge for himself how far, if at all, this is elevated above the level of mere fetish worship.' Perhaps it is that I am not an impartial critic but if I am allowed to be so, I should say that the elevation above mere fetish worship was very considerable.

## PHYSICAL EXCELLENCE

The question whether such and such a course of conduct does or does not do physical harm is the safest test by which to try the question whether it is moral or no. If it does no harm to the body, we ought to be very chary of calling it immoral, while if it tends towards physical excellence, there should be no hesitation in calling it moral. Overwork is as immoral in the case of those who are not forced to overwork themselves (and there are many who work themselves to death for the mere inability to restrain the passion for work which masters them as the craving for drink masters a drunkard) — overwork in these cases is as immoral as over-eating or drinking. This, so far as the individual is concerned; as regards the body politic as a whole it is no doubt well that there should be some men and women so built that they cannot be stopped from working themselves to death, just as it is unquestionably well that there should be some who cannot be stopped from drinking themselves to death, if only that they may keep the horror of the habit well in evidence.

## CONSCIENTIOUSNESS

is a quality which it would be impossible to overrate if it had not been overrated.


## WHEN FATIGUED

I find it rests me to write very slowly with attention to the formation of each letter. I am often thus able to go on when I could not otherwise do so.


## POVERTY

I shun it because I have found it so apt to become contagious; but I find my constitution more seasoned against it now than formerly.


## SIGHT

and all the other senses are only modes of touch.


## FURBER THE VIOLIN-MAKER

From what my cousin [Reginald E. Worsley] and Gogin both tell me I am sure he is one of the best men we have. My cousin did not like to send Hyam to him for a violin: he did not think him worthy to have one. Furber does not want you to buy a violin unless you can appreciate it when you have it.

'He is generally a little tight on a Saturday afternoon, he always speaks the truth, but then it comes pouring out more.'

'His joints [i.e. the joints of the violins he makes] are the closest and neatest that were ever made.'

'He calls the points of a fiddle the corners. Haweis would call them the points. Haweis calls it the neck of a fiddle. Furber always the handle.'

My cousin says he would like to take his violins to bed with him.

Speaking of 'Strad' violins Furber said: 'Rough, rough linings, but they look as if they grew together.'

One day my cousin called and Furber on opening the door before saying, 'How do you do?' or word of any kind said 'The dog is dead', very quietly. The dog's name was Rose.

My cousin, having said what he thought sufficient, took up a violin and played a few notes. Furber evidently did not like it. Rose was still unburied; she was laid out in that very room. My cousin stopped. Then Mrs. Furber came in.

R.E.W. 'I am very sorry, Mrs. Furber, to hear about Rose.'

Mrs. F. 'Well, yes sir, but I suppose it is all for the best.'

R.E.W. 'I am afraid you will miss her a great deal.'

Mrs. F. 'No doubt we shall, sir, but you see she is only gone a little while before us.'

R.E.W. 'Oh, Mrs. Furber, I hope a good long while.'

Mrs. F. (brightening) 'Well, yes sir, I don't want to go just yet though Mr. Furber does say "it is a happy thing to die."'

### MR. DARWIN ON WHAT SELLS A BOOK

I remember when I was at Down we were talking of what it is that sells a book. Mr. Darwin said he did not believe it was reviews or advertisements, but simply 'being talked about' that sold a book. I believe he is quite right here, but surely a good flaming review helps to get a book talked about. I have often inquired at my publishers' after a review, and I never found one that made any perceptible increase or decrease of sale, and the same with advertisements. I think however that the review of *Erewhon* in the *Spectator* did sell a few copies of *Erewhon*, but then it was such a very strong one, and the anonymousness of the book stimulated curiosity.

has a kind of respect and reverence with it. We pay a person the compliment of acknowledging his superiority whenever we lie to him.

### MORAL INFLUENCE AND THE CARACAL

The Caracal lies on a shelf in its den in the Zoological Gardens quietly licking its fur. I go up and stand near it. It makes a face at me. I come a little nearer, it makes a worse face and raises itself up on its haunches. I stand and look. It jumps down from its shelf and makes as if it intended 'going for' me. I move back; the Caracal has exerted a moral influence over me which I have been unable to resist.

Moral influence means persuading another that one can make that other more uncomfortable than that other can make oneself.

### TASTE

comes near to eating, smell less near than taste, touch less near than smell, hearing less near than touch, seeing less near than hearing, but even 'seeing' has some remains of eating with it. So 'Virtue sickens at the sight.'

### PURSE, PERSON AND REPUTATION

A man will feel money losses more keenly than loss even of bodily health so long as he can keep his money. Take his money away, and deprive him of the means of earning any more, and his health will soon break up, but leave him his money, and even though his health breaks up and he dies, he does not mind it so much as we think. Money losses are the worst, bodily pain is next worst, and loss of reputation comes in a bad third. All other things are amusements, provided money, health and good name are untouched.

The Prince was fond of going the rounds with the police, and did so once with a few others, among whom there was a mere lad who, nevertheless, saw all that was to be seen. Before separating they liquored up, and the boy said to the detective who had gone round with them, 'Now you think yourself a very sharp fellow, I know?'

'I don't know about that, but when I've seen a person once I generally know them again.'

'I'll bet you, you don't know who I am.'

'I beg your Ladyship's pardon,' was the rejoinder.

### PLEASURE, ON KNOWING WHAT GIVES US

It is idle to say that this is easily known — it is the highest and most neglected of all arts and branches of education.

### BODY, A SMALL PART OF ONE

Though we think so much of our body, it is in reality a very small part of us; a man's true life lies not in his body but in that which he does with his body. Before birth we get together our tools; in life we use them, and thus fashion our true life which consists not in our tools and tool-box but in the work we have done with our tools. It is Handel's work, not the body with which he did the work, that drags thousands of people on a winter's night from one end of London to another; and this is the true Handel, who is a more living power among us one hundred and twenty-two years after his death than during the time he was amongst us in the body. The body changes hourly — the work changes, but infinitely more slowly.

### NEXT BEST THING TO GETTING IN WITH NICE PEOPLE

I cannot often get in with the kind of people I like. The next best thing is to plague those whom I do not like. This to a certain extent I do.

to keep us this day without being found out!


### PLEASURE

One can bring no greater reproach against a man than to say that he does not set sufficient value upon pleasure and there is no greater sign of a fool than the thinking that he can tell at once and easily what it is that pleases him. A man had better stick to known and proved pleasures, but if he will venture in quest of new ones he should not do so with a light heart.


### CRUCIFYING CHRIST

If I had been born in the times of Jesus Christ, I trust I should not have been among his disciples; I hope I might even have been among those who crucified him, but one must beware of spiritual pride. Who knows but what he himself might have been an apostle if temptation had fallen in his way?


### IMAGINATION

What tricks it plays. Thus, if we expect a person in the street, we transform a dozen impossible people into him while they are still too far off to be seen distinctly; and when we expect to hear a footstep on the stairs — as we will say the postman — we hear footsteps in every sound.


### INTELLIGENCE, OMNIPRESENCE OF
(See Maupertius and Diderot)

A little while ago no one would admit that animals had intelligence. This is now conceded. At any rate, then, vegetables had no intelligence. This is being fast disputed.

Even Darwin leans towards the view that they have intelligence. At any rate, then, the inorganic world has not got an intelligence. Even this is now being denied. Death is being defeated at all points.

## PHILOSOPHER, THE

He should have made many mistakes and been saved often by the skin of his teeth; for the skin of one's teeth is the most teaching thing about one. He should have been or at any rate believed himself a great fool and a great criminal. He should have cut himself adrift from society and yet not be without society. He should have given up all, even Christ himself, for Christ's sake. He should be above fear or love or hate, and yet know all of them extremely well. He should have lost all save a small competence, and know what a vantage ground it is to be an outcast. Destruction and death say they have heard the sound of wisdom with their ears, and the philosopher must have been close up to these if he too would hear it.

## CHRIST

I dislike him very much; still I can stand him. What I cannot stand is the wretched band of people whose profession it is to hoodwink us about him.

## CULTURE

A man should be just cultured enough to be able to look with suspicion upon culture at first, not second hand.

## GODS AND PROPHETS

It is the manner of gods and prophets to begin: 'Thou shalt have none other God or Prophet but me.' If I were to start as a God or a prophet I think I should take the line:

'Thou shalt not believe in me. Thou shalt not have me for a God. Thou shalt worship any d——d thing thou likest except me.' This should be my first and great commandment, and my second should be like unto it.

### BEE IN A WINDOW PANE

When ninety-nine hundredths of one set of phenomena are presented while the hundredth is withdrawn without apparent cause, so that we can no longer do something which according to our past experience we shall find no difficulty whatever in doing — then we may guess what a bee must feel as it goes flying up and down a window-pane. Then we have doubts thrown upon the fundamental axiom of life — i.e. that like antecedents will be followed by like consequents. On this we go mad and die in a short time.

### A PRINCIPLE OF MORALITY

It is more moral to be behind the age than in advance of it.

### ART

All that is not pertinent in art is impertinent.

### DENTISTS AND SOLICITORS

These are the people to whom we always show our best side.

### BOOKS

My main wish is to get my books into other people's rooms, and to keep other people's books out of mine.

## HEAVEN

It is in the essence of heaven that we are not to be thwarted or irritated. This involves absolute equilibrium and absolute equilibrium involves absolute unconsciousness.

## EXTREMES MEET

To be poor is to be contemptible; to be very poor is worse still, and so on, but to be actually at the point of death through poverty is to be sublime. So 'when weakness is utter, honour ceaseth.'

## INDIGESTION

may be due to the naughtiness of the stiff-necked things that we have eaten, or to the poverty of our own arguments, but it may also arise from an attempt on the part of the stomach to be too d.....d clever, and to depart from precedent inconsiderately. The healthy stomach is nothing if it is not conservative. Few radicals have good digestions. See *Life and Habit*.

## DARWIN

Frank Darwin told me his father was once standing near the hippopotamus cage when a little boy and girl aged 4 and 5 came up. The hippopotamus shut his eyes for a minute.

'That bird's dead,' said the little girl; 'come along.'

## EUCLID AND FAITH

Even Euclid cannot lay a demonstrable premise; he requires postulates and axioms which transcend demonstration, and without which he can do nothing. His superstructure is demonstration, his ground is faith. And so his *ultima ratio* is to tell a man that he is a fool by saying 'Which is absurd.' If his opponent chooses to hold out in spite of this, Euclid can do no more. Faith and authority are as necessary for him as for any one else. True he does not want us to believe very much, his yoke is tolerably easy, and he will not call a man a fool till he will have public opinion generally on his side, but none the less does he begin with dogmatism and end with persecution.

### NEEDHAM, HUDIBRAS AND MYSELF

I was completing the purchase of Queen's Villas, and had to sign my name. Mr Needham merely seeing the name and knowing none of my books, said to me, rather rudely but without meaning any mischief: 'Have you written any books like *Hudibras?*' I said promptly: 'Certainly; *Erewhon* is quite as good a book as *Hudibras.*' This was coming it too strong for him, so he thought I had not heard and repeated his question. I said again as before, and he shut up. I sent him a copy of *Erewhon* immediately after we had completed. It was rather tall talk on my part, I admit, but he should not have challenged me unprovoked.

### GOD, TO THE LEXICOGRAPHER

is simply the word that comes next to 'go-cart', and nothing more.

### VITALITY OF CHRISTIANITY

This is held to be an argument for its truth. Surely, then, the vitality of unbelief should count for something? Persecution has been tried against it in vain; it is always being supposed to be killed, but it always comes back again stronger than before.

Gogin was one day going down Cleveland Street and saw an old, lean, careworn man crying over the body of his dog which had been just run over and killed by the old man's own cart. I have no doubt it was the dog's fault, for the man was in great distress; as for the dog itself there it lay, all swelled and livid where the wheel had gone over it, its eyes protruded from their sockets and its tongue lolled out, but it was dead. The old man gazed on it helplessly weeping, for some time, and then got a large piece of brown paper, in which he wrapped up the body of his favourite; he tied it neatly with a piece of string, and placing it in his cart went homeward with a heavy heart. The day was dull, the gutters were full of cabbage stalks, and the air resounded with the cry of costermongers.

On this a Japanese gentleman who had watched the scene lifted up his voice and made the bystanders a set oration; he was very yellow, he had long black hair, and was a typical Japanese, but he spoke English perfectly. He said the scene they had all just witnessed was a very sad one, and that it ought not to be passed over entirely without comment. He explained that it was very nice of the old man to be so sorry about his dog and to be so careful of its remains, and that he and all the bystanders must sympathize with this good man in his grief, to the expression of which sympathy both with the man and with the poor dog he had thought fit with all respect to make them his present speech.

I have not the man's words, but Gogin said they were like a Japanese drawing; that is to say, wonderfully charming, and showing great knowledge, but not done in the least after the manner in which a European would do them. As for the bystanders, they stood open-mouthed and could make nothing of it; they liked it, and the Japanese gentleman liked addressing them. When he left off and went away, they followed him with their eyes, speechless.

## PECKSNIFF OF SCIENCE

I do not see how I can well call Mr. Darwin the Pecksniff of Science, though this is exactly what he is; but I think I may call Lord Bacon the Pecksniff of his age and then, a little later, say that Mr. Darwin is the Bacon of the Victorian era. This will be like passing one item through two different accounts, as though I had made Pecksniff debtor to Bacon and Bacon debtor to Darwin, instead of entering Pecksniff debtor to Darwin at once.

## SPECIALISM AND GENERALISM

Woe to the specialist who is not a pretty fair generalist, and to the generalist who is not also a bit of a specialist.

## MY RANDOM PASSAGES

Emanuel at the Century Club very kindly and hesitatingly ventured to suggest to me that I should get some friend to go over my MS. before printing it; a judicious editor would have prevented me from printing many a bit which it seemed to him was written too recklessly and off-hand. The fact is that the more reckless and random the passage is the more carefully it has been submitted to friends and considered and re-considered; without the support of friends I should never have dared to print one half of what I have printed.

## THE ELECTRIC LIGHT IN ITS INFANCY

I heard a woman in a bus boring her lover about the electric light; she wanted to know this and that, and the poor lover was helpless. Then she said she wanted to know how it was regulated; at last she settled down by saying that she knew it was in its infancy; the word 'infancy' seemed to have a soothing effect upon her, for she said no

93

more, but leaning her head against her lover's shoulder composed herself to slumber.

### RELIGION

Is there any religion whose members can be pointed to as distinctly more amiable and trustworthy than those of any other? If so this should be enough. I find the nicest and best people generally profess no religion at all, but are ready to like the best men of all religions.

### MISS BUCKLEY

She said to me the other day:

'Why don't you write another *Erewhon?*'

I said 'Why Miss Buckley, *Life and Habit* was another *Erewhon.*'

They say these things to me continually to plague me, and make out that I could do one good book, but never any more.

### GRACE AND GOODNESS

There is no true gracefulness which is not epitomized goodness.

### IMAGINATION

I read once of a man who was cured of a dangerous illness by eating his doctor's prescription, which he understood was the medicine itself. So Moorhouse imagined he was being converted to Christianity by reading Burton's *Anatomy of Melancholy*, which he had got by mistake for Butler's *Analogy*, on the recommendation of a friend. But it puzzled him a good deal.

do not let people represent me as one who suffered from misrepresentation and neglect. I was neglected and mis-represented; very likely not half as much as I supposed, but nevertheless to some extent neglected and misrepre-sented. I growl at this sometimes, but, if the question was seriously put to me whether I would go on as I am or be-come famous in my own lifetime, I have no hesitation about which I should prefer. I will willingly pay the few hundreds of pounds which the neglect of my works costs me in order to be let alone and not plagued by the odious people who would come round me if I were known. The probability is that I shall remain after my death as obscure as I am now; if this is so the obscurity will be probably merited, and if it is not a fact, my books will not only work as well without my having been known in my lifetime but a great deal better; my follies and blunders will the better escape notice, to the enhancing of the value of anything that may be found in my books. The only two things I should greatly care about if I had more money, are a few more country outings and a little more varied and better cooked food; nicer things and more expensive things to eat and drink.

PS. March.5.1895. I have long since obtained every-thing that a reasonable man can wish for.

<br>

### WIT

There is no Professor of Wit at either University. Surely they might as reasonably have a professor of wit as of poetry.

<br>

### PRAYERS

I dropped saying them suddenly without malice prepense, once for all. It was the night I went on board ship to start for New Zealand, Sept. 29, 1859. The night before

I had said my prayers and doubted not that I was always going on to say them, as I always had done hitherto. That night I suppose the sense of change was so great that it shook them quietly off. I was not then a sceptic. I had got as far as disbelief in infant baptism, but no further. I felt no compunction of conscience, however, about leaving off my morning and evening prayers — simply I could no longer say them.

## A RECALCITRANT BLACKSMITH

A new curate was explaining to the village blacksmith the nature of miracles. The blacksmith was docile and accepted the story of Jonah in the whale's belly. As the curate put it, he said he saw no difficulty in it, and was ready to believe it. The curate then went on to Shadrach, Meshach and Abednego in the burning fiery furnace. 'Now the furnace,' said the curate, 'was many times larger and hotter than your forge.' This riled the blacksmith; he was proud of his forge which had been his father's before him, besides he could realize a furnace to himself. 'No,' he said, 'I don't believe it, and I don't believe the bloody fish story either.' And so the matter dropped.

## GOD

is a respecter of persons — no one more so.

## EATING, AND ALL THE SENSES

They are all a kind of eating. They are all touch, and eating is touch carried to the bitter end.

## THE GREAT CHARACTERS OF FICTION

live as truly as the memories of dead men. For the life after death it is not necessary that a man or woman should have lived.

As a boy, from twelve years old or so, I always worshipped him; at Cambridge when Sykes began to play Beethoven I would leave the room: I did not like him; little by little I began to like him, and then I played him, and Bach and Mendelssohn's *Songs without Words* and thought them lovely, but I always liked Handel best. Little by little, however, I was talked over to placing him and Bach and Beethoven on a par as the greatest and I thought I did not know which was the best man.

One night, when I was about thirty, I was at an evening party at Mrs Longden's, and met an old West End clergyman of the name of Smalley. I said I did not know which was greatest Handel, Bach or Beethoven; he said: 'I am surprised at that, I should have thought you would have known.'

'Which,' said I, 'is the greatest?'

'Handel,' was the answer.

I knew he was right and have never wavered since. I suppose I was really of this opinion already, but it was not till I got a little touch from outside that I knew it.

## PHILOSOPHY

as a general rule is like stirring mud or not letting a sleeping dog lie. It professes to appease our ultimate 'Why?' In truth it is generally the solution of a *simplex ignotum* by a *complex ignotius*. This at least is my experience of everything that has been presented to me as philosophy. I have often had my 'Why's' answered with so much mystifying matter that I have left off pressing them through fatigue, but this is not having my ultimate 'Why?' appeased. It is being knocked out of time.

## HOLY GHOST IN A HAT

I was with my Aunt Worsley at the National Gallery once, and we were before Van Eyck's picture of John

Arnolfini and his wife (if the picture is, indeed, this). My Aunt mistook it for an Annunciation, and said, 'Dear, dear, what a funny notion to put the Holy Ghost in a hat.'

### EATING, AND SITTING QUIET AFTERWARDS

This is akin to not walking about during service, so as to disturb the congregation. We are catechizing and converting our proselytes, and there should be no row. As you get old, you must digest more quietly still.

### TRÜBNER AND MYSELF

When I went back to Trübner after Bogue had failed I had a talk with him and Mr. Edwardes his partner. I could see they had lost all faith in my literary prospects. Trübner told me I was a 'homo unius libri', meaning Erewhon. He said 'You are in a very solitary position.' I said I knew I was, but it suited me. I said, 'I pay my way; when I was with you before I never owed you money, you find me now not owing my publisher money, but my publisher in debt to me. I never owe so much as a tailor's bill; beyond secured debts, I do not owe £5 in the world and never have' (which is quite true). 'I get my Summer's holiday in Italy every year; I live very quietly and cheaply, but it suits my health and tastes, and I have no acquaintances but those I value. My friends stick by me. If I was to get in with these literary and scientific people I should hate them and they me. I should fritter away my time, and my freedom without getting a quid pro quo: as it is, I am free and I give the swells every now and then such a facer as they get from no one else. Of course I don't expect to get on in a commercial sense at present; I do not go the right way to work for this, but I am going the right way to secure a lasting reputation, and this is what I do care for. You cannot have both — a man must make up his mind which he means going in for. I have gone in for posthumous fame, and I see no step in my literary career which I do not think calculated to promote my being held in esteem when the heat of passion has subsided.'

Trübner shrugged his shoulders. He plainly does not believe that I shall succeed in getting a hearing; he thinks the combination of the religious and cultured world too strong for me to stand against. If he means that the reviewers will burke me as far as they can, no doubt he is right; but when I am dead there will be other reviewers, and I have already done enough to secure that they shall from time to time look me up. They won't bore me then, but they will be just as odious as the present ones.

## MANNERISM

To forbid all mannerism is to forbid form and insist on everything's being thought out afresh *de novo*.

## EATING

An animal that refuses to let another eat it has the courage of its convictions, and if it gets eaten dies a martyr to them.

## BODY AND MIND

We shall never get straight till we leave off trying to separate these two things. Mind is not a thing at all or, if it is, we know nothing about it. It is a function of body. Body is not a thing at all or, if it is, we know nothing about it. It is a function of mind.

### THE ROSSETTI EXHIBITION

I have been to see it and am pleased to find it more odious than I had even dared to hope. I met Rossetti once at Wallis's; there were three besides myself. I disliked them all very much, but Rossetti the most.

### PEOPLE LIKE BIRDS IN THE HEDGES

The people we see going about are like birds we see in the hedges — they look all right, but for the most part they are hard up, or nearly so.

### FATHERS

Those who have never had a father can at any rate never know the sweets of losing one. To most men the death of his father is a new lease of life.

### CRUCIFYING CHRIST

Christ was only crucified once and for a few hours. Think of the hundreds of thousands whom Christ has been crucifying in a quiet way ever since.

### MATTER AND MIND

We have, or at any rate think we have, a fairly definite idea before us when we talk of matter, but I don't think we ever think we have any definite idea about our own meaning when we talk of mind.

### FOUNDATIONS OF MORALITY

are like all other foundations; if you dig too much about them the superstructure will come tumbling down.

turns on whether the pleasure precedes the pain or follows it (provided it is sufficient). Thus it is immoral to get drunk because the headache comes after the drinking, but if the headache came first and the drunkenness afterwards, it would be moral to get drunk.

### A LITERARY MAN'S TEST

Molière's reading to his housemaid has I think been misunderstood as though he in some way wanted to see the effect upon the housemaid and make her a judge of his work. If she was an unusually clever smart girl, this might be well enough, but the supposition commonly is that she was a typical housemaid and nothing more. If Molière ever did read to her it was because the mere act of reading aloud put his work before him in a new light, and by constraining his attention to every line made him judge it more rigorously. I always intend to, and generally do, read what I write aloud to some one — any one almost will do, but he should not be so clever that I am afraid of him. I feel weak places at once when I read aloud where I thought as long as I read to myself only that the passage was all right.

### 'CLEANSE THOU ME FROM MY SECRET SINS'

I heard a man moralizing on this, and shocked him by saying demurely that I did not mind these so much, if I could get rid of those that were obvious to other people.

### WHAT TO LEARN

Never try and find out anything, or try to learn anything till you have found the not knowing it to be a nuisance to you for some time. Then you will remember it, but not otherwise. Let knowledge importune you before you will hear it. Our schools and Universities go on the precisely opposite system.

### DEATH, THE FEAR OF

This is instinctive because in so many past generations we have feared death. But how did we come to know what death is, so that we should fear it? The answer to this is that we do not know what death is and that this is why we fear it.

### UNNATURAL

Men misuse this word as they do the word 'spontaneous' — as though anything which is a part of nature could be 'unnatural'. Whatever is, is natural. Instead of saying 'unnatural' they should say 'unintelligible to myself', 'disgusting', or what not.

### IDENTITY WITH ONE'S ANCESTORS AND CONTEMPORARIES

We are so far identical with our ancestors and our contemporaries that it is very rarely we can see anything that they do not see. It is not unjust that the sins of the fathers should be visited upon the children, for the children committed the sins when in the persons of their fathers; they ate the sour grapes before they were born: true they have forgotten the pleasure now, but so has a man with a sick headache forgotten the pleasure of getting drunk the night before.

### MELCHISEDEC

was a really happy man. He was without father, without mother and without descent; he was an incarnate bachelor. Jones says he was 'a born orphan.'

I know a man, and one whom people generally call a very clever one, who, when his eye catches mine if I meet him at an at home or an evening party, beams upon me from afar with the expression of an intellectual rattlesnake on having espied an intellectual rabbit. Through any crowd that man will come sidling towards me, ruthless and irresistible as fate; while I foreknowing my doom sidle also him-wards, and flatter myself that no sign of my inward apprehension has escaped me.

## MATTHEW ARNOLD ON RIGHTEOUSNESS

According to Mr Matthew Arnold, as we find the highest traditions of grace, beauty and the heroic virtues among the Greeks and Romans, so we derive our highest ideal of righteousness from Jewish sources. Righteousness was to the Jew what strength and beauty were to the Greek, or fortitude to the Roman.

This sounds well, but can we think that the Jews taken as a nation were really more righteous than the Greeks and Romans? Could they indeed be so if they were less strong, graceful, and enduring? In some respects they may have been; every nation has its strong points; but surely there has been a nearly unanimous verdict for many generations, that the typical Greek and Roman is a higher, nobler person than the typical Jew — and this referring not to the modern Jew who may perhaps be held to have been injured by centuries of oppression, but to the Hebrew of the time of the old prophets and of the most prosperous eras in the history of the nation. If three men could be set before us as the most perfect Greek, Roman, and Jew respectively, and if we could choose which we would have our only son most resemble, is it not likely we should find ourselves preferring the Greek or Roman to the Jew? And does not this involve that we hold the two former to be the more righteous in a broad sense of the word?

I dare not say that we owe no benefits to the Jewish nation, I do not feel sure whether we do or do not, but I can see no good thing that I can point to as a notoriously Hebrew contribution to our moral and intellectual well-being, as I can point to our law and say that it is Roman, or to our fine arts and say that they are based on what the Greeks and Italians taught us; on the contrary if asked what feature of post-Christian life we had derived most distinctly from Hebrew sources I should say at once 'intolerance' — the desire to dogmatize about matters whereon the Greek and Roman held certainty to be at once unimportant and unattainable. This, with all its train of bloodshed and family disunion, is chargeable to the Jewish rather than to any other account.

There is yet another vice which occurs readily to any one who reckons up the characteristics which we derive mainly from the Jews — it is one the word for which we have derived from a Jewish sect, and which we call 'Pharisaism.' I do not mean to say that no Greek and Roman was ever a sanctimonious hypocrite; still, sanctimoniousness does not readily enter into our notions of Greeks and Romans and it does so enter into our notions of the old Hebrews. Of course we are all of us sanctimonious sometimes. Horace himself is so when he talks about *aurum irrepertum et sic melius situm*, etc.; as for Virgil he was a prig pure and simple; still on the whole sanctimoniousness was not a Greek and Roman vice, and it was a Hebrew one. True, they stoned their prophets freely, but these are not the Hebrews to whom Mr Arnold is referring; they are the ones whom it is the custom to leave out of sight and out of mind as far as possible, so that they should hardly count as Hebrews at all, and none of our characteristics should be ascribed to them.

Taking their literature, I cannot see that it deserves the

praises that have been lavished upon it. *The Song of Solomon* and the book of *Esther* are the most interesting in the old testament, but these are the very ones that make the smallest pretensions to holiness, and even these are neither of them of very transcendent merit. They would stand no chance of being accepted by Messrs. Cassell and Co., or by any biblical publisher of the present day. Chatto and Windus might take the *Song of Solomon*, but with this exception I doubt if there is a publisher in London who would give a guinea for the pair. *Ecclesiastes* contains some fine things but is strongly tinged with pessimism, cynicism and affectation. Some of the proverbs are good, but not many of them are in common use. *Job* contains some fine passages, and so do some of the *Psalms* — but the psalms generally are poor, and, for the most part they are querulous, spiteful and introspective into the bargain. Mudie would not take thirteen copies of the lot if they were to appear now for the first time — unless indeed their royal authorship were to arouse an adventitious interest in them, or unless their author were a rich man who played his cards judiciously with the reviewers. As for the prophets — we know what appears to have been the opinion formed concerning them by those who should have been best acquainted with them; I can form little idea about the merits of the controversy between them and their fellow-countrymen, but I have read their works, and am of opinion that they will not hold their own against such masterpieces of modern literature as we will say *Pilgrim's Progress*, *Robinson Crusoe*, *Gulliver's Travels* or *Tom Jones*. 'Whether these be prophecyings,' exclaims the Apostle, 'they shall fail;' on the whole I should say that Isaiah and Jeremiah have failed.

I would join issue with Mr Matthew Arnold on yet another point — I understand him to imply that righteousness should be a man's highest aim in life — I do not like setting up righteousness nor yet anything else as an aim in life; a man should have any number of little aims about which he should be conscious, and for which he should have names, but he should have neither name for, nor consciousness concerning the main aim of his life. Whatever we do we must try and do it rightly — this is obvious — but righteousness implies something much more than this — it conveys to our minds not only the desire to get whatever we have taken in hand as nearly right as possible, but also the general reference of our lives to the supposed will of an unseen but supreme power. Granted that there is such a power, and granted that we should obey its will, we are the more likely to do this the less we concern ourselves about the matter, and the more we confine our attention to the things immediately round about us which seem, so to speak, entrusted to us as the natural and legitimate sphere of our activity. I believe a man will get the most useful information on these matters from modern European sources; next to these he will get most from Athens and ancient Rome; Mr Matthew Arnold notwithstanding, I do not think he will get anything from Jerusalem which he will not find better and more easily elsewhere.

### THOUGHTS ON VICE AND VIRTUE

Virtue is something which it would be impossible to over-rate if it had not been over-rated. The world can ill spare any vice which has obtained long and largely among civilized people. Such a vice must have good which cannot be well spared along with its deformities. The question 'How, if every one were to do so and so?' may be met with another 'How, if no one were to do it?' We are a body corporate as well as a collection of individuals.

As a matter of private policy I doubt whether the moderately vicious are more unhappy than the moderately virtuous. 'Very vicious' is certainly less happy than 'tolerably virtuous,' but this is about all. What pass muster as the extremes of virtue probably make people quite as unhappy as extremes of vice do.

The truest virtue has ever inclined toward excess rather than asceticism; that she should do this is reasonable as well as observable, for virtue should be as nice a calculator of chances as other people and will make due allowance for the chance of not being found out.

Virtue knows that it is impossible to get on without compromise, and tunes herself, as it were, a trifle sharp to allow for an inevitable fall in playing. So the psalmist says, 'If thou, Lord, shouldest be extreme to mark what is done amiss', and by this he admits that the highest conceivable form of virtue still leaves room for some compromise with vice. So again Shakespeare writes, 'They say best men are moulded out of faults; And, for the most, become much more the better For being a little bad.'

### A DRUNKARD

would not give money to sober people. He said they would only eat it, and buy clothes and send their children to school with it.

### 'DON'T BE FASTIDIOUS, CHILD'

There was an old woman in Ludlow who gave her servant the key of the house door to unlock the tea-caddy. The maid remonstrated, but her mistress said, 'Don't be fastidious, child, take the key I give you.'[1]

### SUN GOING ROUND THE EARTH

A child asked the same old lady whether the earth went round the sun or the sun round the earth. 'Lor, child,' she

[1] A footnote by Butler identifies this old lady as 'Mrs. Hughes, mother to T. Smart Hughes and to Mrs. Monk, wife to the Bishop of Gloucester.'

said, 'what questions you ask, to be sure. I thought it all over yesterday and I can't think it all over again to-day; what I thought then I think now; sometimes one and sometimes the other.'

### ASSOCIATED IDEAS

When we are impressed by a few only, or perhaps only one of a number of ideas which are bonded pleasantly together, there is hope; when we see a good many there is expectation; when we have had so many presented to us that we have expected confidently and the remaining ideas have not turned up, there is disappointment. So the sailor said in the play:

'Here are my arms, here is my manly bosom, but where's my Mary?'

### PROVIDENCE ITSELF

could not be more absolutely improvident.

### MYSELF AND THE RETURN OF THE JEWS TO PALESTINE

A man called on me last week (Mar. 20, 1883) and proposed to me gravely that I should write a book on an idea which he had hit upon, which should lead to the return of the Jews to Palestine; he said he had called on me because of my literary reputation; he said he knew how he could get the poor Jews back; but that the difficulty lay with the Rothschilds, the Oppenheims, etc. Still with my assistance, it could be done.

I was much flattered, but declined to hear the scheme on the ground that I did not care twopence whether the Rothschilds went back to Palestine or not. This was felt to be an obstacle, but he began to try and make me care, and then I had to get rid of him.

## CLOTHES DRYING ON HINDHEAD

On Hindhead, this Easter we saw a family wash hung out to dry. There were papa's two great nightshirts, and mamma's two lesser nightshirts, and then the children's smaller articles of clothing and mamma's drawers and the girls' drawers all full swollen with a strong north-east wind, but mamma's nightshirt or one of them, was not so well pinned on, and, instead of being full of steady wind like the others it kept blowing up and down as though she were preaching wildly. We stood and laughed for ten minutes. The housewife came to the window and wondered at us, but we could not resist the pleasure of watching the absurdly lifelike gestures which the nightshirt made. I should like a holy family with clothes drying in the back ground.

## NO PLACE TO PUT HIS BREAD AND BUTTER IN AT

After the Crimean War when people took to wearing beards and moustaches I heard of one little girl who would not kiss a friend of her mother's whose mouth was hidden by his moustache, because, as she said, she could not love him; he had no place to put his bread and butter in at.

## ART NOTE. ACCURACY

After having spent years in striving to be accurate, we must spend as many more in discovering when and how to be inaccurate.

## 'THEY DAUBED IT WITH SLIME'

This is one of the few verses in the Bible that I used to like when I was a child.

## HANDEL AND MYSELF

Pauli shaped me more than any man I have ever known, but of all dead men Handel has had the largest place in my thoughts. In fact I should say he and his music have been the central fact in my life ever since I was old enough to know of the existence of either music or life. All day long — whether I am writing or painting or walking — but always — I have his music in my head, and if I lose sight of it and of him for an hour or two as of course I sometimes do, this is as much as I do. I believe I am not exaggerating when I say that I have never been a day since I was thirteen without having Handel in my mind many times over.

### HANDEL AND THE PONTIFEX NOVEL

It cost me a great deal to make Ernest (in *The Way of All Flesh*) play Beethoven and Mendelssohn — I did it simply *ad captandum*, as a matter of fact he played none but early Italian, old English music, and Handel — but Handel most of all.

### DOING THINGS FOR THE WORKING CLASSES

It is only our conceit — as though our way of living and looking at things must be so much better than other people's — which makes us want to 'do things for the working classes'.

### SCIENCE

If it tends to thicken the crust of ice on which, as it were, we are skating, it is all right. If it tries to find, or professes to have found, the solid ground at the bottom of the water it is all wrong.

### BEER AT 4d A POT

I heard a man say to another at Abbey Wood: 'I went to live down there just about the time that beer came down from 5d. to 4d. a pot. That will give you an idea when it was.'

### THE EYE, CREDULOUS, ART NOTE

Painters may remember that the eye as a general rule is a good simple credulous organ — very ready to take things on trust if it be told them with any confidence of assertion.

### DEATH AND BIRTH

We commonly know that we are going to die but we do not know that we are going to be born. Is this so? We may have had the most gloomy forebodings on this head and forgotten all about them. At any rate we know no more about the very end of our lives than about the very beginning. We come up unconsciously, and go down unconsciously.

### THE WORLD AND SELF INTEREST

The world will always be governed by self interest: we should not try and stop this: we should try and make the self interest of cads a little more coincident with that of decent people.

### CRITICISM BY JUDGE AND JURY

Critics generally come to be critics not by reason of their fitness for this, but of their unfitness for anything else. Books should be tried by a judge and jury as though they were a crime, and counsel should be heard on both sides.

### SHADE, COLOUR AND REPUTATION

When a thing is near and in light, colour and form are important. When far and in shadow, they are unimportant. Form and colour are like reputations, which when they become shady are much of a muchness.

### SUBJECT — A FREETHINKING FATHER

A freethinking father has an illegitimate son (which he considers the proper thing) and finds this son taking to immoral ways. He turns Christian, becomes a clergyman and insists on marrying.

### GAINING ONE'S POINT

It is not he who gains the exact point in dispute who scores most in controversy — but he who has shown the better temper.

### CHAIRS AND CAMPSTOOLS

are seats under domestication. Wild seats are seldom comfortable.

### MYSELF AND WASHING UP IN NEW ZEALAND

In New Zealand for a long time I had to do the washing up after each meal. I used to do the knives first, for it might please God to take me before I came to the forks, and then what a sell it would have been to have done the forks rather than the knives.

### IS LIFE WORTH LIVING?

This is a question for an embryo not for a man.

### STOMACH

One's stomach is one's internal environment.

### WILD ANIMALS AND ONE'S RELATIONS

If one would watch them and know what they are driving at, one must keep perfectly still.

## THE LITTLE WOOLLY PIG OF GOD

There was an inland African tribe in a country too hot for sheep, who had therefore no definite idea about a lamb. The missionary who converted them brought the idea somewhat nearer to their comprehension by calling Christ 'the littly woolly pig of God'.

## IMAGINATION

At Ivy Hatch while we were getting beer in the inner parlour we heard a confused melee of voices in the bar, amid which I heard a man say:

'Imagination will do any b—— thing almost.'

I was writing *Life and Habit* at the time and was much tempted to put this passage in. Nothing truer has ever been said about imagination. Then the voice was heard addressing the barman and saying:

'I suppose you wouldn't trust me with a quart of beer would you?'

## THE THIEF

Once committed beyond a certain point he should not worry himself too much about not being a thief any more. Thieving is God's message to him. Let him try and be a good thief.

## DUMB-BELLS

Regard them with suspicion as academic.

## WORDS

are not as satisfactory as we should like them to be, but, like our neighbours, we have got to live with them and must make the best and not the worst of them.

## ANDROMEDA

The dragon was never in better health and spirits than on the morning when Perseus came down upon him. It is said that Andromeda told Perseus she had been thinking how remarkably well he was looking. He had got up quite in his usual health, etc. When I said this to Ballard [a fellow art-student at Heatherley's], and the other thing I said about Andromeda in *Life and Habit*, he said he wished it had been so in the poets. I looked at him and said that I too was 'the poets.'

## MAN

is God's highest present development. He is the latest thing in God.

## TRUTH

Any fool can tell the truth, but it requires a man of some sense to know how to lie well.

## ORGANS

The same skill which now guides them and us in arts and inventions was at one time exercised upon the invention of these very organs themselves. The ligaments which bind the tendons of our feet or the valves of our blood vessels are the ingenious enterprises of individual cells who saw a want, felt that they could supply it, and have thus won themselves a position among the old aristocracy of the body politic.

## PRETENCE OF KNOWLEDGE

I was nearly 40 before I felt how stupid it was to pretend to know things that I did not know, and I still often catch myself doing so.  Not one of my school-masters taught me this, but altogether otherwise.

### GOD IS LOVE
I dare say — but what a mischievous devil love is!

### I HATE THEM WHICH HATE GOD
but I don't find God sufficiently hating them which hate me.

### PORTRAITS OF ONESELF
A man's work whether in music, painting or literature is always a portrait of himself.

### ART NOTE, THE OLD MASTERS AND THEIR PUPILS
The old masters taught, not because they liked teaching, nor yet from any idea of serving the cause of art, nor yet because they were paid to teach by the parents of their pupils.  The parents probably paid no money at first.  They took pupils and taught them because they had more work to do than they could get through, and they wanted some one to help them.  They sold the pupil's work as their own, just as people do now who take apprentices.  When people can sell a pupil's work they will teach the pupil all they know, and they will see he does it.  This is the secret of the whole matter.

### THE SEVEN DEADLY SINS
Want of money, bad health, bad temper, chastity, family ties, knowing that you know things, and believing in the Christian religion.

are water which has had a long talk either with a vine or with a cow, and has been thoroughly satisfied.

### EATING AND PROSELYTIZING

All eating is a kind of proselytizing — a kind of dogmatizing which maintains that the eater's way of looking at things is better than the eatee's. We convert it, or try to do so, to our own way of thinking, and when the food sticks to its own opinion and refuses to be converted, we say it disagrees with us.

### THE PRODIGAL SON

Not very long after his return he probably again felt that he fain would fill his belly with the husks that the swine did eat, but no man gave to him. The veal (which, he said, was taken from some tough old calf) had to be finished.

### MARRIAGE

It is not nice to be wedded to anything — not even to a theory.

### IF GOD WANTS US TO DO A THING

he should make his wishes sufficiently clear. Sensible people will wait till he has done this before paying much attention to him.

### GOD

is not so black as he has been painted — nor yet so white.

## THE CREDIT SYSTEM

The whole world is carried on on the credit system. If every one was to demand payment in hard cash there would be universal bankruptcy. I mean that faith and superstition are at the bases of our very organism.

## GOING TO A DOCTOR

is having such a row with your cells that you refer them to your solicitor. Sometimes you as it were strike against them and stop their food, when they go on strike against yourself. Sometimes you file a bill in chancery against them and go to bed.

## DEATH

There will come a supreme moment in which there will be neither care for ourselves or others, but a complete abandon, a *sans souci* of unspeakable indifference, and this moment will never be taken from us; time cannot rob us of it, but as far as we are concerned will last for ever and ever without flying. So that even for the most wretched and most guilty there is a haven at last where neither moth nor rust doth corrupt and where thieves do not break through nor steal. To himself every one is an immortal. He may know that he is going to die, but he can never know that he is dead.

## TRAGIC EXPRESSION

The three occasions when I have seen a really tragic expression upon a face were as follows.

When Mrs. Inglis in my room at Montreal heard my sausages frying as she thought too furiously in the kitchen, and left me hurriedly, the folds of her dress as she swept out of the room were Niobean.

I saw a certain lady with a tureen of soup before her, and also a plate of the same to which she had just helped herself. There was meat in the soup and I suppose she had got a bit she did not like; instead of leaving it she swiftly, stealthily, picked it up from her plate when she thought no one was looking, and with an expression which Mrs. Siddons might have studied for a performance of Clytemnestra, popped it back into the tureen. I have rarely seen such a look upon any one's face.

I saw an alarm of fire on an emigrant ship in mid-ocean, when I was going to New Zealand, and the women rushed aft with faces as in a massacre of the innocents.

### A SAILOR BOY AND SOME CHICKENS

A pretty girl in the train had some chirping chickens about ten days old in a box labelled 'German egg powders. One packet equal to six eggs.' A handsome sailor boy got in at Basingstoke, a quiet, reserved youth, well behaved and certainly unusually good-looking. By and by the chickens were taken out of the box and fed with biscuit on the carriage seat. This thawed the boy who though he fought against it for some time yielded to irresistible fascination and said:

'What are they?'

'Chickens,' said the girl.

'Will they grow bigger?'

'Yes.'

Then the boy said with an expression of infinite wonder: 'And did you hatch them from they powders?'

We all laughed till the boy blushed and I was very sorry for him. If we had said they had been hatched from the powders he would have certainly believed us.

### THE BEST OF FRIENDS MUST

meet.

They could eat most things, but they drew the line at prophets.

## SOLICITORS

are our money doctors.

## SCIENTISTS

There are two classes, those who want to know, and do not care whether others think they know or not, and those who do not much care about knowing, but care very greatly about being reputed as knowing.

## ART NOTE — BELLINI GIORGIONE AND TITIAN

Think of, and look at, your work as though it were done by your enemy. If you look at it to admire it you are lost.

Any man, no matter how old, will go on improving so long as he is *bona fide* dissatisfied with his work. If he does not see where his work is wrong he will come to do so if he wants to, but unless he wants and pretty badly too — he never will. Think of Giovanni Bellini and Titian and Giorgione. They came to him in the same year as boys of 15 when Bellini was 63 years old — what a day for painting was that! All Bellini's best work was done thence-forward. I know nothing in the history of art so touching as this. (I have changed my mind about Titian. I don't like him.)

## DEATH

Any very great and sudden change is a death.

does not intend people, and does not like people, to be too good. He likes them neither too good nor too bad, but a little too bad is more venial with him than a little too good.

## MEAD

is the lowest of the intoxicants, just as Church is the lowest of the dissipations and caraway seeds the lowest of the condiments.

## AT MRS. SALTER'S

Last week (Oct. 27th, 1883) I went to Basingstoke and met Mrs. Thiselton Dyer. She is a daughter of Sir Joseph Hooker and is very advanced. I said I should go to church in the evening. I said this, partly because I knew she would not like it, and partly to please Miss Burd, who I knew would. Mrs. Dyer did her best to dissuade me. 'Didn't it bore me? And, holding my opinions, ought I not to let people see what I thought?' etc. I said that, having given up Christianity, I was not going to be hampered by its principles. It was the substance of Christianity, and not its accessories of external worship, that I so objected to; and I would be unprincipled whenever and in whatever way I thought convenient. So I went to church out of pure cussedness. She could not make it out at all. But I won't go again, not just yet awhile if I can help it, for it *did* bore me. I had not been for more than seven years.

## TRUTH AND ERROR

There is no such source of error as the pursuit of absolute truth.

## VITALITY OF THE DEAD

The constant tendency of modern invention is to increase the vitality of those who are commonly called dead.

It is seldom very hard to do one's duty when one knows what it is, but it is often exceedingly difficult to find this out.

## TOOLS

A tool is anything whatsoever which is used by an intelligent being for realizing its object.

The idea of a desired end is inseparable from that of a tool. The very essence of a tool is the being an instrument for the achievement of a purpose. We say that a man is the tool of another, meaning that he is being used for the furtherance of that other's ends — and this constitutes him a machine in use.

This being so, the word 'tool' implies also the existence of a living intelligent being capable of desiring the end for which the tool is used — for this is involved in the idea of a desired end. And as few tools grow naturally fit for use (for even a stick or a fuller's teasel must be cut from their places and modified to some extent before they can be called tools) the word 'tool' implies not only a purpose and a purposer, but a purposer who can see in what manner his purpose can be achieved, and who can contrive (or find ready-made and fetch and employ) the tool which shall achieve it.

Strictly speaking nothing is a tool unless during actual use. Nevertheless if a thing has been made for the express purpose of being used as a tool it is commonly called a tool, whether it is in actual use or no. Thus hammers, chisels, etc., are called tools though lying idle in a tool-box. What is meant is that though not actually being used as instruments at the present moment, they bear the impress of their object, and are so often in use that we may speak of them as though they always were so.

Strictly a thing is a tool or not a tool just as it may happen to be in use or not. Thus a stone may be picked up and used to hammer a nail with: the stone is not a tool until picked up with an eye to use; it is a tool as soon as this happens — if thrown away immediately the nail has been driven home the stone is a tool no longer. We see, therefore, matter alternating between a toolish or organic state and an untoolish or inorganic. Where there is intention it is organic, where there is no intention it is inorganic. Perhaps however the word 'tool' should cover also the remains of a tool so long as there are manifest signs that the object was a tool once.

The simplest tool I can think of is a piece of gravel used for making a road. Nothing is done to it, it owes its being a tool simply to the fact that it subserves a purpose. A broken piece of granite used for macadamizing a road is a more complex instrument, about the toolishness of which no doubt can be entertained. It will, however, I think, be held that even a piece of gravel found *in situ* and left there untouched, provided it is so left because it was deemed suitable for a road which was designed to pass over this spot, would become a tool in virtue of the recognition of its utility, while a similar piece of gravel a yard off on either side the proposed road would not be a tool.

The essence of a 'tool', therefore, lies in something outside the tool itself. It is not in the head of the hammer, nor in the handle, nor in the combination of the two that the essence of mechanical characteristics exists, but in the recognition of its utility, and in the forces directed through it in virtue of this recognition.

This appears more plainly when we reflect that a very complex machine if intended for use by children whose aim is not serious ceases to rank in our minds as a tool, and becomes a toy. It is seriousness of aim and recognition of suitability for the achievement of that aim, and not anything in the tool itself, that makes the tool.

The goodness or badness, again, of a tool depends not upon anything within the tool as regarded without relation to the user, but upon the ease or difficulty experienced by the person using it in comparison with what he or others of average capacity would experience if they had used a tool of a different kind. Thus the same tool may be good for one man and bad for another.

It seems to me that all tools resolve themselves into the hammer and the lever, and that the lever is only an inverted hammer or the hammer only an inverted lever whichever one wills, so that all the problems of mechanics are present to us in the simple stone which may be used as a hammer, or the stick that may be used as a lever as much as in the most complicated machine. These are the primordial cells of mechanics. And an organ is only another name for a tool.

## MYSELF IN DOWIE'S SHOP

I always buy ready-made boots and insist on taking those which the shopman says are much too large for me. By this means I keep free from corns, but I have a great deal of trouble generally with the shopman. I had got on a pair once which I thought would do, and the shopman said for the third or fourth time:

'But really, sir, these boots are much too large for you.'

I turned to him and said rather sternly, 'Now, you made that remark before.'

There was nothing in it, but all at once I became aware that I was being watched, and looking up saw a middle-aged gentleman eyeing the whole proceedings with much amusement. He was quite polite but he was obviously exceedingly amused. I can hardly tell why, nor why I should put such a trifle down, but somehow or other an impression was made upon me by the affair quite out of proportion to what such small a matter usually produces.

## IF YOU FEEL STRONGLY

you must persecute, and if you don't feel strongly you will never get on.

I saw my cat undecided in his mind whether he should get up on to the table and steal the remains of my dinner or no; the chair was some eighteen inches from the table, and the back was next the table, so it was a little troublesome for him to get his feet on the bar and then get on the table. He was not at all hungry so he tried, saw it would not be quite easy and gave it up; then he thought better of it and tried again, and again saw that it was not all perfectly plain sailing, and so backwards and forwards with the first-he-would-and-then-he-wouldn'tism of a mind so nearly in equilibrium that a hair's weight would turn the scale one way or the other. I thought again how closely it resembled the action of beer trickling on a slightly sloping table.

## THE RELATIONS BETWEEN THE SEXES

The best opinion of our best medical men, the practice of those nations which have proved most vigorous and comely, the evils that have followed this or that, the good that has attended upon the other, should be ascertained by men who did not care two straws what the conclusion arrived at might be, who were neither moral nor immoral, and whose only desire was to get hold of the best available information. The result should be written down with some fulness and put before the young of both sexes as soon as they are old enough to understand such matters at all. There should be no mystery or reserve. None but the corrupt will wish to corrupt facts; honest people will accept them eagerly whatever they may prove to be, and will convey them to others as accurately as ever they can. On what pretext therefore can it be well that knowledge should be withheld from the universal gaze upon a matter of such universal interest?

It cannot be pretended that there is nothing to be known on these matters beyond what unaided boys and girls can be left without risk to find out for themselves. Not one in a hundred who remembers his own boyhood will say this. How, then, are they excusable who have the care of young people, and yet leave a matter of such vital importance so almost absolutely to take care of itself, although they well know how common error is, how easy to fall into and how disastrous the effects are whether upon the individual or the race?

### RESERVE UPON MONEY MATTERS

Next to sexual matters there are none upon which there is such complete reserve between parents and children as on those connected with money. The father keeps his affairs as closely as he can to himself and is most jealous of letting his children into a knowledge of how he conducts his money. He keeps his children like monks in a monastery as regards money, and calls this training them up with the strictest regard to principle; nevertheless he thinks himself ill-used if his son on entering life falls a victim to designing persons whose knowledge of how money is made and lost is greater than his own.

### MYSELF A LATE DEVELOPER

No one will understand me or my work unless they bear in mind that I was an unusually slow and late grower. I have not developed into much, but I have developed into much more than as a young or middle-aged man I seemed likely to do.

### THE ATHANASIAN CREED

is to me light and intelligible reading in comparison with much that now passes for science.

When I had written *Erewhon* people wanted me at once to set to work and write another book like it. How could I? I cannot think how I escaped plunging into writing some laboured stupid book. I am very glad I did. Nothing is so cruel as to try and force a man beyond his natural pace. If he has got more stuff in him it will come out in its own time and its own way: if he has not — let the poor wretch alone — if he has done one decent book it should be enough. The very worst way to get more out of him is to press him. The more promise a young writer has given the more his friends should urge him not to over-tax himself.

## SUPREME MOMENTS

Our latest moment is always our supreme moment. Five minutes delay in dinner now is more important than a great sorrow ten years gone.

## IMMORTALITY OF ATOMS AND TEACHING

Some things can teach much to some things and little to others; some can be taught much by some things and little by others; some can neither be taught much nor teach much. All depends upon the kind of company into which an atom has got. If it has got into bad hands it will have to part company with them before it can get into better. But all atoms being immortal go on learning and unlearning, combining and separating, appointing, disappointing, and being disappointed for ever and ever.

## 'OMNE INTELLIGENS EX INTELLIGENTE'

is as necessary as 'Omne ovum ex ovo.' It implies every, even the most ultimate atom, intelligent — but how about che increment? A germ of intelligence must come from a pre-existing germ as much as a material germ.

A high intelligence must be the offspring of an intelligence only a little lower than itself, in the same way as an organism cannot be considered as arising from anything but another organism a very little, if any, different from itself. Still there are 'sports' occasionally.

### DEATH IS DISSOLUTION

the dissolving of a partnership the partners to which survive and go elsewhere. Death is certainly the corruption or breaking up of that society which we have called ourselves. The corporation is at an end, both its soul and its body cease as a whole, but the immortal constituents do not cease and never will.

### CAT-IDEAS AND MOUSE-IDEAS

We can never get rid of mouse-ideas completely, they keep turning up again and again, and nibble, nibble — no matter how often we drive them off. The best way to keep them down is to have a few good strong cat-ideas which will embrace them and ensure their not reappearing till they do so in another shape.

### CONVULSIONS

Animal and vegetable organism does not change by large and few convulsions, but by small ones and many of them. So for the most part do states and men's opinions.

### GOD

Men think they mean by God something like what Raffaelle has painted in his transfiguration. Unless this was so Raffaelle would not have painted as he did. But to get at our truer thoughts we should look at our less conscious and deliberate utterances. From these it has been gathered that God is our expression for all forces and powers which we do not understand, or with which we are unfamiliar, and for the highest ideal of wisdom, goodness and power which we can conceive, but for nothing else.

Thus God makes the grass grow, because we do not understand how the air and earth and water near a piece of grass are seized by the grass and converted into more grass, but he does not mow it and make hay of it. It is Apollos and Paul who plant and water — but God who giveth the increase. We never say that God does anything which we can do ourselves, or ask him for anything which we know how to get in any other way. As soon as we understand a thing we remove it from the sphere of God's action.

To understand a thing is to feel as though we could stand under or alongside of it in all its parts and form a picture of it in our minds throughout. We understand how a violin, for example, is made if our minds can follow the manufacture in all its detail and picture it to ourselves. If we feel that we can identify ourselves with the steam and machinery of a steam engine, so as to travel in imagination with the steam through all the pipes and valves, if we can see the movement of each part of the piston, connecting rod, etc., so as to be mentally one with both the steam and the mechanism throughout their whole action and construction, then we say we understand the steam engine, and the idea of God never crosses our minds in connection with it.

When we feel that we can neither do a thing ourselves, nor even learn to do it by reason of its intricacy and difficulty, and that no one else ever can or will, but we see the thing none the less done daily and hourly all round us, then we are not content to say we do not understand how the thing is done, we go further and ascribe the action to God. As soon as there is felt to be an unknown and apparently unknowable element, then, and not till then, does the idea God present itself to us. So at coroners' inquests juries never say the deceased died by the visitation of God if they know any of the more proximate causes.

It is not God, therefore, who sows the corn — we could sow corn ourselves, we can see the man with a bag in his hand walking over ploughed fields and sowing the corn broadcast — but it is God who made the man who goes about with the bag, and who makes the corn sprout, for we do not follow the processes that take place here.

As long as we knew nothing about what caused this or that weather we ascribed it to God's direct action and prayed him to change it according to our wants: now, however, that we know more about the weather there is a growing disinclination among clergymen to pray for rain or dry weather, while laymen look to nothing but the barometer. So people do not say God has shown them this or that when they have just seen it in the newspapers; they would only say that God had shown it them if it had come into their heads suddenly and after they had tried long and vainly to get at this particular point.

### REASON AND FAITH

Reason is no foundation, for it rests in the end on faith. Faith is no foundation for it is founded on reason. We are not won by arguments that we can analyse but by tone and temper, by the manner which is the man himself.

### MAN IS A JELLY

which quivers so much as to run about.

### MEMORY

When asked to remember 'something' indefinitely you cannot: you look round at once for something to suggest what you shall try and remember. I was thinking of this once as I was walking by the side of the Serpentine, and at once looked round and saw some ducks alighting on the water; their feet reminded me of the way the sea-birds used to alight when I was going out to New Zealand and I set to work recalling attendant facts. Without help from outside I should have remembered nothing.

INSTEAD OF SAYING 'I AM VERY MUCH SURPRISED'
we should say, 'I have no organ adapted for the setting up of the special molecular disturbance appropriate to this particular occurrence. I have no nerve fibre suitable for its conveyance even if it were set up. I have no nerve vesicle for it to decompose. Unfortunately the sensation has, by hook or by crook, got inside me, and is like a coal train shunted on to a wrong line, coming into collision with all my ordinary traffic, etc.'

I must either make a new line, and a new station, or re-arrange my existing traffic in some way, or I must bust up the whole concern.

CONVENIENCE

The arrangement of our ideas is as much a matter of convenience as the packing of goods in a druggist's or draper's store and leads to exactly the same kind of difficulties in the matter of classifying them.

FEELING

They say that a living being does not feel unless it knows that it feels. This is true and not true. A man may not be aware of having felt a touch from this or that, but some gesture he has made may make it very plain that he has felt it without being aware either of the feeling or the gesture he has made in consequence. Besides people get tired and do feel things in a lump which they did not in detail.

### SENSE OF HUMOUR

A sense of humour keen enough to show a man his own absurdities as well as those of other people will keep a man from the commission of all sins, or nearly all, save those that are worth committing.

### THE BISHOP OF CARLISLE ON THE FAMILY

On my way down to Shrewsbury some time since I read the Bishop of Carlisle's *Walks in the Regions of Science and Faith*, then just published, and found the following in the essay which is entitled 'Man's Place in Nature;' after saying that young sparrows or robins soon lose sight of their fellow-nestlings and leave off caring for them, the bishop continues:

'Whereas "children of one family" are constantly found joined together by a love which only grows with years, and they part for their posts of duty in the world with the hope of having joyful meetings from time to time, and of meeting in a higher world when their life on earth is finished' (p. 129).

I am sure my great-grandfather did not look forward to meeting his father in heaven — his father had cut him out of his will; nor can I credit my grandfather with any great longing to rejoin my great-grandfather — a worthy man enough, but one with whom nothing ever prospered. I am certain my father did not wish to see my grandfather any more when he was more than forty — indeed long before reaching that age he had decided that Dr. Butler's life should not be written though R. W. Evans would have been only too glad to write it. Speaking for myself I have no wish to see my father any more, and I think it likely that the Bishop of Carlisle would not be more eager to see his than I mine. More than this I know not.

### AN IDYLL. EYES LIKE A COW

I knew a South Italian of the old Greek blood whose sister told him when he was a boy that he had eyes like a cow. Raging with despair and grief he haunted the fountains and looked into the mirror of their waters. 'Are my eyes,' he asked himself with horror, 'are they really like the eyes of a cow?' 'Alas!' he was compelled to answer, 'they are only too sadly, sadly, like them.'

And he asked those of his playmates whom he best knew and trusted whether it was indeed true that his eyes were like the eyes of a cow, but he got no comfort from any of them, for they one and all laughed at him and said that they were not only like, but very like. Then grief consumed his soul and he could eat no food, till one day the loveliest girl in the place said to him:

'Carlino, my grandmother is ill and cannot gather firewood, come with me to the *bosco* this evening and help me to bring her a load or two, will you?' And he said he would go.

So when the sun was well down and the cool night air was sauntering under the chestnuts, the pair sat together cheek to cheek and with their arms round each other's waists.

'Oh Carlino,' she exclaimed, 'I do love you so very dearly. When you look at me your eyes are just like — the eyes' — here she faltered a little — 'of a cow.'

Thenceforth he cared not. . . .

They never married.

### INCOHERENCY OF NEW IDEAS

An idea must not be condemned for being a little shy and incoherent; all new ideas are shy when introduced first among our old ones. We should have patience and see whether the incoherency is likely to wear off or to wear on, in which last case the sooner we get rid of them the better.

We shall never get people whose time is money to take much interest in atoms.


### CLERGYMEN AND CHICKENS

Why, let me ask, should a hen lay an egg which egg can become a chicken in about three weeks, and a full-grown hen in less than a twelvemonth, while a clergyman and his wife lay no eggs, but give birth to a baby which will take three-and-twenty years before it can become another clergyman? Why should not chickens be born and clergymen be laid or hatched? Or why at any rate should not the clergyman be born full grown and in holy orders, not to say already beneficed? The present arrangement is not convenient, it is not cheap; it is not free from danger; it is not only not perfect but is so much the reverse that we could hardly find words to express our sense of its awkwardness if we could observe it with new eyes, or as the cuckoo perhaps observes it. The explanation usually given is that it is a law of nature that children should be born as they are, but this is like the parched pea which St. Anthony set before the devil when he came to supper with him and of which the devil said that it was good as far as it went. We want more; we want to know with what familiar set of facts we are to connect the one in question, which at present dwells apart though in our midst, as a mysterious stranger of whose belongings, reason for coming amongst us, antecedents, and so forth, we believe ourselves to be ignorant, though we know him by sight and name and have a fair idea what sort of man he is to deal with.

We say it is a phenomenon of heredity that chickens

should be laid as eggs in the first instance, and clergymen born as babies, but beyond the fact that we know heredity extremely well to look at and to do business with, we say that we know nothing about it. I have for some years maintained this to be a mistake and have urged in company with Professor Hering of Prague and others that the connection between memory and heredity is so close that there is no reason for regarding the two as generically different, though for convenience sake it may be well to specify them by different names. If I can persuade you that this is so I believe I shall be able to make you understand why it is that chickens are hatched as eggs and clergymen born as babies.

When I say I can make you understand 'why' this is so, I only mean that I can answer the first 'why' that any one is likely to ask about it, and perhaps a why or two behind this. Then I must stop. This is all that is ever meant by those who say they can say 'why' a thing is so and so. No one professes to be able to reach back to the last 'why' which any one can ask and to answer it. Fortunately for philosophers people generally become fatigued after they have heard the answer to two or three 'whys' and are glad enough to let the matter drop. If, however, any one will insist on pushing question behind question long enough, he will compel us to admit that we have come to the end of our knowledge, which it seems is based ultimately upon ignorance. To get knowledge out of ignorance seems almost as hopeless a task as to get something out of any number of nothings, but this in practice is what we have to do, and the less fuss we make over it the better.

When we say that we know 'why' a thing is so and so, we mean that we know its immediate antecedents and connections, and find them familiar to us. I say that the immediate antecedent of, and phenomenon most closely connected with, heredity is memory. I do not profess to show why anything can remember at all, I only maintain that whereas, to borrow an illustration from mathematics, life was an equation, say, of 100 unknown quantities, it is now one of 99 only, inasmuch as memory and heredity have been proved to be one and the same thing. (Extract from a lecture delivered by me Sat. Dec. 2 or 4? 1882, at the Working Men's College, New Ormond Street.)

### PROVIDENCE AND IMPROVIDENCE
We should no longer say put your trust in Providence, but in Improvidence, for this is what we mean.

### GOETHE'S 'WILHELM MEISTER'
I do not think I ever disliked a book so much. I cannot call to mind a single character, or even passage, which does not disgust and depress me. I think I must have got hold of some other *Wilhelm Meister* by some other Goethe.

### THE ANGLO-SAXON RACE AS COLONISTS
They say this race degenerates in the colonies. It does not do so more than, or perhaps so much as, others. All races resume feral characteristics to a certain extent when they find themselves in a new country. Pressure of civilization is taken off them and they are therefore freer to do exactly what they like.

### AMERICA WAS TOO BIG
to have been discovered all at one time. It would have been better for the graces if it had been discovered in pieces of about the size of France and Germany at a time.

### MYSELF AT THE MUSEUM OF NATURAL HISTORY, MONTREAL
I came upon two plaster casts of the Antinous, and the Discobolus, not the good one — but in my poem of course

I intend the good one — stowed away in a neglected corner of a workshop. 'I see,' said I to the keeper who was stuffing birds, 'you have some antiques here; why don't you put them where people can see them?' 'Well, sir,' he answered, 'you see they are rather vulgar.' He then talked a great deal, and said his brother did all Mr Spurgeon's printing.

### A MAN'S STYLE IN WRITING

should be like his dress; should attract as little attention as possible.

### SOME MEN LOVE TRUTH

so much that they seem in continual fear lest she should catch cold on over-exposure.

### TRUTH

is like the use of words, it depends greatly upon custom.

### ART NOTE — TRUTH TO NATURE

goes at once for so much and so little in a picture. Look at some of Titian's dark landscape backgrounds and deep blue skies. They are absolutely untrue, but we like them. Perhaps; but we do not like them as well as the more luminous and truthful landscapes of Giovanni Bellini, Basaiti and Cima da Conegliano.

### THE LIFE WE LIVE IN OTHERS

We have a right to live in others as much as they will let us.

The crouching beasts on whose backs the pillars stand generally have a little one beneath them, or some animal which they have killed, or something in fact to give them occupation; it was felt that though an animal by itself was well, an animal doing something was much better. The mere fact of companionship and silent sympathy is enough to interest, but without this, sculptured animals are stupid, as our lions in Trafalgar Square—which, among other faults, have that of being much too well done.

So Jones's cat, Prince, picked up a little waif in the court and brought it home, and the two lay together, and they were much lovelier than Prince was by himself.

### MR AND MRS HICKS OF NORTHOLT

She and her husband, an old army sergeant who was all through the Indian Mutiny, are two very remarkable people. She owns to 67, I should think she was a full 75, and her husband, say, 65. She is tall, raw-boned, with a great beard and moustaches and has three projecting teeth in her lower jaw, but no more in any part of her mouth; she moves slowly — is always a little in liquor — and singularly dirty in her person. Her husband is like unto her.

For all this, they are hard-working industrious people; keep no servant; pay cash for everything; are clearly going up rather than down in the world; live well. She always shows us what she is going to have for dinner and it is excellent, 'And I made the stuffing over night and the gravy first thing this morning.' Each time we go we find the house a little more done up. She doats on Mr Hicks; we never go there without her wedding day being referred to. She has earned her own living ever since she was ten years old, and lived 29 and a half years in the house from which Mr Hicks married her. 'I am as happy,' she said, 'as the day is long.' She dearly loves a joke and a little flirtation.

I always say something perhaps a little impudently broad to her, and she likes it extremely. Last time she sailed smilingly out of the room, doubtless to tell Mr Hicks, and came back still smiling. When we come, we find her as though she had 'lien among the pots,' but as soon as she has given us our beer she goes upstairs and puts on a cap and a clean apron and washes her face — that is to say, she washes a round piece in the middle of her face, leaving a great glory of dirt showing all round it. It is plain the pair are respected, by the manner in which all who come in treat them. Last time I was there she said she hoped she should not die yet. 'You see,' she said, 'I am beginning now to know how to live.'

These were her own words, and considering the circumstances under which they were spoken they are enough to stamp the speaker as a remarkable woman. She has got as much from age and lost as little from youth as woman can well do; nevertheless, to look at she is like one of the witches in *Macbeth*.

### IF I DIE PREMATURELY

at any rate I shall be saved from being bored to death by my own success.

### BY FAITH

a man can even read Herbert Spencer.

### MYSELF AND THE GENERAL CONFESSION

I cannot repeat this unreservedly — I should say rather: 'I have left unsaid much that I am sorry I did not say, but I have said little that I am sorry for having said, and I am pretty well on the whole, thank you.'

### LIFE AND DEATH

No one can be expected to like two such opposite things at one and the same time.

### LIFE AND DEATH

Life is the gathering of waves to a head — at death they break into a million fragments, each one of which, however, is absorbed at once into the sea of life and helps to form a later generation, which comes rolling on till it too breaks.

### CHRISTIANS SAY THAT CHRISTIANITY

has stood so many attacks for so long that it cannot be false. That is just what we say about rationalism.

### IT IS NOT THE CHURCH IN A VILLAGE

that is the source of the mischief, but the rectory. I would not touch a church from one end of England to the other.

### WHEN THE VIRTUOUS MAN

turneth away from the virtue which he hath committed, and doeth that which is unlawful and nice, it shall sometimes be a good deal better both for him and everyone else.

### FURBER

My cousin says he hardly knows any one by their real name. He identifies them by some nickname in connection with the fiddles they buy from him or get him to repair, or by some personal peculiarity.

'There is one man,' said my cousin, 'whom he calls "diaphragm" because he wanted a fiddle made with what he called a diaphragm in it. He knows Dando, and Carrodus, and Jenny Lind, but hardly any one else.'

'Who is Dando?' said I.

'Why, Dando? Not know Dando? He was George the Fourth's music master, and is now one of the oldest members of the profession.'

### A CLIFFORD'S INN EUPHEMISM

People, when they want to get rid of their cats and do not like killing them, bring them to the garden of Clifford's Inn, drop them there, and go away. In spite of all that is said about cats being able to find their way so wonderfully, they seldom do find it, and once in Clifford's Inn the cat generally remains there. The technical word among the laundresses in the Inn for this is, 'losing' a cat:

'Poor thing, poor thing,' said one old woman to me a few days ago, 'it's got no fur on its head at all, and no doubt that's why the people she lived with lost her.'

### MR. GARNETT AND OUR NEXT CANTATA

He asked me what we thought of doing when we had finished our present cantata. I said we should perhaps next try a sacred subject. He looked very proper and asked what one we had in view. I said demurely that we were thinking of the Woman taken in Adultery. Mr. Garnett did not quite like this.

### CONSCIENTIOUSNESS

The first duty of a conscientious person is to have his or her conscience absolutely under his or her own control.

## SUCCESS

All success is built from a scaffolding of conceit. All actual out of something which is not actual.

## SETTING ONE'S HOUSE IN ORDER

If a man should do this when he is going to die, surely much more should he do it if he is going to live. But if things are in a great mess let him thoroughly tidy up a very little at a time.

## WHAT TO LEARN

Let this question be solved by finding out what there is, in practice, that you can no longer get on comfortably without.

## THE OBSCURITY IN WHICH I LIVE

should help me by making my faults more easily forgotten. Unfortunately I am my own enemy in this respect for I write so much about myself that I betray myself.

## WORDSWORTH

If a thing made such a noise (like a skylark, for example) that one could attend to nothing else, Wordsworth could hear it, and immediately thought he was the only person in the world who could.

## THOUGHT READING

is like the circulation of the blood. We are all thought readers only we don't pay attention to it.

are taking the place of those for charitable purposes. They will be as mischievous or more so, and will no less surely have one day to be restricted if not forbidden.

## INTERVALS OF REST

No matter what it is that we have just done we don't want to do the same directly afterwards. We vary it as soon as we can. Every action is a discharge. The gun must be reloaded before there is another.

## SNAILS AND SLUGS

The snail's shell is a superstition. Slugs have no shells and thrive just as well. But a snail without a shell would not be a slug unless it had also the slug's indifference to a shell.

## UNITY AND SEPARATENESS

In the closest union there is still some separate existence of component parts; in the most complete separation there is still a reminiscence of union. When they are most separate the atoms seem to bear in mind that they may one day have to come together again. When most united they still remember that they may come to fall out some day and do not give each other full unreserved confidence.

The difficulty is how to get 'unity' and separate 'separateness' at one and the same time. The two main ideas underlying all action are desire for closer unity, or desire for more separateness. 'Nature' is the puzzled sense of a vast number of things which feel they are in an illogical position, and should be more either of one thing or the other than they are. So they will first be this and then that, and act and re-act, and keep the balance as near equal as they can, yet knowing all the time that it isn't right, and as they incline one way or the other, they will love or hate.

When we love, we draw what we love closer to us; when we hate a thing we fling it away from us. All disruption and dissolution is a mode of hating; and all that we call affinity is a mode of loving.

The puzzle which puzzles every atom is the same which puzzles ourselves — a conflict of duties — our duty towards ourselves, and our duty as members of a body politic. It is swayed by its sense of being a separate thing — of having a life to itself which nothing can share; it is also swayed by the feeling that in spite of this it is only part of an individuality which is greater than itself and which absorbs it. Its action will vary with the predominance of either of these two states of opinion.

### THE GEOGRAPHY OF EREWHON

Up as far as the top of the pass where the statues are keeps to the actual geography of the upper Rangitata district except that I have doubled the gorge. There was no gorge up above my place [Mesopotamia], and I wanted one, so I took the gorge some ten or a dozen miles lower down and repeated it, and then came upon my own country again, but made it bare of grass and useless instead of (as it actually was) excellent country. Baker and I went up the last saddle we tried, and thought it was a pass to the West Coast, but found it looked down on to the headwaters of the Rakaia: however we saw a true pass opposite, just as I have described in *Erewhon* only that there were no clouds, and we never went straight down as I said I did, but took two days going round by lake Heron. And there is no lake at the top of the true pass. This is the pass which in consequence of our report Whitcombe was sent over and got drowned on the other side. We went up to the top of the pass, but found it too rough to go down without more help than we had.  I rather think I have told this in my New Zealand book, but am so much ashamed of that book that I dare not look to see.  I don't mean to say that the later books are much better, still they are better.

They shew a lot of stones on the Hokitika pass, so Mr Slade told me, which they call mine, and say I intended them in *Erewhon* [for the statues].  I never saw them, and knew nothing about them.

## DEATH

is only a larger kind of going abroad.

## ADOPTION OF A SON

It takes more trouble and as much risk to adopt a son as to get one in the ordinary way.

## BUSINESS

should be like religion and science; it should know neither love nor hate.

## ART NOTE — RELATIVE IMPORTANCES AND AVERAGE TRUTHS

It is all a question of relative importances and average truths; the study of art resolves itself simply into this.

## DEATH

When I was young I used to think the only certain thing in life was that I should one day die.  Now I think the only certain thing about life is that there is no such thing as death.

Our own death is a premium as it were which we pay for the far greater benefit we have derived from the fact that so many people have not only lived but also died before us. For if the old ones did not in course of time go, there would have been no progress; all our civilization is due to the arrangement whereby no man shall live for ever, and to this huge mass of advantage we must each contribute our mite; that is to say, when our turn comes we too must die.

## INTRODUCTION OF PLEASING FOREIGN PLANTS

I have brought back some mountain auriculas and blue salvia seed and Fusio tiger-lily seed this year, and mean sowing the seeds in Epping Forest and elsewhere round about London. I wish people would more generally bring back the seed of nice plants and introduce them broadcast, sowing them by our waysides and in our fields, or in whatever situation is most likely to suit them. It is true, this would puzzle botanists, but there is no reason why botanists should not be puzzled.

## THE TWO WORLDS AND DEATH

Even the world admits that there are two worlds; that there is a kingdom, veritable and worth having, which nevertheless is invisible and has nothing to do with any kingdom such as we now see. All men who deserve the name admit that there is, and that its wisdom is foolishness here on earth, and *vice versa* that the wisdom of the world is foolishness in the kingdom of heaven; and we all in our hearts admit that the kingdom of heaven is the higher and better worth living for and better worth dying for of the two, if it be sought steadfastly and in singleness of heart; we are also agreed that if it is to be won, it must be sought by those who put all else on one side and shrink from no sacrifice and are ready to give up all facing any amount of shame, poverty and torture here, rather than abandon the hope of the prize of their high calling. Nobody who doubts this is worth talking with. The question is, where is the heavenly kingdom to be found? What way are we to take to find it? And here happily the answer is more easy than appears, for you are not likely to go wrong if you heartily, in all simplicity, humility and good faith, desire to find it, and follow the dictates of ordinary common-sense.

### SAINTS GRUMBLING

Saints are always grumbling because the world will not take them at their own estimate, so they cry out upon this place and upon that, saying it does not know the things belonging to its peace, and that it will be too late soon, and that they will be very sorry later on that they did not make more of the grumbler, whoever he may be, inasmuch as he will make it hot for them and pay them out generally. All this means: 'Put me in a better social and financial position than I now am; give me more of the good things of this life (if not actual money yet authority, which is better loved by most men than even money itself) to reward me because I am to have such an extraordinary good fortune and high position in the world which is to come.' When the world does not see this, and tells them that they can't expect to have it both ways, they lose their tempers, shake the dust from their feet, and go sulking off into the wilderness. This is as regards themselves; to their followers they say: 'You must not expect to be able to make the best of both worlds. The thing is absurd, it cannot be done. You must choose which you prefer and go in for either one or the other, for you cannot have both.' When Christ said that the Jews did not know the things belonging to their peace, what he really meant was they did not know sufficiently to care about the things belonging to his own peace.

are as heat and cold, as life and death, certainty and uncertainty, unity and separateness. There is no absolute heat, life, certainty, union, etc., nor absolute cold, death, uncertainty or separateness.

We can conceive of no ultimate limit beyond which a thing cannot become either hotter or colder, there is no limit; there are degrees of heat and cold, etc., but there is no heat so great that we cannot fancy its becoming a little hotter, that is to say but we cannot fancy it to have still a few degrees of cold in it which can be extracted; heat and cold are always relative to one another, they are never absolute; so with life and death, there is neither perfect life nor perfect death but in the highest life there is some death and in the lowest death there is still some life; the fraction is so small that in practice it may and must be neglected, but it is neglected not as of right, but as of grace, and the right to insist on it is never finally and indefeasibly waived.

## GREATNESS

He is greatest who is most often in men's good thoughts.

## DEATH

I do not doubt that a person who will grow out of me as I now am, but of whom I know nothing now, and in whom therefore I can take none but the vaguest interest, will one day undergo so sudden and complete a change that his friends must notice it and call him dead; but as I have no definite ideas concerning this person, not knowing whether he is a man of forty-nine or seventy-nine or any age between these two — so this person will, I am sure, have forgotten the very existence of me as I am at the moment. If it is said that no matter how wide a difference of condition may exist between myself for the moment and myself at the moment of death, nor again how complete the forgetfulness of connection on either side, yet the fact of the one's having grown out of the other by an infinite series of gradations makes the second personally identical with the first, then I say that the difference between the corpse and the till recently living body is not great enough, either in respect of material change, nor of want of memory concerning the earlier existence, to bar personal identity and prevent us from seeing the corpse as alive and a continuation of the man from whom it was developed, though now having very different tastes, etc. from those it had while it was a man.

From this point of view there is no such thing as death, I mean as the death which we have commonly conceived of hitherto. A man is much more alive when he is what we call alive than when he is what we call dead; but no matter how much he is alive he is still in part dead, and no matter how dead he is still in part alive, and his corpsehood is connected with his living bodyhood by gradations which even at the moment of death are extraordinarily subtle; and the corpse does not forget the living body more completely than the living body has forgotten a thousand or a hundred thousand of its own previous states — so that we should see the corpse as a person, of greatly and abruptly changed habits it is true, but still of habits of some sort, for hair and nails grow for some time after death, and with an individuality which is as much identical with that of the person from whom it has arisen, as this person was with himself as an embryo of a week old, or indeed more so.

If we have identity between the embryo and the octogenarian, we must have it also between the octogenarian and the corpse, and do away with death except as a rather striking change of thought and habit, greater indeed, in degree, but still in kind substantially the same as any of the changes which we have experienced from moment to moment throughout that fragment of that existence which we commonly call our lives, so that in sober seriousness there is no such thing as absolute death, any more than absolute life. Either this, or we must keep death at the expense of personal identity, and deny identity between any two states which present considerable differences and neither of which has any fore-knowledge of, or recollection of the other. In this case, if there be death at all it is someone else who dies and not we inasmuch as long as we are alive we are not dead, and as soon as we are dead we are no longer ourselves. So that it comes in the end to this, that either there is no such thing as death at all, or else that if there is, it is someone else who dies and not we.

We cannot blow hot and cold with the same breath. If we would retain personal identity at all, we must continue it beyond what we call death; in which case death ceases to be what we have hitherto thought it, that is to say, the end of our being. We cannot have both personal identity and death too.


MONEY

It is curious that money which is the most valuable thing in life *exceptis excipiendis*, should be the most fatal corrupter of music, literature and art. As soon as any of these things are pursued with a view to money, then farewell in ninety-nine cases out of a hundred all hope of genuine good work. If a man has money at his back he may touch these things and do something which will live a long while, and he may be very happy in doing it; if he has no money he may do good work, but the chances are he will be killed in doing it, and for having done it; or he may make himself happy by doing bad work and getting money out of it, and there is no great harm in this, provided he knows his work is bad and rates it for its commercial value only, still, as a rule a man should not touch either music, literature or art — I mean not as a creator, unless he has a '*discreta posizionina*' behind him.

The hardship is not that people should undergo that change which we commonly call death but that interested persons should scare them into thinking that change to be the desperate business which it is commonly made out to be. Undesirable of course it must always be to those who are fairly well off — but that is about all.

## MYSELF AND MY COUNTRY

When I read such articles about myself as one I have just read in the *Monthly Journal of Science* (Nov. 1884) I feel tempted to exclaim that I do not fare well at the hands of my own generation; and this is true up to a certain point. Certainly I play pretty assiduously, but I am received with more hisses than applause. If I look at what my contemporaries do for me personally, I am afraid I must admit that I consider myself not too handsomely dealt with; this, however, is only what one must expect; no sensible man will suppose himself to be of so much importance that his contemporaries should be at much pains to get at the truth concerning him. There is happily another and much more pleasant way of looking at the relations between myself and my country, and if I ask what has my country done for me, and what does my own generation do for me, I can answer 'everything that makes life worth living. It gives me London and its infinite sources of pleasure and amusement, good theatres, concerts, exhibitions, newspapers, a comfortable dwelling, railways, and above all the society of the friends I value; this surely gives it a claim on me that I should give it the best I can whether it uses me as I think particularly well or not in return.'

## THE 'WRITER' AT EYNSFORD

I saw a man painting there the other day but passed his work without looking at it, and sat down some hundreds of yards off. In course of time he came strolling round to see what I was doing, and I not knowing but what he might paint much better than myself was apologetic, and said I was not a painter by profession.

'What are you?' said he.

I said I was a writer.

'Dear me,' said he. 'Why that's my line, I'm a writer.'

I laughed and said I hoped he made it pay better than I did. He said it paid very well, and asked me where I lived and in what neighbourhood my connection lay. I said I had no connection but only wrote books.

'Oh! I see. You mean you are an author. I'm not an author, I didn't mean that; I paint people's names up over their shops, and that's what we call being a writer.' Then he said, 'There isn't a touch on my work as good as any touch on yours.'

I was gratified at so much modesty and on my way back to dinner called to see his work; I am afraid that he was not far wrong — it was awful.


### 'MEDIO TUTISSIMUS IBIS'

A boy in examination translated it thus: 'In the middle of them all stalks the Ibis, most cautious of birds'; and he put a note, as follows: 'By this translation I have endeavoured to give the full value of the superlative.'


### OMNE IGNOTUM PRO MAGNIFICO

This holds with painters perhaps more than elsewhere; we never see a man sketching, or even carrying a paint-box without rushing to the conclusion that he can paint very well. There is no way of getting a reputation cheaper than that of going about with easel, paint-box, etc., provided one can ensure no one's seeing one's work. And the more traps one carries the cleverer people think one.

## PORTRAIT

A great portrait is always as much a portrait of the painter as of the painted. When we look at a portrait by Holbein or Rembrandt it is of Holbein or Rembrandt we think more than of the subject of their picture. Even a portrait of Shakespeare by Holbein or Rembrandt could tell us very little about Shakespeare. It tells us a great deal, however, about Holbein and Rembrandt.

## SWINBURNE ON CHARLES LAMB AND GEORGE WITHER

There is an article on them in this month's *Nineteenth Century* by Swinburne. Lamb was, like Mr. Darwin, 'a master of happy simplicity'. Sometimes, of course, he says very good things; at any rate some very good things have been ascribed to him; but more commonly he is forced, faint, full of false sentiment and prolix. I believe he and his sister hated one another as only very near relations can hate. He made capital out of his supposed admirable treatment of her. Aunt Sarah likes him; so do most old maids who were told what they ought to like about fifty-five years ago; but I never find men whom I think well of admire him, and as for Ainger's *Life* — well, my sisters like it. (January, 1885.)

## THE CORPSE'S BROTHER

At a funeral the undertaker came up to a man and said to him, 'If you please, sir, the corpse's brother would be happy to take a glass of sherry with you.'

## NEW LANGUAGES

English will be the universal language, but each profession will, by and by, come to have a subordinate dialect of its own which will be hardly understood by those of another profession. The longer we can delay this the better.

Bodily offspring I do not leave, but mental offspring I do. Well, my books do not have to be sent to school and college, and then insist on going into the church, or take to drinking, or marry their mother's maid.

## WORDS

We want them to do more than they can. We try to do with them what comes to very much like trying to mend a watch with a pickaxe or to paint a miniature with a mop.

Words are parvenu people as compared with thought and action. What we should read is not the words, but the man whom we feel to be behind the words.

## CONSCIOUSNESS, AND BRAIN AND NERVES

A postman knows nothing of the contents of the letters he carries. These contain all manner of varied stimuli and shocks, yet to him — the nerve that conveys them — they are all one, except as regards mere size and weight. I should think, therefore, that the nerves and ganglia really do see no difference in the stimuli that they convey. And yet the postmen do see some difference, they know a business letter from a valentine at a glance, and practice teaches them to know much else which escapes ourselves. Who then shall say what the nerves and ganglia know, and what they do not know? True, to us, as we think of a piece of brain inside our own heads, it seems as absurd to consider that it knows anything at all as it does to consider a hen's egg as knowing this or that, but if the brain could see us, perhaps the brain might say it was absurd to suppose that that thing could know anything. Besides what is the self of which we say that we are self-conscious? We say that we are self-conscious, but no one can say what it is that we are conscious of. This is one of the things which lie altogether outside the sphere of words.

As for the postman, he can open a letter if he likes and know all about the stimulus he is conveying, but if he does this he is diseased *qua* postman. So, maybe, a nerve may open a letter or two on the way sometimes, but it would not be a good nerve.

## THOUGHT

There is nothing so unthinkable as thought, unless it be the entire absence of thought.

## ENTERTAINING ANGELS UNAWARES

It is always we who are to entertain the angels, and never they us. I cannot, however, think that an angel would be a very entertaining person, either as guest or host.

## AN APOLOGY FOR THE DEVIL

It must be remembered that we have only heard one side of the case. God has written all the books.

## MYSELF AND FETTER LANE

If I were asked what part of London I was most identified with after Clifford's Inn itself, I should say Fetter Lane, every part of it. Just by the Record Office is one of the places where I am especially prone to get ideas, so also is the other end about the butcher's shop near Holborn. The reason in both cases is the same, namely that I have about had time to settle down to reflection after leaving, on the one hand, my rooms in Clifford's Inn and, on the other, Jones's in Barnard's Inn. The subject being approached anew after an interval and a shake, some new idea in connection with it often strikes me. But long before I knew Jones, Fetter Lane was always a street which I was more in than perhaps any other in London. Leather Lane, the road through Lincoln's Inn Fields to the Museum, the Embankment, Fleet Street, Strand, Charing Cross come next.

It is right to say that heredity and memory are one and the same thing. It is right to say that heredity is a mode of memory, or it is right to say that heredity is due to memory, if it is intended that animals can only grow in virtue of their being able to recollect. Memory and heredity are the means of preserving experiences, of building them together, of uniting a mass of often confused detail into homogeneous and consistent both mind and matter; but they do not originate one single one of the raindrops which go to form the full flowing river of the life of a complex organism.

Memory and heredity deal with the conservation and utilization of that which design, or accident designedly turned to account, have furnished.

It is therefore not right to say, as some have supposed me to mean, that we can do nothing which we do not remember to have done before. We can do nothing very difficult or complicated which we have not done before, unless as by a *tour de force* once in a way under exceptionally favourable circumstances, but our whole conscious life is the performance of acts either imperfectly remembered or not remembered at all. There are rain-drops of new experiences in every life which are not within the hold of our memory or past experience, and, as each one of these raindrops before it passed into the hold of memory came originally from something outside, the whole river of our life has in its inception nothing to do with memory, though it is only through memory that the raindrops of new experience can ever unite to form a full flowing river of variously organized life and intelligence.

## ACADEMICISM AND MYSELF

The more I see of Academicism the more I distrust it. If I had approached painting as I have approached book-writing and music, that is to say, by beginning at once to do what I wanted, or as near as I could to what I could find out of this, and waiting till a difficulty arose in practice before troubling myself about it, letting, in fact, the arising of any difficulty be the occasion on which that particular matter should be attended to, if I had approached painting in this way I should have been all right, as it is I have been all wrong, and it was South Kensington and Heatherley's that set me wrong. In 1864 immediately on my return from New Zealand I began a picture which I called Family Prayers, and which is certainly one of the very funniest things I have seen outside Italian votive pictures. I never finished it but have kept it, and hope it will not be destroyed at my death. I could neither paint nor draw nor compose; I knew nothing of perspective or very little but if I had gone on doing things like this and doing them entirely out of my own head without models or nature (except by way of residuary impression) I should have long since obtained so many and such accurate residuary impressions as to be able to paint pretty much what I liked. As it was I listened to the nonsense about how I ought 'to study' before beginning to paint and about never painting without nature, and the result was that I learned to study, but not to paint. Now I have got too much to do and am too old to do what I might easily have done, and should have, if I had found out earlier what writing *Life and Habit* was the chief thing to teach me. This and more general experience.

So I painted study after study as a priest reads his breviary and at the end of ten years knew no more what the face of nature was like, unless I had it immediately before me, than I did at the beginning. I am free to confess that in respect of painting I am a failure. I have spent far more time on painting than I have on anything else, and have failed at it more than I have failed in any other respect almost solely for the reasons given above. I tried very hard, but I tried the wrong way.

Fortunately for me there are no academies for teaching people how to write books or I should have fallen into them as I did into those for painting, and instead of writing should have spent my time and money in being told that I was learning how to write. By the time I had discovered I could write music I was old enough to have found out all about this, so having written one minuet which showed me that I could write, I wrote another because it amused me and to make sure that there was no mistake; then I wrote a Gavotte because it came into my head, and a Corante because I am so fond of the Suites de Pièces, and then I began a grand Oratorio with Jones which is now two thirds done. I did three exercises of one line each in two part note against note counterpoint, and one in two notes against one, and this is all the studies and exercises I have ever done. If Jones and I had one thing to say to students before we died, I mean, if we were told we had got to die, but might tell students one thing first we should say:—

'Don't learn to do, but learn in doing. Let your falls not be on a prepared ground, but let them be *bona fide* falls in the rough and tumble of the world; only of course let them be on a small scale in the first instance till you feel your feet safe under you. Act more, in fact, and rehearse less.'

### CONTRADICTION IN TERMS

This is not only to be excused but there can be no proposition which is not more or less a contradiction in terms. It is the fact of there being contradictions in terms which have to be smoothed away and fused into harmonious acquiescence in their surroundings, which makes life and consciousness possible at all. Unless the unexpected was sprung upon us continually to enliven us, we should pass life as it were in sleep. To a living being no 'it is' can be absolute; wherever there is an 'is' there is an 'is not,' as skeleton in its cupboard. When there is absolute absence of 'is not' the 'is' goes too. And the 'is not' does not go completely till the 'is' is gone along with it.

### DUNKETT'S RAT-TRAP[1]

At dinner at Seebohm's I met Skertchley, who told me about a rat-trap invented by Dunkett, Mr. Tylor's coachman.

Dunkett found all his traps fail one after another, and was in such despair at the way the corn got eaten that he resolved to invent a rat-trap. He began by putting himself as nearly as possible in the rat's place.

'Is there anything,' he asked himself, 'in which, if I were a rat, I should have such complete confidence that I could not suspect it without suspecting everything in the world and being unable henceforth to move fearlessly in any direction?'

He pondered for a while and had no answer, till one night the room seemed to become full of light, and he heard a voice from Heaven saying, 'Drain-pipes'.

Then he saw his way. To suspect a common drain-pipe would be to cease to be a rat. Here Skertchley enlarged a little, explaining that a spring was to be concealed inside, but that the pipe was to be open at both ends; if the pipe were closed at one end, a rat would naturally not like going into it, for he would not feel sure of being able to get out again; on which I interrupted and said: 'Ah, it was just this which stopped me from going into the Church.'

### WORDS ARE LIKE MONEY

There is nothing so useless in themselves, unless when in actual use.

[1] This note is an amalgamation of two of Butler's MS notes

I suspect I am rather a disappointing person, for every now and then someone makes a fuss and I am to meet some one who would very much like to make my acquaintance, or some one writes me a letter and says he has long admired my books and may he come and see me, etc.? Of course I say 'Yes,' but experience has taught me that it always ends in turning some one who was more or less inclined to run me into one who considers he has a grievance against me for not being a very different kind of person from what I am. These people (and this happens on an average once or twice a year) however do not come solely to see me; they generally tell me all about themselves, and the impression is left upon me that they have really come in order to be praised. I am as civil to them as I know how to be, but enthusiastic I never am, for they have never any of them been nice people, and it is my want of enthusiasm for themselves as much as anything else which disappoints them. They seldom come again. Mr Alfred Tylor was the only acquaintance I have ever made through being sent for to be looked at, or letting some one come to look at me, who turned out a valuable ally, but then he sent for me through mutual friends in the usual way.

### THE VOICE OF THE LORD

is the voice of common sense which is shared by all that is.

### EPIGRAM

The following epigram is going about [1885] apropos of Mr. Gladstone's having 'kindly consented to join the Committee of the Gordon Memorial' —

> Judas died desperate, his crime confessed;
> Had Judas flourished in our age and city,
> He'd be alive and figure with the rest
> Upon the Christ Memorial Committee.[1]

[1] A footnote by Butler gives the author's name as Richard Crawley.

## TRUTH

He who can best read men best knows all truth that need concern him; for it is not what the thing is, apart from man's thought in respect of it, but how to reach the fairest compromise between men's past and future opinions; that is the fittest object of consideration, and this we get by reading men and women.

## BE VIRTUOUS

— and you will be vicious.

## MY FATHER AND SHAKESPEARE AND TENNYSON

My father is one of the few men I know who say they do not like Shakespeare. He says 'Shakespeare is so very coarse.' I could forgive my father for not liking Shakespeare if it was only because Shakespeare wrote poetry, but this is not the reason. He says he likes Tennyson and this gravely aggravates his offence.

## HANDEL

We were talking about Handel one night, and I said the great prevailing feeling caused by everything he ever wrote was 'man'. Jones agreed, and said he was first man, then poet, and then musician; whereas Beethoven was first poet, then musician, and never man at all. We settled that Bach was first mechanician, then musician, then man (but not very much of one), and never poet at all. Mendelssohn was first hairdresser, then poetaster, and then musician; or, first hairdresser, then musician, and then poetaster.

## THE SINEWS OF ART AND LITERATURE

like those of war, are money.

There is no excuse for this being bad. Amateurs often excuse their shortcomings on the ground that they are not professionals. The professional could plead with greater justice that he is not an amateur; he has not, he might well say, the leisure and freedom from money anxieties which will let him devote himself to his art in singleness of heart, telling of things as he sees them without fear of what man shall say unto him; he must think not of what appears to him right and loveable, but of what his patrons will think and of what the critics will tell his patrons to say they think; he has got to square everyone all round, and will assuredly fail to make his way unless he does this; if then, he betrays his trust he does so under temptation, whereas the amateur who works with no higher aim than that of immediate recognition betrays it from the vanity and wantonness of his spirit. The one is naughty because he is needy, the other from natural depravity. Besides, the amateur can keep his work to himself, whereas the professional man must exhibit or starve.

The question is what is the amateur an *amateur* of? What is he really in love with? Is he in love with other people, thinking he sees something nice which he would like to show them, which he feels sure they would enjoy if they could only see it as he does, which he is therefore trying as best he can to put before the few nice people whom he knows? If this is his position he can do no wrong, the spirit in which he works will ensure that his defects will be only as bad spelling or bad grammar in some pretty saying of a child. If, on the other hand, he is playing for social success and to get a reputation for being clever, then no matter how dexterous his work may be, it is but another mode of the speaking with the tongues of men and angels without charity; it is as sounding brass and tinkling cymbals full of sound and fury signifying nothing.

## AIMEZ VOUS DONC LES BEAUTÉS DE LA NATURE?

A man told me that at some Swiss hotel he had been speaking enthusiastically about the beauty of the scenery and a Frenchman said to him:

'Aimez-vous donc les beautés de la nature? Pour moi je les abhorre.'


## HOURS IN PUBLIC HOUSES

She was a very Gothic woman looking like the crooked old crusader who lay in the church transept, and one would almost expect to find her body scrawled all over with dates, ranging from 400 back to the present day like the marble figure itself. (This was at Dorchester near Oxford.)


## HANDICAPPED PEOPLE

sometimes owe success to the misfortune which weights them. They seldom know beforehand how far they are going to reach, and this helps them, for if they knew the greatness of the task before them they would not attempt it. He who knows he is infirm and who would yet climb, does not think of the summit which he believes beyond his reach, but climbs slowly onwards, taking very short steps, looking below as often as he likes but not above him, never trying his powers, but seldom stopping; and then, sometimes, behold! he is on the top, which he would never have even aimed at could he have seen it from below. It is only in novels and sensational biographies that handicapped people, 'are fired by a knowledge of the difficulties that others have overcome, resolve to triumph over every obstacle by dint of sheer determination, and in the end carry everything before them.' In real life the person who starts thus almost invariably fails. This is the worst kind of start.

The greatest secret of good work whether in music, literature or art lies in not attempting too much; if it is asked, 'What is too much?' the answer is, 'Anything that we find difficult or unpleasant.' We should not ask whether others find this same thing difficult or no. If we find the difficulty so great that the overcoming it is a labour not a pleasure, we should either change our aim altogether, or aim, at any rate for a time, at some lower point.

It must be remembered that no work is required to be more than right as far as it goes. The greatest work cannot get beyond this and the least comes strangely near the greatest if this can be said of it.

### MYSELF AT THE WILLIAM ROSSETTIS

I have just come back from an At Home at the William Rossettis. I did not know them, but Mrs. Rossetti sent me an invitation and said her father, Madox Brown (the painter), would be there and would much like to see me. I used to know the Madox Browns, but found that, if they gave me a bun at all, they wanted me to climb my pole too much and too often before they would let me have it, and it was not a good bun when it came; so on my return from America I did not call, but let the acquaintance drop.

In the meantime Oliver Madox Brown had died, and I was supposed not to be so sorry as I ought to have been, the fact being that I hardly knew him at all beyond his calling on me sometimes and reading me his MS. novels, which bored me very much. I don't mind reading my own MSS. to people but I don't like being read to, and I did not like either young Brown or his novels; besides, as soon as I began to read any of my MSS. he used to go, and, indeed, this was the only way I had of getting rid of him. Perhaps, then, I did not feel his loss so acutely as I ought to have done.

However, two years or so ago old Madox Brown, the father, wrote me a letter asking if I had any letters of his son's as they wanted them for a biography. I don't know whether he ever wrote me a letter or no, at any rate I had none; but I took the opportunity to write prettily about the loss literature had sustained, etc., and the old man wrote me back an answer which showed that my letter had pleased him, and said something about 'silent equivoques'. I did not quite understand it, but he spelt the word with a k (equivokes), and it was rather touching, for I knew he had been very proud and hopeful about his son. So when Mrs. Rossetti wrote me this, I thought I ought to go, and did.

There was old Madox Brown, and I went up and said how glad I was to meet him, but he did not respond as I had expected; in fact, he snubbed me; he would not know who I was, and I had to tell him, and remind him of our correspondence.

'Oh yes', he said, 'I remember there was something but I forget how it all ended.' And his manner was distinctly repellent, so I immediately left him.

Either Mrs. Rossetti had never consulted her father about the matter, or he had had me sent for on purpose to be rude to me — I should think the former. She probably wanted me to come to her At Home, and knew that what she said would be an appeal, as it were, to my feelings which I should not find it easy to resist, and so said it without more ado.

Then I found myself knowing no one in the room, introduced to no one, and accordingly very soon went. Before I did so, I had a few words with William Rossetti. I said how beautiful his pictures were; in reality I hated them, but I did all as I should, and it was accepted as about what I ought to have said. There was a portrait of Professor Fawcett on the walls and I, referring to it, said something about the loss we had all sustained in his recent death. Rossetti did not quite catch that I was talking about Professor Fawcett and immediately turned it on to Oliver Madox Brown, so I let it stand thus and listened to a sustained panegyric on the great 'might have been'. Then I went away bored and ruffled. I left a card a few days later, but did not go in, and have not been asked since.

### THE BETTER PART OF VALOUR
is indiscretion.

### RIGHT OR WRONG
I do not greatly care whether I have been right or wrong on any point, but I care a good deal about knowing which of the two I have been.

### HANDEL FESTIVAL JOTTINGS
The large sweeps of sound passed over the orchestra as the wind playing upon a hillside covered with young heather.

I wonder which of the Alpine passes Handel went over on his various journeys into Italy, what time of year was it? What kind of weather did he have? Were the spring flowers out? Did he walk the greater part of the way as we do now? And what did he hear? For he must sometimes have heard music inside him — and that too, probably as much above what he has written down as what he has written down is above all other music. No man can catch all nor always the best of what is put for the moment or two within his reach. Handel took as much and as near the best, doubtless, as mortal man can do, but he must have had moments and glimpses which were given to him alone and which he could tell no man.

### HANDEL FESTIVAL JOTTINGS
I dreamed of a world as of a great orchestra filled with angels whose instruments were of gold, and I saw the organ

as it were on the top of the axis round which all should turn, but nothing turned and nothing moved, and the angels stirred not and played not, and all was as still as a stone, and I was myself also like the rest, as still as stone. — Then I saw some huge, cloud-like forms nearing, and behold it was the Lord holding two of his children by the hand.

'O papa!' said one, 'isn't it pretty?'

'Yes, my dear,' said the Lord, 'and if you drop a penny into the box the figures will work.'

Then I saw that what I had taken for the keyboard of the organ was no keyboard but only a slit, and one of the little Lords dropped a plaque of metal into it, and then the angels played and the world turned round, and the organ made a noise, and the people began killing one another, and the little Lord clapped his hands and was delighted.

### EDITING LETTERS

It is a mistake to think you are giving letters most faithfully by printing them as they were written without the smallest alteration, for you do not give the letters unless you reproduce their environment, and this cannot be done. He who undertakes to edit letters undertakes to translate them from one set of surroundings to other very different ones. It is the essence of a private letter that the audience should be few and known to the writer. It is the essence, generally, of a published letter that the audience should be large and unknown to the writer. Few readers as much as ever attempt to make allowance for the fact that a published letter is no longer what it was when the writer wrote it; nine out of every ten will regard published letters as things intended by the writer to be seen as the reader now sees them, whereas nothing was farther from his intention, and very little would have been allowed to stand without alteration if the writer had had any idea that his or her letter was going to be laid before the public. Granted that an editor should, like a translator, keep as religiously close to the original text as he can reasonably do, and in every alteration should consider what the writer would have wished and done if he or she could be consulted, but subject to these limitations he should be free to alter, according to his discretion or indiscretion.

## MYSELF

I said somewhere about myself, but I forgot where: 'I attacked the foundations of morality in *Erewhon*, and nobody cared two straws. I tore open the wounds of my Redeemer as he hung upon the Cross in *The Fair Haven*, and people rather liked it. But when I attacked Mr. Darwin they were up in arms in a moment.'

## HOLMAN HUNT AGAIN

I have unintentionally run up against this gentleman, I mean in the spirit, more than once lately. Last night I dined at Mrs. Tylor's and she told us how Holman Hunt had called on them one winter's afternoon, and had been talking of his picture 'The Light of the World', and the house in which it was painted.

'How I should like', he exclaimed, 'to see that house again.'

Then they asked him where it was, and when he told them they found it belonged to them, and was now un-tenanted.

'So off we all went', said Mrs. Tylor in her most reginal manner, 'then and there, and got to Chelsea' (I suppose from Queen Anne's Gate) 'soon after dark. Then we could not get the keys, and it was found they were at Mr. Morse's and they had to be fetched; and then, when at last they came, we could not unlock the door, so we caught a little street boy and put him over the wall and he got into the house and let us in; and then Holman Hunt led the way holding a lanthorn in his hand, looking — oh, so like "The Light of the World", you know — his own picture' ('just as if', I thought to myself, 'Holman Hunt would miss a point like that. Doubtless he said to himself "Now they are thinking I am so like 'The Light of the World' " '). 'And he led the way upstairs and brought us to the room in which he had painted his great picture; and there in that very room he gave us the history of his whole past career as an artist.'

'And were there any chairs in the room?' I thought, irreverently, but of course I said how interesting it must have been.

### THE 'WILL BE' AND THE 'HAS BEEN'

touch us more nearly than the 'is'; so we are more moved by children and very old people than by those in the prime of life.

### THE DISLIKE OF DEATH NECESSARY

We cannot like both life and death at once; if we like life we must dislike death and if we leave off disliking death we shall soon die. Death will always be more avoided than sought. For living involves effort, perceived or unperceived, central or departmental, and this will only be made by those who dislike the consequences of not making it more than the trouble of making it. A race, therefore, which is to exist at all must be a death-disliking race, for it is only at the cost of death that we can rid ourselves of all aversion to the idea of dying, so that the hunt after a philosophy which shall strip death of his terrors is like trying to find the philosopher's stone, which cannot be found, and if found would defeat its own object.

Moreover, as a discovery which should rid us of the fear of death would be the vainest, so also it would be the most immoral of discoveries, for the very essence of morality is involved in the dislike (within reasonable limits) of death.

Morality aims at a maximum of comfortable life and a minimum of death; if, then, a minimum of death and maximum of life were no longer held worth striving for, the whole fabric of morality would collapse, as indeed we have it on record that it is apt to do among classes that from one cause or another have come to live in disregard and expectation of death.

However much we may abuse death for robbing us of our friends — and there is no one who is not sooner or later hit hard in this respect — yet time heals these wounds sooner than we like to own; if the heyday of grief does not shortly kill outright, it passes, and I doubt whether most men, if they were to search their hearts, would not find that, could they command death for some single occasion, they would be more likely to bid him take than restore. Moreover, death does not blight love as the accidents of time and life do. Even the fondest grow apart if parted; they cannot come together again not in any closeness or for any long time. Can death do worse than this? The memory of a love that has been cut short by death remains still fragrant though enfeebled but no recollection of its past can keep sweet a love that has dried up and withered through accidents of time and life.

ONE MAN'S GNAT

is another man's camel.[1]

'SIR CUSSHA SWEESONG TWAR'

Jones went to an evening party and said there was a lady there who sang a song (as he at first thought) about an Indian potentate named Sir Cussha Sweesong Twar, but he discovered presently that the song was French ('Ce que je suis sans toi').

[1] Butler adds:—'Jones told me this as having been said by Herbert Clarke who writes poems and stories in *Home Chimes.*'

When Edgar Paine's last baby was born he explained to his eldest daughter, aged about six, that she had a little sister, and told her how nice it all was. The child said it was delightful, and added:

'Does Mamma know? Let's go and tell her.'

### SIR G. A. MACFARREN

said that the penalties of genius were labour and study. Labour and study are not penalties; the penalties which musical genius must undergo are the determined hostility of the Sir G. A. Macfarrens and Sir G. Groves of its time.

### A DIRECTION

We asked a man to show us the way on one of our Sunday walks and he said, 'You oughted to have went down the path, straight up through.'

### QUICKNESS

comes from long sustained effort after rightness, and comes unsought. It never comes from effort after quickness.

### JONES AND I

went last night to the Philharmonic, we sat in the shilling orchestra, just behind the drums, so that we could see and hear what each instrument was doing. The concert began with Mozart's G Minor Symphony. We liked this fairly well, especially the last movement, but we found all the movements too long and speaking for myself, if I had a tame orchestra for which I might write programmes I should probably put it down once or twice again not from any spontaneous wish to hear more of it, but as a matter of duty that I might judge it with fuller comprehension — still, if each movement had been half as long I should probably have felt cordially enough towards it, except of course in so far as that the spirit of the music is alien to that of the early Italian school with which alone I am in genuine sympathy, and of which Handel is the climax.

Then came a terribly long-winded recitative by Beethoven, and an air with a good deal of 'Che farò' in it. I do not mind this, and if it had been 'Che farò' absolutely I should I daresay have liked it better. I never want to hear it again and my orchestra should never play it.

The Concerto for violin and orchestra (op. 61) which followed was longer and more tedious still. I have not a single good word for it. If the subject of the last movement was the tune of one of Arthur Roberts' comic songs or of any music-hall song it would do very nicely and I daresay we should often hum it. I do not mean at the opening of the movement but about half way through, where the character is just that of a common music-hall song, and so far good.

Part II opened with a suite in F Major for orchestra op. 39. by Moszkowski. This was much more clear and in every way interesting than the Beethoven; every now and then there were passages that were pleasing, not to say more. Jones liked it better than I did, still one could not feel that any of the movements were the mere drivelling show stuff of which the concerto had been full. But it, like everything else done at these concerts is too long, cut down one-half it would have been all right and we should have liked to have heard it twice. As it was, all we could say was that it was much better than we had expected. I did not like the look of the young man who wrote it and who also con-ducted. He had long yellowish hair and kept tossing his head to fling it back on to his shoulders, instead of keeping it short like Jones and I keep ours.

Then came Schubert's 'Erl König' which I daresay is

very fine but with which I have absolutely nothing in common.

And finally there was a tiresome characteristic overture by Berlioz, which if Jones could by any possibility have written anything so dreary I should certainly have begged him not to publish.

The general impression left upon me by the concert is that all the movements were too long, and that no matter how clever the development may be it spoils even the most pleasing and interesting subject if there is too much of it. Handel knew when to stop and when he meant stopping he stopped much as a horse stops, with little if any peroration. Who can doubt that he kept his movements short because he knew that the worst music within a reasonable compass is better than the best which is made tiresome by being spun out unduly? I only know one concerted piece of Handel's which I think too long, I mean the overture to *Saul*, but I have no doubt that if I were to try to cut it down I should find some excellent reason that had made Handel decide on keeping it as it is.

### HENRY HOARE'S TORN FINGER-NAIL

When Hoare was a young man of about five-and-twenty, he one day tore the quick of his finger-nail — I mean, he separated the fleshy part of the finger from the nail — and this reminded him that many years previously while quite a child he had done the same thing. Thereon he fell to thinking of that time, which was impressed upon his memory partly because there was a great disturbance in the house about a missing five-pound note, and partly because it was while he had the scarlet fever.

Having nothing to do he followed the train of thought aroused by his torn finger, and asked himself how he tore it. After a while it came back to him that he had been lying ill in bed as a child of about seven years old at the house of an aunt who lived in Hertfordshire. His arms often hung out of the bed and as his hands wandered over the wooden frame of the bed he felt that there was a place where a nut had come out so that he could stuff his fingers in; one day, in trying to stuff a piece of paper into this hole, he stuffed it so far and so tightly that he tore the quick of his nail. The whole thing came back so vividly, though he had not thought of it for twenty years, that he could see the room in his aunt's house, and remembered how his aunt used to sit by his bedside writing at a little table from which he had got the piece of paper which he had stuffed into the hole.

So far so good; but then there flashed upon him an idea that was not so pleasant. I mean it came upon him with irresistible force that the piece of paper he had stuffed into the hole in the bedstead was the missing five-pound note about which there had been so much disturbance. At that time he was so young that a five-pound note was to him only a piece of paper; when he heard that five pounds were missing he had thought it was five sovereigns; or perhaps he was too ill to know anything, or to be questioned. I forget what I was told about this — at any rate he had no idea of the value of the piece of paper he was stuffing into the hole but now that the matter had recurred to him at all he felt so sure it was the note that he immediately went down to Hertfordshire where his aunt was still living, and asked to the surprise of every one to be allowed to wash his hands in the room he had occupied as a child. He was told there were friends staying with them who had the room at present, but, on his saying he had a reason, and particularly begging to be allowed to remain alone a little while in this room, he was taken upstairs and left there.

He immediately went to the bed, lifted up the chintz which then covered the frame, and found his old friend the hole.

A nut had been supplied and he could no longer get his fingers into it.

He rang the bell and, when the servant came, asked for a bed-key. All this time he was rapidly acquiring the reputation of being a lunatic throughout the whole house, but the key was brought, and by the help of it Hoare got the nut off. When he had done so, there sure enough, by dint of picking with his pocket-knife, he found the missing five-pound note.

See how the return of a given present brings back the presents that have been associated with it.

### IMAGINARY COUNTRIES

Why should we be at such pains to describe adventurous journeys to these? Surely we have not far to go before we find them. They are like the Kingdom of Heaven —'within us.'

### LISZT AND ROSSINI

It is said, with what truth I know not, that Liszt got Verdi to give him a letter of introduction to Rossini and went to call on him. Rossini was exceedingly polite, asked him to play, and when he had done inquired what the piece was. Liszt said, 'It is a march I have written on the death of Meyerbeer, how do you like it, maestro?' Rossini said he liked it very much, but presently added, 'Do you not think it would have been better if it had been you who had died, and Meyerbeer who had written the music?'

### 'TEACH ME TO LIVE THAT I MAY DREAD

the grave as little as my bed.' This is from the evening hymn that all respectable children are taught. It sounds well, but it is not moral; it is not desirable that any living being should live in habitual indifference to death; this should be kept for worthy occasions, and even then, though death is gladly faced, it is not healthy that it should be faced as though it were a mere undressing and going to bed.

### GOD AND NOTHING AND EVERYTHING

God is the unknown, and hence the nothing *qua* us. He is also the ensemble of all we know, and therefore the everything *qua* us. So that the most absolute nothing and the most absolute everything are extremes that meet (like all other extremes) in God.

### SOME MEN'S SOULS

transmigrate in great part into their children, but there is a large alloy in respect both of body and mind through sexual generation. The souls of other men migrate into books, pictures, music, or what not, and every one's mind migrates somewhere whether remembered and admired or the reverse. The living souls of Handel, Rembrandt and Bellini appear and speak to us in their works with less alloy than they could ever speak through their children; but men's bodies disappear absolutely on death except they be in some measure preserved in their children, and in so far as harmonics of all that has been remain.

### PERSONALITY

It is this which most interests us in music, painting or literature: when we feel that we have got well hold of this we can let the rest go. I mean, of course, we care comparatively little about the history of the work, or what it means, or even its technique; we can enjoy it without thinking of more than its beauty, and of how much we like the artist. If, however, the work does not attract us to the workman, neither does it attract us to itself.

as all who know him must admit, is one of the most amiable and benign of men; he is also very tall. One day I saw him stretching himself to his utmost to reach one of the top shelves of the Reading Room reference library, so I said, 'Why, Mr. Garnett, you are the very embodiment of Milton's line "Of linked sweetness long drawn out".' He was much pleased.

## CRYSTALS

know a lot, and they occur early in the scale of evolution. Look at snow crystals.

## THE LILIES SAY

'Consider the Solomons in all their glory; they toil not neither do they spin, yet verily I say unto you that not a lily among you all is arrayed like one of these.'

## EVERYTHING KNOWS SOMETHING

and has had some experiences; and everything is a record of its own experiences; knowledge and condition are as convertible as force and heat. They say that knowledge is power. Is, then, knowledge a mode of heat, since force and heat are convertible? May we not say that knowledge is not only a power, but the power of all powers.

All things in which any power resides know something; and where is there a thing in which there is no *insita vis* of any kind?

But some things know more than others. Some have had larger experience and made more of it. Their forms and qualities are the expression of this experience, in so far as it has affected them.

are the first, or are among the first, great experiments in the social subdivision of labour.

### MYSELF AND THE BISHOP OF CHICHESTER

At Faido last summer I met Mrs Reader, who remembered me in New Zealand, and her children; good people, all of them; they had friends coming to them, a certain Mr Prebendary Mount and his sister (I suppose I ought to call him Canon Mount) and there was a talk that the Bishop of Chichester might possibly come too. In the course of time Canon Mount and his sister came and Miss Mount was put to sit next me at dinner. At first she was below zero and her brother opposite me was hardly less freezing; but as dinner wore on they thawed, and from regarding me as the monster which in the first instance they clearly did, began to see that I agreed with them in much more than they had thought possible. By and by they were reassured, became cordial and proved on acquaintance to be most kind and good. They soon saw that I liked them, and the Canon let me take him where I chose. I took him to the place where the Woodsias grow and found some splendid specimens. I took him to Mairengo and showed him the double chancel; coming back he said I had promised to show him some Alternifolium. I stopped him and said: 'Here is some;' for there happened to be a bit in the wall by the side of the path. This quite finished the conquest, and before long I was given to understand that the Bishop really would come, and we were to take him pretty near the Woodsias and not tell him, and he was to find them out for himself. I have no doubt that the Bishop had meant coming with the Mounts, and had written to the Readers. The Readers said in their reply that I was there. This would not do for the Bishop at all; at any rate Canon Mount must exploit me first and see how bad I was; then the Mounts said I was all right, and in a couple of days or so the Bishop and his daughters arrived.

The Bishop did not speak to me at dinner, but after dinner in the Salon he made an advance in the matter of the newspaper and, I replying, he began a conversation which lasted the best part of an hour, and during which I hope I behaved discreetly. Then I bade him good-night and left the room.

Next morning I saw him eating his breakfast and said good-morning to him. He was quite ready to talk. We discussed the Woodsia Ilvensis and agreed that it was a mythical species. He said it was said in botany books to grow near Guildford. We dismissed this assertion, but he said it was extraordinary in what odd places we sometimes did find plants; he knew a single plant of Asplenium Trichomanes which had no other within thirty miles of it; it was growing on a tombstone, which had come from a long distance and from a trichomanes country; it almost seemed as if the seeds and germs were always going about in the air and grew wherever they found a suitable environment. I said it was the same with our thoughts; the germs of all manner of thoughts and ideas are always floating about unperceived in our minds, and it was astonishing sometimes in what strange places they found the soil which enabled them to take root and grow into perceived thought and action. The Bishop looked up from his egg and said: 'That is a very striking remark,' and then he went on with his egg as though if I were going to talk like that he should not play any more. Thinking I was not likely to do better than this I retreated immediately and went away down to Claro where there was a confirmation, and so on to Bellinzona.

In the morning I had asked the waitress how she liked the Bishop. She said 'Oh! beaucoup, beaucoup, et je trouve son nez vraiment noble.'

### THE VANITY OF HUMAN WISHES

There is only one thing vainer than this, and that is the having no wishes.


### JONES SAID THAT WHEN PYJAMAS

came into general use, the angels would be sure to use them.


### UNMARRIED MEN

very rarely speak the truth about the things that most nearly concern them; married men, never.


### THE BEST MUSIC SHOULD BE PLAYED AS THE BEST

men and women should be dressed — neither so well nor so ill as to attract attention to itself.


### MY GRANDFATHER'S PRESENTATION PLATE

My father left this to me, and I immediately sold it. It cost altogether nearly a thousand pounds, but I did not want it and, though I could only get old silver price for it, I determined to sell it. I took it to a silversmith's in the Strand, or rather made them send someone to see it; he said it was very good, but of a period (1837) now out of fashion.

'There is one especial test of respectability in plate,' he said; 'we seldom find it but, when we do, we consider it the most correct thing, and the best guarantee of solid prosperity that anything in plate can give. When there is a silver venison dish we know that the plate comes from an owner of the very highest respectability.'

My grandfather had a silver venison dish.

On the night the plate came to Clifford's Inn, the porter and I unpacked it in the cellar where we put it for safety. The cellar was dark and, as we only had one candle, we looked like a couple of burglars counting our swag. I had an especially guilty feeling because a good many people told me I ought not to sell the plate at all, but should keep it, out of respect for my grandfather's memory. People will talk like this and it made me uncomfortable, though I did not mean paying any attention to it.

While we were unpacking the plate, or repacking it, I forget which, I saw a dilapidated old book lying on the knife-board with a blacking bottle on it and an old tin tallow candlestick. I knew there was something in the book that made it go in counterpoint with the surroundings, so I took the blacking bottle off it and opened it. It was an early copy of my grandfather's *Atlas of Ancient and Modern Geography*. I daresay people will think that I invented this; I can only say that I did not, and indeed could not invent anything so perfectly in keeping with itself. But it frightened me.

PS. When I wrote the above, I knew nothing about my grandfather except that he had been a great schoolmaster — and I did not like schoolmasters; and then a bishop — and I did not like bishops; and that he was supposed to be like my father. Of course when I got hold of his papers, I saw what he was, and fell head over ears in love with him. Had I known then what I know now, I do not think I could have sold the plate; but it was much better that I should, and I have raised a far better monument to his memory than ever the plate was.

### MRS. CATHIE AND THE MOUSE DIRTS

She said she had been having a great clean out and found everything in a deplorably neglected state. 'There was the same old fluff gathered in all the corners and the mouse dirts was cruel.' (Song, 'Oh, cruel, cruel mouse dirts.')

### WATTS'S PICTURES

I went to Christie's to see these one day last week and I read what the *Times* said about them (April, 1887).

I never saw a more feeble, contemptible lot of pictures got together. You could see weak brag — such weakness, and such brag — in every picture, that it is difficult to understand how even in this press-ridden age Watts could have attained his reputation. Certainly he never could have attained it in an age in which men and women looked at pictures with their own eyes and not with those of other people. As, however, it is questionable how far there ever has been an age or ever will be, in which people will be at the pains of forming their own opinions, it is probable that there always have been and always will be both Wattses and buyers of Watts's pictures.

The 'Return of the Dove to the Ark' was the best picture because there was least in it; flat sky, flat sea, a great deal of both, and both as near empty as they could be, a tiny, tiny little ark, as cheap as cheap could be, and then one very poorly painted bird which I suppose may pass for a dove. It sold for about £700.

LYING IN WAIT (AS BY MY REMBRANDT)

As an example of the evenness of the balance of advantages between the principles of staying still and taking what comes, and going about to look for things, I might mention my small Rembrandt of the Robing of Joseph before Pharaoh. I have wanted a Rembrandt all my life, and I have wanted not to give more than a few shillings for it. I might have travelled all Europe over for no one can say how many years, looking for a good well-preserved forty-shilling Rembrandt (and this was what I wanted), but on two occasions of my life, cheap Rembrandts have run right up against me. The first was a head cut out of a ruined picture that had only in part escaped destruction when Belvoir Castle was burned down at the beginning of the century. I did not see the head but have little doubt it was genuine; it was offered me for a pound but I was not equal to the occasion and did not at once go to see it as I ought, and when I attended to it some months later the thing had gone. My only excuse must be that I was very young.

I never got another chance till a few weeks ago when I saw what I took, and take, to be an early, but very interesting, work by Rembrandt in the window of a pawnbroker opposite St. Clement Danes Church in the Strand. I very nearly let this slip too. I saw it, was very much struck with it, but knowing that I am a little apt to be too sanguine, distrusted my judgment; in the evening I mentioned the picture to Gogin who went and looked at it; finding him not less impressed than I had been with the idea that the work was an early one by Rembrandt, I bought it, and the more I look at it the more satisfied I am that we are right.

People talk as though the making the best of what comes was such an easy matter, whereas nothing in reality requires more experience and good sense. It is only those who know how not to let the luck that runs against them slip, who will be able to find things, no matter how long and how far they go in search of them. (1887.)


### THE TWO BARRISTERS AT YPRES

When Gogin and I were taking our Easter holiday this year we went among other places to Ypres. We went to the Hôtel Tête d'Or and found it exquisitely clean, comfortable and cheap with a charming old world last century feeling prevailing throughout. It was Good Friday, so we were to dine *maigre*; this was clearly *de rigueur*, so we did not venture even the feeblest protest. When we came down to dinner we were told there were two other gentlemen, also English, who were to dine with us, and in due course they appeared — the one a man verging towards 58, a kind of cross between Cardinal Manning and the late Mr John Parry; the other some ten years younger, amiable-looking, and I should say not so shining a light in his own sphere as his companion was. These two sat on one side of the table, and we opposite them on the other. There was an air about both which said 'you are not to try to get into conversation with us; we shall not let you if you do; we dare say you are very good sort of people, but we have nothing in common; so long as you keep quiet we will not hurt you, but if you so much as ask us to pass the melted butter we will shoot you.' We saw this and so during the first two courses talked *sotto voce* to one another, and made no attempt to open up communications. With the third course, however, there was a new arrival in the person of a portly gentleman of about 55 or from that to 60, who was told to sit at the head of the table and accordingly did so. This gentleman had a decided manner and carried all as many guns as the two barristers (for barristers they were) who sat opposite to us. He had rather a red nose, he dined *maigre* because he had to, but he did not like it. I do not think he dined *maigre* often; he had something of the air of a half, but not wholly, broken-down blackguard of a gambler, who had seen much, had moved in good society, and been accustomed to have things more or less his own way. This gentleman, who before we went gave us his card, from which it appeared that he was the Marchese Ferdinando Lotario Del Lottaringhi from Florence, immediately opened up conversation both with us and our neighbours, addressing his remarks alternately and impartially to both. He said he was an Italian who had the profoundest admiration for England. I said at once —

'Lei non puo piu amare l'Inghilterra ch' io amo ed ammiro l'Italia.' The Manning-Parry barrister looked up with an air of slightly injured surprise; conversation was continued between both parties and the Italian — who acted, as Gogin said afterwards, like one of those stones in times of plague on to which people from the country put their butter and eggs, and people from the town their money. By and by dealings became more direct between us and at last, I know not how, I found myself in full discussion with the elder barrister, as to whether Jan Van Eyck's picture in the National Gallery commonly called 'Portrait of John Arnolfini and his wife' should not more properly be held to be a portrait of Van Eyck himself (which by the way, I suppose there is no doubt that it should not, though I have never gone into the evidence for the present inscription). Then they spoke of the tricks of light practised by de Hooghe, so we rebelled, and said de Hooghe had no tricks; no one less; and that what they called trick was only observation and direct rendering of nature. Then they applauded Tintoretto, and so did we, but still as men who were bowing the knee to Baal; we put in a word for Gaudenzio Ferrari, but they had never heard of him; then they played Raffaelle as a safe card, and we said he was a master of line and a facile decorator but nothing more. On this all the fat was in the fire, for they had invested in Raffaelle as believing him to be the three per cents of artistic securities. Did I not like the Madonna di S. Sisto? I said no. I said the large photo looked well at a distance because the work was so concealed under a dark and sloppy glaze that any one might see into it pretty much what he chose to bring, while the small photo looked well because it had gained so greatly by reduction. I said the child was all very well as a child, but a failure as a Christ, as all infant Christs must be to the end of time. I said the Pope and female saint, whoever she was, were commonplace, as also the angels at the bottom. I admitted the beauty of line in the virgin's drapery and also that the work was an effective piece of decoration, but I said it was not inspired by devotional or serious feeling of any kind, and for impressiveness could not hold its own with even a very average Madonna by Giovanni Bellini. They appealed to the Italian, but he said there was a great reaction against Raffaelle in Italy now, and that few of the younger men thought of him as their fathers had done. Gogin of course backed me up, so they were in a minority; it was not at all what they expected or were accustomed to; I yielded

184

wherever I could, and never differed without giving a reason which they could understand; they must have seen that there was no malice prepense, but it always came round to this in the end that I did not agree with them.

Then they played Leonardo Da Vinci, and I had not intended saying how cordially I dislike him; but presently they became enthusiastic about the head of the virgin in the 'Vierge aux rochers' in our gallery. I said Leonardo had not succeeded with this head, he had succeeded with the angel's head lower down to the right (I think) of the picture, but had failed with the Madonna. They did not like my talking about Leonardo Da Vinci as now succeeding and now failing, just like other people. I said it was perhaps fortunate that we knew the Last Supper only by engravings, and might fancy the original to have been more full of individuality than the engravings are. I said I greatly questioned whether I should have liked the work if I had seen it as it was when Leonardo left it. As for his caricatures he should not have done them, much less preserved them; the fact of his having set store by them was enough to show that there was a screw loose about him somewhere, and that he had no sense of humour; still, I admitted that I liked him better than I did Michael Angelo.

Whatever we touched upon the same fatality attended us, fortunately neither evolution nor politics came under discussion. Nor yet happily music, or they would have praised Beethoven and very likely Mendelssohn too; they did begin to run Nuremberg and it was on the tip of my tongue to say, 'Yes, but there's the flavour of *Faust* and Goethe,' however I did not. In course of time the séance ended though not till nearly ten o'clock and we all went to bed. Next morning we saw them at breakfast, and they were quite tame. As Gogin said to me afterwards:

'They sat on our fingers, and ate crumbs out of our hands.' (1887.)

was only a very strong and singularly well-timed Salvation Army movement that happened to receive help from an unusual and highly dramatic incident. It was a Puritan reaction in an age when, no doubt, a Puritan reaction was much wanted; but like all sudden violent reactions, it soon wanted reacting against.

## ON NOT KNOWING WHEN ONE IS BEATEN

This is all very well, but one of the first businesses of a sensible man is to know when he is beaten, and to leave off fighting at once. Not to know when one is beaten is made an excuse for some of the most unjustifiable conduct that can be imagined, as, for example, in the case of the Liberal party at the present moment.

## JOHN MORLEY, SIR GEORGE TREVELYAN, AND MYSELF

When I was at Cambridge I met Trevelyan once or twice at Raikes's rooms. I was told he was a genius; and feeling myself still weak, formless, and all uncertain of my ground, I was overawed by one who I thought really did know things of which I well knew that I was myself mainly intent on trying to conceal my ignorance. I had neither strength nor imagination to suspect that Trevelyan might be just as weak, formless, and intent on concealing ignorance as I was; besides he played his part better and took in a good many people, whereas I took in but few.

Henry Hoare and Marriott used to tell me I should try and be like Trevelyan, and I believed them. Nevertheless, it never got beyond a sense of duty; I knew I did not want to be like Trevelyan, and could not, even though I tried. When I met him I expected to be dazzled as well as over-awed. I was overawed, but not dazzled, for Trevelyan said hardly anything, and this, while making me uncomfortable, frightened me; for it made me think he must know himself to be so strong. I came away with a sense that I had been uncomfortable, but still too weak to venture on rebellion even in my thoughts, and always spoke of Trevelyan as the genius my friends and neighbours said he was.

At that time I used still to echo my poor mother who called that old fool Professor Kennedy a genius. I have since found that this silence trick is common with people who would get reputation cheaply. Rossetti, the painter, played it when I met him in Wallis's rooms shortly after *Erewhon* appeared; he sat still, moody, impenetrable; but this was the best part of twenty years later, and though still very ignorant and timid I was beginning to feel my feet, and to be more rebellious in my own mind. Now, I am free to confess, I feel fairly strong, though whether I really am so or not is a matter on which I know that my opinion goes for little. To return, however, to Trevelyan, or rather to John Morley, who was the other man whom Hoare and Marriott used to hold up to me as one whom I ought to attempt to follow in all humility, no matter at how great a distance.

When *Erewhon* came out Hoare and Marriott kept urging me to try and imitate John Morley's style, so I got his *Voltaire* and disliked it very much. Then I was to meet Morley. Marriott was to give a dinner and Morley and I were to be brought together. This came off; Marriott gave a splendid feed, which I regret to say I have never to this day returned, and Morley and I were put to sit in the middle of the table side by side, and there was to be a feast of reason and a flow of soul — a part of the programme which did not come off. Morley talked a great deal, and so, I have no doubt, did I; but I cannot, happily, remember one syllable that was said by either of us; all I remember is that I disliked and distrusted Morley. In those days I was even more intolerant of Liberals than I am now, and I knew him to be a Liberal, as was Marriott, who had not yet got into Parliament, much less joined the Conservative party. I met Morley again a year or two later at Marriott's, and again we did not like each other, but by this time my short-lived laurels had begun to fade, and *Erewhon* was passing for a book of which a good deal too much had been made. Whether on account of this change in the public mind or no I don't know, but Morley would hardly speak to me.

I may say in passing that I do not wonder at people's saying that *Erewhon* had been made too much of. I believe *Erewhon* to be all very well as a beginning, but nothing more. Of my later books I think to the full as well as anyone else does. I do not doubt that *Erewhon* owed its success in great measure to its having appeared anonymously; my Uncle Philip to this day is fond of telling me that this was so. I do not like my Uncle Philip, but believe him to be right in saying what he does. The reviewers did not know but what the book might have been written by a somebody whom it might not turn out well to have cut up, and whom it might turn out very well to have praised.

### 'GOD IS LOVE'

It should be 'God is love and hate.' God is a never ending and never beginning sense of desire towards, and of aversion from, this or that; these states of mind are made manifest to us, so far as they can be made manifest at all, in change, and ultimately come most home to us in that special-ized form of change which we associate with organic matter as growth and decay.

### STUDYING FROM NATURE

When is a man studying from nature, and when is he only flattering himself that he is doing so because he is painting with a model or lay-figure before him? A man may be working his eight or nine hours a day from the model and yet not be studying from nature. He is painting but not studying. He is like the man who looks at himself in a glass in the Bible and goeth away forgetting what manner of man he was. He will know no more about nature at the end of twenty years than he did at the beginning. Unless he gets what he has seen well into his memory, so as to have it at his fingers' ends as familiarly as the characters with which he writes a letter, he can be no more held to be familiar with, and to have command over, nature than a man who only copies his signature from a copy kept in his pocket, as I have known French Canadians do, can be said to be able to write. It is painting without nature that will give a man this, and not painting directly from her. He must do both the one and the other, and the one as much as the other.

Indeed the man who never has a model but studies the faces of people as they sit opposite him in an omnibus, and goes straight home and puts down what little he can of what he has seen, dragging it out piecemeal from his memory, and going into another omnibus to look again for what he has forgotten as near as he can find it — that man is studying from nature as much as he who has a model four or five hours daily — and probably more.

### THE ELEVENTH PLAGUE OF EGYPT

The tenth plague was no good at all. The Egyptians would have been strangely unlike any papas and mammas that I have ever known if they had emancipated their slaves merely because one of their children died. What made them let the Jews go was an eleventh plague in consequence of which their papas and mammas were endowed with immortality. On this they let the Jews go immediately.

is but as when a servant changes his situation.

### THE HOLY GHOST

It is all very well to say that wisdom cannot be gotten for gold, but gold or the value that is equivalent to gold lies at the root of wisdom; granted that wisdom cannot be gotten for gold still less can it be got without it.

So with the Holy Spirit, which is only another term for wisdom, or the fear of the Lord. Gold enters largely into the very essence of the Holy Ghost, so that 'no gold, no Holy Ghost' may pass as an axiom, and yet it is not easy to buy it — perhaps for this reason — I mean, because it is almost impossible to sell it. It is a very unmarketable commodity, as those who have received it truly know at once to their own great bane and boon.

### STAMPS AND COINS

Re preliminary training and academicism we have spent hundreds of thousands, or more probably of millions, on national art collections and schools of art, without wanting anything in particular, but when the nation did at last try all it knew to make a new sixpence, it failed. The other coins were all very well in their way, and so are the stamps — the letters get carried, and the money passes; but both stamps and coins would have been just as good, and very likely better, if there had not been an art school in the country. (1888.)

### HENS HAVING NO OCCASION TO LAY

A rich lady whose husband had made his money in trade was asked whether her hens were laying. She said,

'Oh dear no, with our position, you know, they have no occasion to lay.'


## WORDSWORTH

How thankful we ought to feel that he was only a poet, and not a musician. Fancy a symphony by Wordsworth. Fancy having to sit it out. And fancy what it would have been if he had written fugues.


## PROGRESS

All progress is based upon a universal innate desire on the part of every organism to live beyond its income.


## GOD

He might begin the Day of Judgment, but he would probably find himself in the dock long before it was over.


## GOD AND THE DEVIL

You cannot take all the devil out of a thing without taking all the God too. There must be harmonics of God in the Devil, and of the Devil in God.


## PUBLIC OPINION

People say how strong it is; and indeed it is strong while it is in its prime. In its childhood and old age it is as weak as any other organism. I try to make my own work belong to the youth of a public opinion. The history of the world is the record of the weakness, frailty and death of public opinions, as the geological record is that of the decay of those bodily organisms in which those opinions have found material expression.

HONOUR THY FATHER AND MOTHER

For the most part this is all very well, especially from the parental point of view. I should say the Ten Commandments were written by a parent, and by one who had long lost his own father and mother. But even this writer did not tell us to honour our uncles and aunts, nor our grandfathers and grandmothers.


## FLYING

Whatever any other organism has been able to do man should surely be able to do also, though he may go a different way about it.


## MY BOOKS

I never make them: they grow; they come to me and insist on being made, and on being made such and such. I did not want to write *Erewhon*; I wanted to go on painting, and I found it an abominable nuisance being dragged willy-nilly into writing a book. At the same time, of course I liked it. So with *Luck or Cunning, Ex Voto* or with this life of my grandfather which I am now writing: they are none of them subjects of my own choosing, but pressed upon me with more force than I could resist. If I had not liked the subjects in spite of much unwillingness to write another book, I should have kicked, and nothing would have got me to do it at all. As I did like the subjects and the books came and said they were to be written, I grumbled a little and wrote them.


## THE EASY NONCHALANT WAY IN WHICH A PRIEST
### CROSSES HIMSELF

I always cross myself and genuflect when I go into a Roman Catholic church, but Gogin says that I don't do it like an old hand. How rudimentary is the action of an old priest. I saw one in the dining-room of the Hotel la Luna once who crossed himself by a rapid motion of his fork, just before he began to eat, and Miss Thomas told me she saw a lady at Varallo cross herself with her fan.

### MRS. CATHIE AND JACK THE RIPPER

When the last of his murders was known Mrs. Cathie, my laundress, gave me the following account of it.

'They asked him what he had got in his bag and he said it was something the ladies did not like, so I suppose they were too sharp for him, or perhaps it was not to be their fate, and that's another thing. He must have been in a dreadful disguise, and her a'singing "Sweet Violets" at half-past eight that very morning, poor creature.'

### SORROWS WITHIN SORROWS

He was in reality damned glad; he told people he was sorry that he was not more sorry, and here began the first genuine sorrow, for I believe he was really sorry that people would not believe he was sorry that he was not more sorry.

### THOUGHT

All the most essential and thinking part of thought is done without words, or consciousness. It is not till doubt and consciousness enter that words become possible. Thought pure and simple is as near to God as we can get, it is through this that we are linked with God.

Words are an attempt to grip and dissect that which in ultimate essence is as ungrippable as a shadow.

### WARBURG'S OLD FRIEND

He said to Warburg one day, talking about his wife, who was ill, 'If God were to take one or other of us, I should go and live in Paris.'

### A LIVING WORK
The only living works are those which have drained much of the author's own life into them.

### COLOUR
is like nature; you may pitchfork it out as you will, but it will always find its way back. I mean, cover a building with Portland cement, and it will, ere long, get lichen-grown and in good colour again.

### RELIGION
We no more deny the essential value of religion because we hold most religions false, and most professors of religion liars, than we deny that of science because we can see no great difference between men of science and theologians.

### LIFE AND DEATH
If life is an illusion, then so is death — the greatest of all illusions.

If life must not be taken too seriously — then so neither must death.

### TO KNOW GOD BETTER
is only to realize more fully how impossible it is that we should ever know him at all. I know not which is more childish — to deny him, or to define him.

### ALL THINGS TO ALL MEN
I suppose this was all right; but there can be no doubt about being all things to all women.

## SKELETON IN THE CUPBOARD

It does not matter much how many cupboards we may have with how many skeletons in them, if they will only keep to the cupboards and not find their way outside them. It is more serious when the skeletons insist on answering the hall-door bell, button-holing everyone who comes to the house, and telling them all about it.

## MEN SHOULD NOT TRY TO

overstrain their goodness more than any other faculty, bodily or mental.

## THERE IS ONLY ONE THING CERTAIN

namely that we can have nothing certain; and therefore it is not certain that we can have nothing certain. We are as people who would insist on looking over the brink of a precipice. Some few can gaze into the abyss without losing their heads, but most men will grow dizzy and fall.

## GENIUS

I should say it was best defined as hereditary aptitude — the inheritance, without conscious trouble, of a faculty acquired by an ancestor. It is instinctive, and like other instincts is hard to repress.

## TO KNOW

is to know the things belonging to one's peace.

## IDEAS

of all kinds, serviceable and the reverse, are like mushroom spawn, always in the air, and catch on to the minds most fitted to receive them.

is a matter about which we are lost if we reason either too much or too little.

### MYSELF

At Biella a clergyman was bullying me. He asked if I was a Roman Catholic. I said quite civilly that I was not a Catholic. He replied that he had not said a Catholic but Roman Catholic. What was I? Was I an Anglican Catholic? So seeing that he meant to argue I said I did not know; I was a Londoner and was of the same religion that people generally are at London.

This made him angry. He snorted:

'Oh, that's nothing at all;' and almost immediately left the table.

### MEMORY AND FORGETFULNESS

are so like life and death — each of these is so much involved in the other, and is so much a process of the other — that as it is almost fair to call death a process of life, and life a process of death, so it is to call memory a process of forgetting, and forgetting a process of remembering. So with black and white, and heat and cold. You never can get either all the light, or all the heat, out of anything; so with God and the Devil; so with everything.

### DISEASED SOLICITOR

A man exercises the same kind of discretion or indiscretion in preparing his limbs that he exercises in after life in the articles he buys, the tools he prefers to work with, the tradesmen with whom he elects to deal, or the professional men whom he employs. So he dies sometimes through disease of his solicitor or failure of his bank's action.

## LUCKY AND UNLUCKY

People are lucky and unlucky not according to what they get absolutely, but according to the ratio between what they get and what they have been led to expect.

## FREE-WILL IN ATOMS

The element of free-will, spontaneity, individuality, so omnipresent, so essential, yet so unreasonable and so inconsistent with the other element not less omnipresent and not less essential, I mean necessity — this element of free-will which comes from the unseen kingdom within which the writs of our thoughts run not, must be carried down to the most tenuous atoms, whose action is supposed most purely chemical and mechanical; it can never be held as absolutely eliminated, for if it be so held there is no getting it back again, and that it exists even in the lowest forms of life cannot be disputed. Its existence is one of the proofs of the existence of an unseen world, and a means whereby we know the little that we know at all.

## THE FIRMEST LINE

that can be drawn upon the smoothest paper has still jagged edges if seen through a microscope. This does not matter until important deductions are made on the supposition that there are no jagged edges.

## UNION

may be strength, but it is mere blind brute strength unless wisely directed.

## THE UNSEEN WORLD

I believe that there is an unseen world about which we know nothing, as firmly as any one can believe it.

I see things coming up from it into the visible world and going down again from the seen world to the unseen, but my unseen world is to be *bona fide* unseen, and so far as I say I know anything about it, I stultify myself.

### INTUITION AND EVIDENCE

seem to have something of the same relation that faith and reason, luck and cunning, free-will and necessity, and demand and supply have. They grow up hand in hand and no man can say which comes first.

### TEACHING AND EATING

I said in *Luck or Cunning*, that the only way (at least I think I said so) in which a teacher can thoroughly imbue an unwilling learner with his own opinions, is for the teacher to eat the pupil up, and thus assimilate him — if he can — for it is possible that the pupil may continue to disagree with the teacher. And as a matter of fact school-masters do live upon their pupils, and I, as my grandfather's grandson, continue to batten upon old pupil.

### CONFLICT OF OPINION

This is apt to generate a material conflict; and there is no material conflict without attendant clash of opinion. Opinion and matter act and react as do all things else, they come up hand in hand out of something which is both and neither but so far as we can catch sight of either first on our mental horizon, it is opinion that is the prior of the two.

### CHANGE AND IMMORALITY

Every discovery, and indeed every change of any sort is immoral as tending to unsettle men's minds, and hence their custom and hence their morals, which are the net residuum of their 'mores' or customs. Wherefrom it should follow that there is nothing so absolutely moral as stagnation.


## ROBBING PETER TO PAY PAUL

Nature is conducted on the principle of robbing Peter to pay Paul. He giveth them their meat in due season. Yes, by taking the meat from the mouth of something else that would be glad enough to have it. Or again, He giveth them as meat to something else in due season; or he giveth their meat in due season to something else.


## CHRISTIANITY

If there is any moral in Christianity, if there is anything to be learned from it, if the whole story is not profitless from first to last, it comes to this that a man should back his own opinion against the world's — and this is a very risky and immoral thing to do, but the Lord hath mercy on whom he will have mercy.


## EVACUATIONS. ANALOGY BETWEEN THE

There is a resemblance, greater or less, between the pleasure we derive from all these. Without specifying them I believe that in all cases the pleasure arises from rest — rest, that is to say, from the considerable, though in most cases unconscious labour of retaining that which it is a relief to us to be rid of. In ordinary cases the effort whereby we retain those things that we would get rid of is unperceived by the central government — being, I suppose department-ally made; we — as distinguished from the subordinate personalities of which we are composed — know nothing about it, though the subordinates in question doubtless do; but when the desirability of removing is abnormally great we know about the effort of retaining it perfectly well, and the gradual increase in our perception of the effort suggests strongly that there has been effort all the time, descending to conscious and great through unconscious and normal, from unconscious and hardly any at all. It is the relaxation of this effort that causes the sense of refreshment that follows all healthy discharges. So I am told that on death people void their excrements, as no longer making the effort necessary to retain them, and in this case we may imagine that death, so far as it can be perceived at all, must, in its more advanced stages, be at least as pleasant as the reverse.

I explain the dominancy of the pleasure that attends sexual intercourse, through the fact that all our limbs and sensual organs, in fact our whole body and life, is but an accretion round and a fostering of those spermatozoa that the male emits. They are the real 'he'. His eyes, ears, tongue, legs and arms, are but so many organs and tools that minister to the protection, education, increased intelligence and multiplication, of these spermatozoa; so that our whole life is in reality a series of complex efforts in respect to these, conscious or unconscious according to their comparative commonness. They are the central fact in our existence, the point towards which all effort is directed; relaxation of effort here, therefore, is the most complete and comprehensive of all relaxations and as such the supreme gratification — the most complete rest we can have, short of sleep and death.

MYSELF AND MY HUMOUR

The thing to say about me just now is that my humour is forced. This began to reach me in connection with my 'Quis Desiderio . . .?' article a year and a half ago [*Universal Review*, 1888] and is now [1889], I understand, pretty generally perceived even by those who had not found it out for themselves. I am not aware of forcing myself to say anything that has not amused me, which is not apposite, and which I do not believe will amuse a neutral reader, but I may very well do so without knowing it. As for my humour, I am like my father and grandfather, both of whom liked a good thing heartily enough if it was told them, but I do not often say a good thing myself. Very likely my humour what little there is of it, is forced enough. I do not care, so long as it amuses me, such as it is, I shall vent it in my own way and at my own time.

### JONES'S TWO RULES OF LIFE

Jones said there were two great rules in life, the one general and the other particular. The first is that every one can in the end get what he wants if he only tries. This is the general rule. The particular rule is that every individual is more or less of an exception to the general rule.

### CLOTHES

Our minds want clothes as much as our bodies.

### ALFRED, THE WORLD AND MYSELF

I have found the world like Alfred — a delightful play-fellow to live with, but like Alfred it does not like my trying to teach it anything.

### TRUTH

We can neither define what we mean by truth, nor be in doubt as to our meaning. And this I suppose must be due to the antiquity of the instinct that on the whole directs us towards truth. We cannot self-vivisect ourselves in respect of such a vital function, though we can discharge it normally and easily enough so long as we do not think about it.

## PARENTAL SERVITUDE

Some people seem compelled by unkind fate to parental servitude for life. There is no form of penal servitude much worse than this.

## MAN A CONSUMING FIRE

Man must always be a consuming fire, or be consumed. As for Hell, we are in a burning fiery furnace all our lives — for what is life but a process of combustion?

## TRUTH

Whenever we push her hard she runs to earth in contradiction in terms, that is to say, in falsehood. An essential contradiction in terms meets us at the end of every enquiry.

## CONSIDER THE LILIES, ETC.

But in the first place the lilies do toil and spin after their own fashion, and in the next it was not desirable that Solomon should be dressed like a lily of the valley.

## TASTE

People care more about being thought to have taste than about being thought either good, clever, or amiable.

## BEGINNINGS AND ENDINGS

We say 'everything has a beginning.' This is one side of the matter. There is another, according to which nothing has a beginning. According to this, beginnings and endings are but as it were steps cut in a slope of ice without which we could not climb it. They are for convenience and the hardness of men's hearts makes an idol of classification, but they are nothing apart from our sense of our own convenience.

## THING AND THINK

A thing is the thing it is because we think it so, and we think it so because it is the thing that it is. So that thing is father to think, and think father to thing at one and the same time. This is like sexual generation, according to which two different and apparently irreconcileable stories are fused in practice into a single version.

## SETTLEMENT — UNION BANK

There is a settlement in the Union Bank building, Chancery Lane, which has made three large cracks in the main door steps. I remember these cracks some three or four and twenty years ago just after the bank was built, as mere thin lines and now they must be some half an inch wide and are still slowly widening. They have grown very gradually but not an hour or a minute has passed without a groaning and travailing together on the part of every stone and piece of timber in the building to settle how a *modus vivendi* shall be arrived at. This is why the crack is said to be caused by a settlement — some parts of the building willing this and some that, and the battle going on, as even the steadiest and most unbroken battles must go, by fits and starts; which though to us appearing as an even tenor, would, if we could see them under a microscope prove to be a succession as it were of bloody engagements between regiments that sometimes lost and sometimes won. Sometimes doubtless strained relations have got settled by peaceful arbitration and reference to the solicitors of the contending parts without open visible rupture, at others again, discontent has gathered on discontent as the snow upon a subalpine slope, flake by flake, till the last is one too many, and the whole comes crashing down, whereon the cracks have become some minute fraction of an inch wider.

Of this we see nothing. All we note is that ten or twenty years have gone by and that the cracks are rather wider. So doubtless if the materials of which the bank is built could speak they would say they knew nothing of the varied interests that sometimes coalesce and sometimes conflict within the bank. The joys of the rich depositor, the anguish of the bankrupt are nothing to them; to them the stream of people coming in and going out is as steady, continuous a thing as a blowing wind or river to ourselves; all they know or care about is that they have a trifle more weight of books and clerks and bullion than they once had, and that this hinders them somewhat in their effort after a permanent settlement.

### MEN OF SCIENCE

If they are worthy of the name, are indeed about God's path and about his bed and spy out all his ways.

### ON BORROWING IN MUSIC

In books it is easy to make mention of the forgotten dead to whom we are indebted, and to acknowledge an obligation at the same time and place that we incur it. The more original a writer is, the more pleasure will he take in calling attention to the forgotten work of those who have gone before him. The conventions of painting and music, on the other hand, while they admit of borrowing no less freely than literature does, do not admit of acknowledgement; it is impossible to interrupt a piece of music, or paint some words upon a picture to explain that the composer or painter was at such and such a point indebted to such and such a source for his inspiration, but it is not less impossible to avoid occasionally borrowing, or rather taking, for there is no need of euphemism, from earlier work; where, then, is the line to be drawn between lawful and unlawful adoption of what has been done by others? This question is such a nice one that there are almost as many opinions upon it as there are painters and musicians.

To leave painting on one side, if a musician wants some forgotten passage in an earlier writer, is he, knowing where this sleeping beauty lies, to let it sleep on unknown and unenjoyed, or shall he not rather wake it and take it — as likely enough the earlier master did before him — with, or without modification? It may be said this should be done by republishing the original work with its composer's name, giving him his due laurels. So it should, if the work will bear it; but more commonly times will have so changed that it will not. A composer may want a bar, or bar and a half, out of, say, a dozen pages; he may not want even this much without more or less modification; is he to be told that he must republish the ten or dozen original pages within which the passage he wants lies buried, as the only righteous way of giving it new life? No one should be allowed such dog-in-the-manger-like ownership in beauty, that because it has once been revealed to him therefore none for ever after shall enjoy it unless he be their cicerone. If this rule were sanctioned, he who first produced anything beautiful would sign its death warrant for an earlier or later date, or at best would tether that which should forthwith begin putting girdles round the world.

Beauty lives not for the self glorification of the priests of any art, but for the enjoyment of priests and laity alike. He is the best art-priest who brings most beauty most home to the hearts of most men. If any one tells an artist that part of what he has brought home is not his but another's, 'Yea let him take all,' should be his answer. He should know no self in the matter; he is a fisher of men's hearts from love of winning them, and baits his hook with what will best take them without much heed where he gets it from. He can gain nothing by offering people what they know or ought to know already, he will not therefore take from the living or lately dead; for the same reason he will instinctively avoid anything with which his hearers will be familiar, except as recognized common form, but beyond these limits he should take freely even as he hopes to be one day taken from.

True, there is a hidden mocking spirit in things which ensures that he alone can take well who can also make well, but it is no less true that he alone makes well who takes well. A man must command all the resources of his art, and of these none is greater than knowledge of what has been done by predecessors. What, I wonder, may he take from these — how may he build himself upon them and grow out of them — if he is to make it his chief business to steer clear of them? A safer canon is that the development of a musician should be like that of a fugue or first movement, in which, the subject having been enounced, it is essential that thenceforward everything shall be both new and old at one and the same time — new, but not too new — old, but not too old.

Indeed no musician can be original in respect of any large percentage of his work. For independently of his turning to his own use the past labour involved in musical notation, which he makes his own as of right without more thanks to those who thought it out than we give to him who invented wheels when we take a cab, independently of this, it is surprising how large a part even of the most original music consists of common form scale passages and closes. *Mutatis mutandis*, the same holds good with even the most original book or picture; these passages or forms are as light and air, common to all of us; but the principle having been once admitted that some parts of a man's work cannot be original

— not, that is to say, if he has descended with only the reasonable amount of modification — where is the line to be drawn? Where does common form begin and end?

The answer is that it is not mere familiarity that should bar borrowing, but familiarity with a passage as associated with special surroundings. If certain musical progressions are already associated with many different sets of antecedents and consequents, they have no special association except in so far as they may be connected with a school or epoch; no one, therefore, is offended at finding them associated with one set the more; familiarity beyond a certain point ceases to be familiarity, or at any rate ceases to be open to the objections that lie against that which, though familiar, is still not familiar as common form. Those on the other hand who hold that a musician should never knowingly borrow will doubtless say that common form passages are an obvious and notorious exception to their rule, and one the limits of which are easily recognized in practice however hard it may be to define them neatly on paper.

It is not suggested that when a musician wants to compose an air or chorus, he is to cast about for some little known similar piece, and lay it under contribution. This is not to spring from the loins of living ancestors but to batten on dead man's bones. He who takes thus will ere long lose even what little power to take he may have ever had. On the other hand there is no enjoyable work in any art, which is not easily recognized as the affiliated outcome of something that has gone before it. This is more especially true of music, whose grammar and stock in trade (twelve semitones) are so much simpler than those of any other art; he who loves music will know what the best men have done, and hence will have numberless passages from older writers floating at all times in his mind, like germs in the air, ready to hook themselves on to anything of an associated character. Some of these he will reject at once, as already too strongly wedded to associations of their own; some are tried and found not so suitable as was thought; some one, however, will probably soon assert itself as either suitable, or easily altered so as to become exactly what is wanted; if, indeed, it is the right passage in the right man's mind, it will have modified itself unbidden already; how, then, let me ask again, is the musician to comport himself towards those uninvited guests of his thoughts? Is he to give them shelter, cherish them, and be thankful? or is he to shake them rudely off, bid them begone, and go out of his way so as not to fall in with them again?

Can there be a doubt what the answer to this question should be? As it is fatal deliberately to steer on to the work of other composers, so it is no less fatal deliberately to steer clear of it; music to be of any value must be a man's freest and most instinctive expression. Instinct in the case of all the greatest artists, whatever their art may be, bids them attach themselves to, and grow out of those predecessors who are most congenial to them. Beethoven grew out of Mozart and Haydn, adding a leaven which in the end leavened the whole lump, but in the outset adding little; Mozart grew out of Haydn, in the outset adding little; Haydn grew out of Domenico Scarlatti and Emmanuel Bach, adding, in the outset, little. These men grew out of John Sebastian Bach, for much as both of them admired Handel I cannot see that they allowed his music to influence theirs. Handel even in his own lifetime was more or less of a survival and protest; he saw the rocks on to which music was drifting, and steered his own good ship wide of them; as for his musical parentage he grew out of the early Italians and out of Purcell. The more original a composer is the more certain is he to have made himself a strong base of operations in the works of earlier men, striking his roots deep into them, so that he, as it were, gets inside them and lives in them, they in him, and he in them; then, this firm foothold having been obtained, he sallies forth as opportunity directs, with the result that his works will reflect at once the experiences of his own musical life and of those musical progenitors to whom a loving instinct has more particularly attached him.

The fact that his work is deeply imbued with their ideas and little ways is not due to his deliberately taking from them. He makes their ways his own, as children model themselves upon those older persons who are kind to them. He loves them because he feels they felt as he does, and looked on men and things much as he looks upon them himself; he is an outgrowth in the same direction as that in which they grew; he is their son, bound by every law of heredity to be no less them than himself; the manner, therefore, which came most naturally to them, will be the one which comes also most naturally to him as being their descendant. Nevertheless no matter how strong a family likeness may be (and it is sometimes, as between Handel and his forerunners, startlingly close), two men of different generations will never be so much alike that the work of each will not when viewed as a whole, have a character of its own — unless indeed the one is masquerading as the other, which is not tolerable except on rare occasions and on a very small scale. No matter how like his father a man may be we can always tell the two apart, but this once given, so that he has a clear life of his own, then a strong family likeness to some one else is no more to be regretted or concealed if it exists, than to be affected if it does not.

It is on these terms alone that attractive music can be written, and it is a musician's business to write attractive music. He is, as it were, tenant for life and trustee for the estate of that school to which he belongs. Normally that school will be the one which has obtained the firmest hold upon his own countrymen. An Englishman cannot successfully write like a German or a Hungarian, nor is it desirable that he should try. If, by way of variety, we want German or Hungarian music we shall get a more genuine article by going direct to German or Hungarian composers; for the most part, however, the soundest Englishmen will be stay-at-homes, in spite of their being much given to Summer flings upon the Continent. Whether as writers, therefore, or as listeners, Englishmen should stick for the most part to Purcell, Handel, and Sir Arthur Sullivan. True, Handel was not an Englishman by birth, but no one was ever more thoroughly English in respect of all the best and most distinguishing features of Englishmen. As a young man, though Italy and Germany were open to him, he adopted the country of Purcell, feeling it, doubtless, to be as far as he was concerned, more Saxon than Saxony itself. He chose England; nor can there be a doubt that he chose it because he believed it to be the country in which his music had the best chance of being appreciated; and what does this involve, if not that England, take it all round, is the most musically minded country in the world? That this is so, that it has produced the finest music the world has known, and is therefore the finest school of music in the world, cannot be reasonably disputed.

To the born musician, it is hardly necessary to say, neither the foregoing remarks nor any others about music, except those that may be found in every text book, can be of the smallest use. Handel knew this and no man ever said less about his art — or did more in it. There are some semi-aprocryphal rules for tuning the harpsichord that pretend, with what truth I know not, to hail from him, but here his theoretical contributions to music begin and end. The rules begin 'In this chord' (the tonic major triad) 'tune the fifth pretty flat, and the third considerably too sharp'. There is an absence of fuss about these words which suggests Handel himself. The work of great painters or musicians who can talk or write is seldom lasting — artists are a dumb inarticulate folk, whose speech is in their hands not in their tongues. They look at us like seals, but cannot talk to us. To the musician, therefore, what has been said above is useless, if not worse; its object will have been attained if it aids the uncreative reader to criticize what he hears with more intelligence.

P.S. I once told Rockstro I liked to know where I was cribbing my ideas from; I said, 'It is a wise tune that knows its own father.'

### GENIUS

Genius is akin both to madness and inspiration, and as every one is both more or less inspired and more or less mad, every one has more or less genius. When, therefore, we speak of genius we do not mean an absolute thing which some men have and others have not, but a small scale-turning overweight of a something which we all have but which we cannot either define or apprehend — the quantum which we all have being allowed to go without saying.

This small excess weight has been defined as a supreme capacity for taking trouble, but he who thus defined it can hardly claim genius in respect of his own definition — his capacity for taking trouble does not seem to have been abnormal. It might be more fitly described as a supreme capacity for getting its possessors into pains of all kinds, and keeping them therein so long as the genius remains. People, indeed, who are credited with genius have been sometimes very painstaking, but they would often show more signs of genius if they had taken less. 'You have taken too much trouble with your opera,' said Handel to Gluck. It is not likely that the Hailstone chorus or Mrs Quickly cost their creators much pains, indeed we commonly feel the ease with which a difficult feat has been performed to be a more distinctive mark of genius than the fact the performer took great pains before he could achieve it. Pains can serve genius, or even mar it, but they cannot make it.

We can rarely, however, say what pains have or have not been taken in any particular case, for over and above the

211

spent pains of a man's early efforts, the force of which may carry him far beyond all trace of themselves, there are the still more remote and invisible ancestral pains, repeated we know not how often, nor in what fortunate correlation with pains taken in some other and unseen direction. This points to the conclusion that though it is wrong to suppose the essence of genius to lie in a capacity for taking pains, it is right to hold that it must have been rooted in pains, and that it cannot have grown up without them.

Genius, again, might perhaps almost as well be defined as a supreme capacity for saving other people from having to take pains, if the highest flights of genius did not seem to know nothing about pains one way or the other. What trouble can *Hamlet* or the *Iliad* save to any one? Genius can, and does, save it sometimes, the genius of Newton (if he had genius — which I am much inclined to question) may have saved a good deal of trouble one way or the other, but it has probably engendered as much new as it has saved old. This, however, is all a matter of chance, for genius never seems to care whether it makes the burden or bears it. The only certain thing is that there will be a burden, for the Holy Ghost has ever tended towards a breach of the peace, and the New Jerusalem, when it comes, will probably be found so far to resemble the old as to stone its prophets freely. 'The world thy world is a jealous world, and thou shalt have none other worlds but it.' Genius points to change, and change is a hankering after another world, so the old world suspects it. It disturbs order; it unsettles *mores* and hence it is immoral. On a small scale it is intolerable, but genius will have no small scales; and it is even more immoral to be too far in front than to lag too far behind. The only absolute morality is absolute stagnation; but this is unpractical, so a peck of change is permitted to every one, but it must be a peck only, whereas genius would have ever so many sacks full. There is a myth among some Eastern nation that at the birth of Genius an unkind fairy marred all the good gifts of the other fairies, by depriving it of the power of knowing where to stop.

Nor does genius care more about money than about trouble. It is no respecter of time, trouble, money, or persons, the four things round which human affairs turn most persistently. It will not go a hair's breadth from its way either to embrace fortune, or to avoid her. It is, like Love, 'too young to know the worth of gold.' It knows indeed both love and hate, but not as we know them for it will applaud and fly for help to its bitterest foe, or attack its dearest friend in the interests of the art it serves.

Yet this genius, which so despises the world, is the only thing of which the world is permanently enamoured, and the more it flouts the world, the more the world worships it, when it has once well killed it in the flesh. Who can understand this eternal crossing in love, and contradiction in terms which warps the woof of actions and things from the atom to the universe? The more a man despises time, trouble, money, persons, place and everything on which the world insists as most essential to salvation, the more pious will this same world hold him to have been. What a fund of universal unconscious scepticism must underlie the world's opinions. For we are all alike in our worship of genius that has passed through the fire. Nor can this universal instinctive consent be explained otherwise than as the welling up of a spring whose sources lie deep in the conviction that great as this world is it masks a greater, wherein its wisdom is folly, and which we know as blind men know where the sun is shining, certainly, but not distinctly. This should in itself be enough to prove that such a world exists, but there is still another proof in the fact that so many come among us showing instinctive and ineradicable familiarity with a state of things which has no counterpart here, and cannot, therefore, have been acquired here.

From such a world we come, every one of us but some seem to have a more living recollection of it than others.

Perfect recollection of it no man can have, for to put on flesh is to have all one's other memories jarred beyond power of recognition. And it must put on flesh; for it is only by the hook and crook of taint and flesh, that tainted beings like ourselves can apprehend it. It is only in and through flesh that it can be made manifest to us at all, and yet it is this same flesh which cloaks it at the very time that it reveals it. It seems as though the flesh must have gone clean off it before it can be seen; and also that we must stand a long way from it; for the world grows more and more myopic as it grows older — on which there comes another trouble — for by the time the flesh has gone off it enough, and it is far enough off for us to see it without glasses, the chances are we shall have forgotten its very existence, and lose the wish to see at the very moment of becoming able to do so. Hence one sees no remedy for the oft repeated complaint that the world knows little. How can it be expected to do so? And how can the greatest men be expected to know more than a very little of the world? At any rate, they very seldom do, and it is just because they cannot, and do not, that if they ever happen to be found out at all they are recognized as the greatest, and the world weeps and wrings its hands that it cannot know more about them.

Lastly, if genius cannot be bought with money, still less can it sell what it produces. The only price that can be paid for genius is suffering, and this is the only wages it can receive. The only work that has any considerable permanence is written more or less consciously in the blood of the writer, or in that of his or her forefathers. Genius is like money, or again like crime, every one has a little, if it be only a halfpenny, and he can beg or steal this much if he has not got it; but those who have little are rarely very fond of millionaires; people generally like and understand best those who are of much about the same social standing and money status as their own; and so it is for the most part as between those who have only the average amount of genius and the Homers, Shakespeares and Handels of the race.

And yet so paradoxical is everything connected with genius, that it almost seems as though the nearer people stood to one another in respect either of money or genius, the more jealous they become of one another. I have seen it said that Thackeray was one day flattening his nose against a grocer's window and saw two bags of sugar, one marked 10¾d. and the other 11d (for sugar has come down since Thackeray's time). As he left the window he was heard to say, 'How they must hate one another.' So it is in the animal and vegetable worlds. The war of extermination is generally fiercest between the most nearly allied species — for these stand most in one another's light. So here again the same old paradox and contradiction in terms meets us like a stone wall in the fact that we like best those who are in the main like ourselves, but when they get too like we hate them, and so again we hate most those who are unlike ourselves, but if they become unlike enough, we may often be very fond of them.

But however this may be, genius must make those that have it think apart, and to think apart is to be an idiot, for an idiot is one who insists on taking his own view of things and who knows not the blessedness of thinking as every man thinks. He knows what others do not, and he does not know what others know; hence the *belli causa*; for he cannot serve two masters, the God of his own inward light, and the Mammon of common sense at one and the same time. How can a man think apart and not apart? But if he is a genius this is the riddle he must solve. The uncommon sense of genius and the common sense of the rest of the world are thus as husband and wife to one another; they are always quarrelling, and common sense, who must be taken as the husband, always fancies himself the master — nevertheless genius is generally admitted to be the better half.

He who would know more of genius must turn to what

he can find in the poets or to whatever other sources he can discover, for I can help him no further.

### ART AND TRADE

People confound literature and article-dealing because the plant in both cases is similar, but no two things can be more distinct. Neither the question of money nor that of friend or foe can enter into literature proper. Here, right feeling — or good taste, if this expression be preferred — is alone considered. If a *bona fide* writer thinks a thing wants saying, he will say it as tersely, clearly and elegantly as he can. The question whether it will do him personally good or harm, or how it will affect this or that friend, never enters his head, or, if it does, it is instantly ordered out again. The only personal gratifications allowed him (apart, of course, from such as are conceded to every one, writer or no) are those of keeping his good name spotless among those whose opinion is alone worth having and of maintaining the highest traditions of a noble calling. If a man lives in fear and trembling lest he should fail in these respects, if he finds these considerations alone weigh with him, if he never writes without thinking how he shall best serve good causes and damage bad ones, then he is a genuine man of letters. If in addition to this he succeeds in making his manner attractive, he will become a classic. He knows this. He knows, although the Greeks in their mythology forgot to say so, that Conceit was saved to mankind as well as Hope when Pandora clapped the lid on her box.

With the article-dealer, on the other hand, money is, and ought to be, the first consideration. Literature is an art; article-writing, when a man is paid for it, is a trade and none the worse for that; but pot-boilers are one thing and genuine pictures are another. People have indeed been paid for some of the most genuine pictures ever painted, and so with music, and so with literature itself — hard-and-fast lines ever cut the fingers of those who draw them — but, as a general rule, most lasting art has been poorly paid, so far as money goes, till the artist was near the end of his time, and, whether money passed or no, we may be sure that it was not thought of. Such work is done as a bird sings — for the love of the thing; it is persevered in as long as body and soul can be kept together, whether there be pay or no, and perhaps better if there be no pay.

Nevertheless, though art disregards money and trade disregards art, the artist may stand not a little trade-alloy and be even toughened by it, and the tradesmen may be more than half an artist. Art is in the world but not of it; it lives in a kingdom of its own, governed by laws that none but artists can understand. This, at least, is the ideal towards which an artist tends, though we all very well know we none of us reach it. With the trade it is exactly the reverse; this world is, and ought to be, everything, and the invisible world is as little to the trade as this visible world is to the artist.

When I say the artist tends towards such a world, I mean not that he tends consciously and reasoningly but that his instinct to take this direction will be too strong to let him take any other. He is incapable of reasoning on the subject; if he could reason he would be lost *qua* artist; for, by every test that reason can apply, those who sell themselves for a price are in the right. The artist is guided by a faith that for him transcends all reason. Granted that this faith has been in great measure founded on reason, that it has grown up along with reason, that if it lose touch with reason it is no longer faith but madness; granted, again, that reason is in great measure founded on faith, that it has grown up along with faith, that if it lose touch with faith it is no longer reason but mechanism; granted, therefore, that faith grows with reason as will with power, as demand with supply, as mind with body, each stimulating and augmenting the other until an invisible, minute nucleus attains colossal growth — nevertheless the difference between the man of the world and the man who lives by faith is that the first is drawn towards the one and the second towards the other of two principles which, so far as we can see, are co-extensive and co-equal in importance.

### THE WORLD'S GREATEST MEN

It is said the world knows nothing (or little?) of its greatest men; it might be added that its greatest men have known very little of the world. Indeed they never can, for they and the world have nothing, or at any rate very little, in common, and cannot understand each other.

### THE LIMITS OF THE BODY

These seem well defined enough as definitions go, but appearances mislead here as elsewhere. A man's banker or solicitor are so much parts of him that commonly he can no more cut them off from himself and grow new ones than he can cut off his legs and arms and furnish himself with a new pair. Neither must he wound his solicitor. A wound in the solicitor is a very serious thing.

### RELIGIOUS LIGHT

A light cannot be religious if it is not dim. Religion belongs to the twilight of our thoughts, just as business of all kinds to their full daylight. So a picture which may be impressive while seen in a dark light will not hold its own in a bright one.

The Greeks and Romans did not enquire into the evidences on which their belief that Minerva sprang full-armed from the brain of Jupiter was based. If they had written books of evidences to show how certainly it all happened, etc. — well, I suppose if they had an endowed Church with some considerable prizes, they would have found means to hood-wink the public.

### VIRTUE

If virtue had everything her own way she would be as insufferable as dominant factions generally are. It is the function of vice to keep virtue within reasonable bounds.

### THE PEACE THAT PASSETH UNDERSTANDING

Yes. But as there is a peace more comfortable than any understanding so also there is an understanding more covetable than any peace.

### I SAW A WIDOW ONCE

with a crape umbrella. She was what St. Paul calls 'a widow indeed.'

### 'PASTOR IGNAVUS DORMIT SUPINUS'

This was translated in the old Eton grammar, 'The idle shepherd sleeps with his face upwards.' I took this, when a child, as an interesting fact in natural history, and believed I could always now distinguish an idle from an industrious shepherd by observing whether he slept with his face downwards or upwards. I was sure that Frick, Mr. Vincent Hall's shepherd, always slept with his face downwards, but if you really wanted to know about a shepherd you must watch.

### JAEL

was a remarkably nervous woman in private life; she screamed if she saw a mouse and fainted at the sight of a cut finger.

will only, in the end, follow those who have despised as well as served it.

### THE HUMBLE AND MEEK

I really do not see much use in exalting the humble and meek; they do not remain humble and meek long when they are exalted.

### GREAT WORKS

These have always something of the 'de profundis' about them. They must be written with heart's blood and with tears as well as laughter.

### BELIEF

like any other moving body follows the path of least resistance.

### GOD AND MEN'S WIVES

are indeed about their beds and about their paths and spy out all their ways.

### WHEN THE RIGHTEOUS MAN

turneth away from the righteousness that he hath committed and doeth that which is neither quite lawful nor quite right, he will generally be found to have gained in amiability what he has lost in holiness.

### THE COURSE OF

true anything never does run smooth.

### THE RIDICULOUS AND THE SUBLIME

As there is but one step from the sublime to the ridiculous, so also there is but one from the ridiculous to the sublime.

## MONEY AND LANGUAGE

Gold and silver coins are only the tokens, symbols, outward and visible signs and sacraments of money. When not in actual process of being applied in purchase they are no more money than words not in use are language. They are potential money as words are potential language, but it is the power and will to apply the counters that alone give life to money, and when these are in abeyance the money lies dead as a log.

## FAITH

The reason why the early Christians held faith in such account was because they felt it to be a feat of such super-human difficulty.

## OPINIONS

have vested interests just as men have.

## THE DEAD BEING THE MAJORITY

it is natural that we should have more friends among these than among the living.

## THE MOST IMPORTANT

service rendered by the press and the magazines is that of educating people to approach printed matter with distrust.

## PUBLIC OPINION

The public buys its opinions as it buys its meat, or takes in its milk, on the principle that it is cheaper to do this than to keep a cow. So it is, but the milk is more likely to be watered.

### MYSELF AND THESE NOTES

I make them under the impression that I may use them, but I never do, unless they come into my head. When I wrote my recent article 'Ramblings in Cheapside' [in the *Universal Review*, reprinted in *Essays on Life, Art and Science*], the last foregoing note would have come in admirably; it was in my pocket, in my little black note-book, but I forgot all about it till I came to post this note-book into my ledger.

### LIFE

is the art of drawing sufficient conclusions from insufficient premises.

### TASTE

Everything is a matter of taste — the form of one's organs as much as of one's dress. The most profound and permanent instinct or structure had its inception in a fancied preference, sometimes highly eccentric.

### HEAVEN

At any rate there will be no wedding presents.

### TRUTH AND KINDNESS

Truth generally is kindness, but where the two diverge and collide, kindness should override truth.

is dead men's bones and dead men's souls. The money that men make lives after them.

### THE VATES SACER

So Jones, Gogin, my cousin Reginald and Pauli are all men of more insight, quicker wit, more playful fancy, and, in all ways, abler men than I am, but you will find ten of them for one of me. I note what they say, think it over, adapt it and give it permanent form. They throw good things off as sparks; I collect them and turn them into warmth. But I could not do this if I did not sometimes throw out a spark or two myself.

### THE DEAD

The dead should be judged like criminals, impartially, but they should be allowed the benefit of a doubt. When no doubt exists they should be hanged out of hand for about a hundred years. After that time they may come down and move about under a cloud. After about 2000 years they may do what they like. If Nero murdered his mother — well, he murdered his mother and there's an end. The moral guilt of an action varies inversely as the squares of its distances in time and space, social, psychological, physiological or topographical, from ourselves. Not so its moral merit: this loses no lustre, through time and distance.

Good is like gold, it will not rust nor tarnish and is rare, but there is some of it everywhere. Evil is like water, it abounds, is cheap, soon fouls, but runs itself clear of taint.

### COMMON STRAIGHTFORWARDNESS AND KINDLINESS

are, of course, the highest points that man or woman can reach, but they should be no more made matters of conversation than should the lowest vices. Extremes meet here, as elsewhere, the extremes of vice and virtue are alike very common, and alike unmentionable.

## THE RELATIONS BETWEEN THE SEXES

must always involve friction.

## WORK

with some men is as besetting a sin as idleness with others.

## PRUDENCE

There is nothing so imprudent or so improvident as over-prudence or over-providence.

## BREVITY

Talking with Gogin last night, I said that in writing it took more time and trouble to get a thing short than long. He said it was the same in painting. It was harder not to paint a detail than to paint it — easier to put in all that one can see than to judge what may go without saying, omit it and range the irreducible *minima* in due order of precedence. Hence we all lean towards prolixity.

The difficulty lies in the nice appreciation of relative importances and in the giving each detail neither more nor less than its due. This is the difference between Gerard Dow and Metsu. Gerard Dow gives all he can, but un-reflectingly; hence it does not reflect the subject effectively into the spectator. We see it, but it does not come home to us. Metsu on the other hand omits all he can, but omits intelligently, and his reflection excites responsive enthusiasm in ourselves. We are continually trying to see as much as we can, and to put it down. More wisely we should consider how much we can avoid seeing and dispense with.

So, added Jones, it is also in music. Cherubini says the number of things that can be done in fugue with a very simple subject is endless, but that the trouble lies in knowing which to choose from all these infinite possibilities.

As regards painting, anyone can paint anything in the minute manner with a little practice, but it takes an exceedingly able man to paint so much as an egg broadly and simply. Bearing in mind the shortness of life and the complexity of affairs, it stands to reason that we owe most to him who packs our trunk for us, so to speak, most intelligently, neither omitting what we are likely to want, nor including what we can dispense with, and, at the same time, arranges things so that they will travel most safely and be got at most conveniently. So we speak of composition and arrangement in all arts.

### POETRY

The highest whether in music or literature is ineffable. It must be felt from one person to another but cannot be articulated. The greatest poets never wrote poetry. The Homers and Shakespeares are not the greatest, they are only the best that we can know. And so with musicians, but I do not think that this holds good with painting.

### SUBJECT AND TREATMENT

People often say that treatment is more important than subject, but no treatment can make a repulsive subject not repulsive. It can make a trivial or even a stupid subject interesting, but a really bad flaw in the subject cannot be treated out.  Happily the man who has sense enough to treat a subject well will generally have sense enough to choose a good one, so that the case of a really repulsive subject treated in a masterly manner does not often arise.  It is often said to have arisen, but in nine cases out of ten the treatment will be found to have been overpraised.

## THE BASIS OF LIFE

We may say what we like, but it is, *au fond*, sensual.

## REASON

is the penultimate test of truth, but not the ultimate of truth nor is it the court of first instance.

For example: A man questions his own existence; he applies first to the court of mother-wit and is promptly told that he exists; he appeals to reason and, after some wrangling, is told that the matter is very doubtful; he proceeds to the equity of that reasonable faith which inspires and transcends reason, and the judgment of the court of first instance is upheld while that of reason is reversed.

Nevertheless it is folly to appeal from reason to faith unless one is pretty sure of a verdict and, in most cases about which we dispute seriously, reason is as far as we need go.

## MY NOTES

They always grow longer if I shorten them.  I mean the process of compression makes them more pregnant and they breed new notes.  I never try to lengthen them, so I do not know whether they would grow shorter if I did. Perhaps that might be a good way of getting them shorter.

### EVERYTHING MUST BE STUDIED

from two points of view i.e. in itself as near as we can get to this, and in its relations as near as we can get to them. If we try to see it absolutely in itself, unalloyed with relations, we shall find by and by that we have as it were whittled it away. If we try to see it in its relations to the bitter end, we shall find that there is no corner of the universe into which it does not enter. Either way the thing eludes us if we try to grasp it with the horny hands of language and conscious thought. Either way we can think it perfectly well — so long as we don't think about thinking about it. The pale cast of thought sicklies over everything.

Practically everything should be seen as itself pure and simple as far as we can comfortably see it, and at the same time as not itself, so far as we can comfortably see it, and then the two views should be combined, as far as we can combine them without discomfort. If we cannot comfortably combine them we should think of something else.

### A LITTLE LEVITY

will save many a good heavy thing from sinking.

### CLOTHES ON A CLOTHES LINE

A story might be told by a series of sketches of the clothes of a given family hanging out to dry. A love story might be told in the washes hung out in adjacent gardens. Then there should be three washes and a gentleman nightshirt and a lady nightshirt should be alone. By and by there should be some little nightshirts.

might be tempted, on seeing the little nightshirt, to think that the old nightshirts had made it. What we do is much the same, for the body of a baby is not much more made by the two old babies, after whose pattern it has cut itself out, than the little nightshirt is made by the old ones. The thing that makes either the little nightshirts or the little babies is something about which we know nothing whatever at all.

## GOD

The course of true God never did run smooth. God to be of any use must be made manifest, and he can only be made manifest in and through flesh. And flesh to be of any use (except for eating) must be alive, and it can only be alive by being inspired of God. The trouble lies in the getting the flesh and the God together in the right proportions. There is lots of God and lots of flesh, but the flesh has always got too much God or too little, and the God has always too little flesh or too much.

## SHAKESPEARE'S COMMONPLACE BOOK

Why did not Shakespeare make a few odd notes now and again about anything he saw or heard and anything that came into his head? If we could have one such volume of rubbish shot anyhow from Shakespeare or Homer we would give up three parts of the *Iliad*, and at least two of the plays — say *Hamlet* and *Othello*.

Only whoever makes such notes should write them in copying ink, and send the other copy to a friend.

### THE TEST OF MUSIC

To know whether you are enjoying a piece of music or not you must see whether you find yourself looking at the advertisements of Pears' soap at the end of the libretto.

### LANGUAGE

There was a time when language was as rare an accomplishment as writing was in the days when it was first invented. Probably talking was originally confined to a few scholars as writing was in the Middle Ages, and gradually became general. Besides speech is still growing. Poor folks cannot understand the talk of educated people. Perhaps reading and writing will indeed one day come by nature.

### SILENCE AND TACT

Silence is not always tact and it is tact that is golden, not silence.

### 'THE ANCIENT MARINER'

I think I have said that the Ancient Mariner would not have taken so well if it had been called 'The Old Sailor,' so that Wardour Street has its uses.

### THOUGHT

There are two kinds; there is a thinking which we can watch fairly well in others, and understand, and feel confident that the thinker is doing what we know ourselves to do. This we call thought. But there is another thinking which we cannot follow or watch, and which has so little analogy to our own mainly verbose thought that we cannot think along with it. This we say is not thought. So that the distinction between thought and non-thought with us lies in our own ability to follow the thought, but this is rather small. If we can think it too, it is thought; if we cannot think it too, no matter how much anyone else can think it, it is not thought.

### ENDLESS SUFFERING

All mythologies and religions are based on the supposition that an endlessness of pain and disappointment is as agreeable an object of human contemplation as an endlessness of happiness.

### LOGIC AND FAITH

Logic is like the sword — those who appeal to it, shall perish by it. Faith is appealing to the living God, and one may perish by that too, but somehow one would rather perish that way than the other, and one has got to perish sooner or later.

### HAPPINESS AND MISERY

consist in a progression towards better or worse; it does not matter how high up or low down you are, it depends not on this, but on the direction in which you are tending.

### NEW IDEAS

Every new idea has something of the pain and peril of childbirth about it.

is all very well as long as you can keep on climbing or stick at the top; but it is hard to come down it without tumbling off.

### FOR THE RAMBLINGS IN CHEAPSIDE ENLARGED

There are Canterbury Pilgrims every Sunday in summer, who start from close to the old Tabard, only they go by the South-Eastern railway and come back the same day for five shillings. And, what is more, they are just the same sort of people.

If they do not go to Canterbury they go by the *Clacton Belle* to Clacton on the sea. There is not a Sunday the whole summer through, but you may find all Chaucer's pilgrims, man and woman for man and woman, on board the *Lord of the Isles* or the *Clacton Belle*. Why, I have seen the Wife of Bath on the *Lord of the Isles* myself. She was eating her luncheon off an *Ally Sloper's Half-Holiday* that was spread out upon her knees. Whether it was I who had had too much beer or she, I cannot tell, God knoweth; and whether or no I was caught up into Paradise, again I cannot tell; but I certainly did hear unspeakable words which it is not lawful for a man to utter, and that not above fifteen years ago but the very last Sunday that ever was. The Wife of Bath heard them too, but she never turned a hair. Luckily I had my detective camera with me, so I snapped her there and then. She put her hand up to her mouth at that very moment and rather spoiled herself, but not much. (1891.)

### BREVITY

is not only the soul of wit, but the soul of making oneself agreeable, and of getting on with people, and indeed of everything that makes life worth having. So precious a thing, however, cannot be got without more expense of trouble than most of us have the moral wealth to lay out. It takes much less trouble to be long than short.

### KNOWLEDGE

descends with modification like everything else. And just as there is no organism that has not descended from others nearly like it, so there is no knowledge but has sprung from the loins of past knowledge not greatly different.

### GOD

And so there is no God but has been in the loins of past gods.

### MYSELF AND BOREDOM

I do not object to being bored if I am paid for it, but I never am paid for it. So many people have run up such long scores with me in this respect, and never paid me, that I will give no more credit. I must have cash down before I will be bored at all, but my figure is very low; so long as I get paid at all I will give people as much fun for their money, by way of letting them bore me, as anyone is likely to do.

### RELIGION

We must first learn to distinguish between this and vested interests.

### LIFE IS A DREAM

and that is why the greatest men have always been dreamers.

Science is being daily more and more personified and anthropomorphized into a god. By and by they will say that science took our nature upon him, and sent down his only begotten son, Charles Darwin, or Huxley, into the world so that those who believe in him, etc.; and they will burn people for saying that science, after all, is only an expression for our ignorance of our own ignorance.

## ON TEMPTATION

For example, I am acrossing from Calais to Dover and there is a well-known popular preacher, say Archdeacon Farrar, on board.

I have my camera in my hand, and though the sea is rough the sun is brilliant. I see the Archdeacon come on board at Calais looking as if he had just stepped out of a band-box, and seat himself in an excellent light on the upper deck. Can I be expected to resist the temptation of snapping him? Suppose that between Boulogne and Calais I had said 'lead us not into temptation' any number of times — is it likely that the Archdeacon would have been made to take some other train, or been induced to stay in Calais, or that I myself should have been led into some other temptation, though perhaps smaller, by being delayed upon my homeward journey? Had I not better snap him and have done with it? Is there enough chance of good result to make it worth while to try the experiment? The general *consensus* of opinion is that there is not.

And as for praying for strength to resist temptation — granted that if, when I saw the archdeacon sitting like a band-box I had immediately prayed for strength, I might have been enabled to put the camera from me for a time; how long would this have been likely to last when I saw his face growing saintlier and saintlier? I am an excellent sailor myself, but he is not, and when I see him there with his eyes closed and his head thrown back like a sleeping St. Joseph with a shovel hat on, and a basin beside him, can I expect to be saved from snapping that Archdeacon by such a formula as 'deliver us from evil?' Is it in photographer's nature to do so? Is it likely that I shall leave off snapping him phase by phase as long as I have a plate left in my slides? When David found himself in the cave with Saul, he cut off one of Saul's coat-tails; if he had had a camera and there had been light enough he would have photographed him; but would it have been in flesh and blood for him neither to cut off the coat-tail nor to snap him?

There is a photographer in every bush, going about like a roaring ramping lion and seeking what he may devour.

### THE ARTIST AND THE SHOPKEEPER

Most artists, whether in religion, music, literature, painting, or what not, are shopkeepers in disguise. They hide their shop as much as they can, and keep pretending that it does not exist, etc., but they are essentially shopkeepers and nothing else. Why do I try to sell my books and feel regret at never seeing them pay their expenses, if I am not a shopkeeper? Of course I am, only I keep a bad shop — a shop that does not pay.

In like manner, the professed shopkeeper has generally a taint of the artist somewhere about him which he tries to conceal as much as the professed artist tries to conceal his shopkeeping.

The business man and the artist are like matter and mind. We can never get either pure and without some alloy of the other.

### FOR EREWHON REVISITED

An art-class in which the first thing insisted on is that the pupils should know the price of all the leading modern pictures that have been sold during the last twenty years at Christie's, and the fluctuations in their values. Give an examination paper on this subject. The artist being a picture-dealer, the first thing he must do is to know how to sell his pictures, and therefore how to adapt them to the market. What is the use of being able to paint a picture unless one can sell it when one has painted it? (Add that the secret of the success of modern French art lies in its recognition of values.)

### IT IS MADNESS NOT TO TRY TO KNOW

but it is almost as much madness to try to do so. God will not have any human being know what will sell, nor when anyone is going to die, nor even whether or no it is going to rain. Sometimes publishers, hoping to buy the Holy Ghost with a price, fee such men as Andrew Lang, Haweis or Canon Ainger to read for them, but this is the vain tossing of insomnia. I do not say that the impossibility of being ever confident about the future was designed, but it is as complete as though it had been not only designed but designed exceedingly well.

### HE WILL VISIT THE VIRTUES

of the fathers upon the children, etc. to the third and fourth generations. How often do we not see children ruined through the virtues, real or supposed, of their fathers and mothers? The most that can be truly said for virtue is that there is a considerable balance in its favour, and that it is a good deal better to be for it than against it, but it lets people in very badly sometimes.

### PERFECT LOVE

only casts out fear when there is perfect knowledge at the same time. Otherwise it creates as much fear as it destroys.

It is more true to say of perfect hate that it casts out fear, than of perfect love.

### AMENDES HONORABLES

There is hardly an offence so great but if it be frankly apologized for it is easily both forgotten and forgiven. There is hardly an offence so small but it rankles if he who has done it does not express proportionate regret. If a man habitually indulges his own selfishness in this respect at the expense of what is due to other people, to me he is no better than a drunkard or debauchee, and I have no more respect for him than I have for the others.

We all like to forgive, and love best not those who offend us least, nor who have done most for us, but those who make it most easy for us to forgive them.

### FAD

There is but one step from the Academy to the Fad.

### MIND

Being either too quick or too slow in making up one's mind is generally a sign that one has not got much mind. The rate at which a mind works soundly is a most important gauge of its strength. If it works correctly at once, this is greatness; but as a general rule if it is found to work rapidly, it will be incorrectly.

### J. S. BACH

It is imputed to him for righteousness that he goes over the heads of the general public and appeals mainly to musicians. But the greatest men do not go over the heads of the masses, they take them rather by the hand. The true musician would not snub so much as a musical critic. His instinct is towards the man in the street rather than the Academy. Perhaps I say this as being a man in the street myself as regards music. I do not know, but I know that Bach does not appeal to me and that I do appeal from Bach to the man in the street and not to the Academies, because I believe the first of these to be the sounder.

Still, I own Bach does appeal to me sometimes. In my own poor music I have taken passages from him before now, and have my eye on others which I have no doubt will suit me somewhere. Whether Bach would know them again when I have worked my will on them, and much more whether he would own them, I neither know nor care. I take or leave as I choose, and alter or leave untouched as I choose. I prefer my music to be an outgrowth from a germ whose source I know, rather than a waif and stray which I fancy to be my own child when it was all the time begotten of a barrel organ. It is a wise tune that knows its own father, and I like my music to be the legitimate offspring of respectable parents. Roughly, however, as I have said over and over again if I think something that I know and greatly like in music, no matter whose, is appropriate — I appropriate it. I should say I was under most obligations to Handel, Purcell and Beethoven.

For example, anyone who looked at my song 'Man in Vain' would say it was taken from 'Batti, batti'. I should like to say it was taken from, or suggested by, a few bars in the opening of Beethoven's pianoforte sonata op. 78, and by Purcell's duet 'Hark how the Songsters'. (From *Timon of Athens*)

I am not aware of having borrowed more in the song than what follows as natural development of these two passages.

## MYSELF AND THESE NOTES

I hope no one will think I thought all the stupid titles and subjects I have jotted down in these notes to be good or even tolerable. I put them down as things to start from and make tolerable, but I confess I often cannot see what I once saw in them. Sometimes, no doubt, there was a context and development in my mind which I have forgotten.

## CONTRADICTION IN TERMS

So in the utmost purity there is impurity, and *vice versa*.

## FOR EREWHON REVISITED

Refer to the agony and settled melancholy with which unborn children in the womb regard birth as the extinction of their being, and how some declare that there is a world beyond the womb and others deny this. 'We must all one day be born.' 'Birth is certain,' etc., just as we say of death. Birth involves with it an original sin. It must be sin — for the wages of sin are death and assuredly the wages of birth are death.

## SUFFERING OR PAIN

It is as important that we should learn to look on these with fortitude, as to bear them bravely in our own persons.

## ABSOLUTE UNCERTAINTY

We can no more have this than we can have absolute certainty, and so with truth and untruth.

MONEY

It has such an inherent power to run itself clear of taint
that human ingenuity cannot devise the means of making it
work permanent mischief, any more than means can be
found of torturing people beyond what they can bear. Even
if a man founds a College of Technical Instruction, the
chances are ten to one that no one will be taught anything
and that it will have been practically left to a number of
excellent professors who will know very well what to do
with it.

## INACCURACY

I do not mind being bowled over in inaccuracy, which I
have tried to verify myself. It makes me careful, but if I
have not tried to verify and then turn out wrong, this, if
I find it out, upsets me very much and I pray that I may be
found out whenever I do it.

## EREWHON REVISITED

They have a Professor of Mischief. They found that
people always did harm when they meant well and all the
professorships founded with an avowedly laudable object
failed, so they aim at mischief in the hope that they may go
wrong here as when they aimed at what they thought advan-
tageous and curiously enough they find it much less easy to
do mischief than they expected. They thought they would
do any amount in no time but it all seemed to come to
nothing when they tried.

## EREWHON REVISITED

The Professor of Worldly Wisdom had plucked a man
for having bought an egg that had a date stamped upon it.

## FOUNDATIONS

Everything is founded and grows out of either avowed mystery or mystery hidden under chicane. In either case the more we occupy ourselves with what lies on the surface, and the less we dig about foundations, the better for us.

## EREWHON REVISITED

A man plucked for being too often and too seriously in the right.

The man who got the prize declined to answer a single one of the questions set. He said he saw they were more intended to show off the ingenuity of the examiner than either to assist or test the judgment of the examined. He observed, moreover, that the view taken of his answers would in great measure depend on what the examiner had had for dinner. Since, then, it was not in his power to control this, he was not going to waste time where the result was at best so much a matter of chance. Briefly, his view of life was that the longer you lived, and the less you thought or talked about it the better. He should go pretty straight in the main himself, because it saved trouble on the whole; and he should be guided mainly by a sense of humour in deciding when to deviate from the path of technical honesty. Anyhow his errors should be on the side of excess rather than asceticism.

## SILENCE AND TACT

may or may not be the same thing.

## KNOWLEDGE IS POWER

Yes — but it must be practical knowledge. There is nothing less powerful than knowledge unattached, and incapable of application. That is why what little knowledge I have has done myself personally so much harm. I do not know much, but if I knew a good deal less than that little I should be much more powerful. The rule should be never to learn a thing till one is pretty sure one wants it or that one shall want it before long so badly as not to be able to get on without it. This is what sensible people do about money, and there is no reason why people should throw away their time and trouble more than their money. There are plenty of things that most boys would give their ears to know — these and these only are the proper things for them to sharpen their wits upon.

If a boy is idle and does not want to learn anything at all, the same principle should guide those who have the care of him i.e. that he is never to be made to learn anything till it is pretty obvious that he cannot get on without it. This will save trouble both to boys and teachers, moreover it will be far more likely to increase a boy's desire to learn. I know in my own case no earthly power could make me learn till I had my head given me; and nothing has been able to stop me from incessant study from that day to this.

### CONTRADICTION IN TERMS

So there is nothing which at once affects a man so much and so little as his own death.

### DEATH

It is a case in which the going-to-happen-ness of a thing is of greater importance than the thing. The thing itself cannot be of importance to anyone; for death cuts its own throat in the matter of hurting people. It so overdoes the thing as to defeat its object; it is as a bee that can sting but once and in the stinging dies, so death is dead to him who is dead already. As long as it keeps to shaking his wings at a man only, there is *brutum fulmen* but the man goes on living; he may be hit by pain and sickness but not by death; death may frighten but yet can never hurt.

The pains of Tantalus, Sisyphus and all the rest of them — pains which show what an instinctive longing there is in all men both for end and endlessness of both good and ill — these are but mockery as compared with the fruitless chase to which poor death has been condemned for ever and ever. Does it not seem as though he must have committed some crime for which his sentence is to be for ever grasping that which becomes non-existent the very moment that he grasps it? But then I suppose it would be with him as with the rest of them, he must either die himself, which he has not done, or become used to it and enjoy the frightening as much as the actual killing.

It always is so. They minded it very much for the first six months or perhaps twelve — but after that it was like shelling peas on a hot afternoon in July. They began by finding out (no doubt long after the fact had been apparent enough to everyone else) that they had not been noticing what they were doing so much as usual, and that they had been even thinking of something else — from this moment, the automatic stage of action having once commenced, the progress towards always thinking of something else was very rapid, and now, I am informed, it is a hard matter to make Sisyphus and the Danaids understand that they are really rolling stones uphill and filling empty sieves at all.

'At any rate,' said one of Danaids to my informant, 'for goodness sake don't say anything about it, or we may be put to some other work; you see we must be doing something and it may just as well be this as anything else. We have not got to make our lives by it and what in the name of reason can it matter to us whether the sieves get full or not? I suppose since you say so, that we really are holding funnels under a running pump. I have sometimes thought my feet did get a little damp occasionally, it may be so or not, I know nothing about it. I should have said myself that we passed our time chiefly in gossip with other shades as we pass by, in laughing at the absurd airs assumed by Aga-memnon and Ajax, and in watching Sisyphus roll his stone downhill. Now that you have called my attention to it I see that I do keep on making as though I were trying to fill this odd funnel-like sieve with water. How very strange. Why should any animal have such an organ as a sieve, and why should it spend its whole life in pumping it full and empty-ing it again? Much the same as what you do yourselves in breathing? Still I do not know what you are talking about. If the pump were to cease pumping or my funnel were to get choked it would be the death of me. We murder any-body? What do you mean? Egyptus? I do not even know the gentleman's name. Argos? Where's that? I have been here with my sisters at this pump as long as I can remember anything at all, and here, please Jupiter, I mean to stay till I can find one that runs better or can get a larger funnel.'

And so the poor wretch rattled on. As for Sisyphus, he was perfectly aware of what he was doing and found the utmost delight in timing the downward rush of his stone so as to inflict the greatest possible scare on any unwary shade who might be wandering below. The amusement and interest of this was so great and so varied that his labour, though it cost him no effort, never reached the stage of unconscious-ness and automatism or reflex action, which I understand is the name applied by men of science to all actions that are done without reflection. He was a pompous ponderous old gentleman, very irritable, and always thinking that the other shades were laughing at him or trying to take advantage of him. There were two, however, whom he hated with a fury that seemed to torment far more seriously than anything else did — the first of these was Archimedes who had constituted a series of experiments in regard to various questions connected with mechanics and had conceived a scheme by which he could turn Sisyphus' stone into a motive power for the purpose of lighting Hades by electricity. The other was Agamemnon who took good care to keep out of the stone's way when it was more than a quarter of the way up the slope, but who delighted in teasing Sisyphus so long as he considered it safe to do so. As for the other shades they delighted in gathering together about stone time and on betting how far it would roll.

Then to Tantalus. He got plenty both to eat and drink. Water stuck to the hairs on his body and he gathered it up in his hand — and he got many an apple when the wind was napping as it had to do sometimes. Perhaps he would have liked more, but he got enough to keep him going.

So on then to Tityus: what does a crow matter in the liver of a man who covers nine acres? It was a gentle stimulant.

Then go to Mt Olympus and find the everlasting happiness of the gods as great a failure as everlasting torment had been down below. Hercules found Hebe a fool and he could not get her off his everlasting knee. It was all very well as long as they could get about among mankind, but all that had been stopped long ago, and there was nothing now to relieve the monotony of their existence.

Then Jove thought it all over and said, 'I see it is no use trying to make people either very happy or very miserable for long together. The thing cannot be done. Hades and Mt Olympus are both failures, and they both fail for the same reason: that they suppose pain and happiness to be absolute, not relative. Any pain through which a man can live at all becomes unfelt as soon as it becomes habitual. Pain consists not in that which is now endured, but in the strong memory of something better that is still recent. And so hopefulness lies in the memory of a recent worse and the expectation of a better that is to come shortly', etc.

It is all very well to insist upon the cunning side of
living action, more especially now when it has been so
persistently ignored, but though the fortunes of birth and
surroundings have all been built up by cunning, yet it is by
ancestral, vicarious cunning, and this, to each individual,
comes to much the same as luck pure and simple; in fact,
luck is seldom seriously intended to mean a total denial of
cunning, but is for the most part only an expression whereby
we summarize and express our sense of a cunning too complex and impalpable for conscious following and apprehension.

When we consider how little we have to do with our
parentage, country and education, or even with our genus
and species, how vitally these things affect us both in life
and death, and how, practically, the cunning in connection
with them is so spent as to be no cunning at all, it is plain
that the drifts, currents, and storms of what is virtually
luck will be often more than the little helm of cunning can
control. And so with death. Nothing can affect us less,
but at the same time nothing can affect us more; and how
little can cunning do against it? At the best it can only defer
it. Cunning is nine-tenths luck, and luck is nine-tenths
cunning; but the fact that nine-tenths of cunning is luck
leaves still a tenth part unaccounted for.

### MYSELF AND UNCONSCIOUS HUMOUR

'Unconscious humour' is the one contribution I have
made to the current literature of the day. I am continually
seeing 'unconscious humour' (without quotes) alluded to in
*Times* articles and other like places, but I never remember
to have come across it as a synonym for dullness, till I
wrote *Life and Habit*.

When I take my Sunday walks in the country, I try and buy a few really new-laid eggs warm from the nest. At this time of the year they are very hard to get and I have long since invented a sick wife who has implored me to try and get her a few eggs laid not earlier than the self-same morning. Of late, as I am getting older, it has become my daughter who has just had a little baby and this will generally draw a new-laid egg if there is one about the place at all.

At Harrow Weald it has always been my wife who for years has been a great sufferer, and who finds a really new-laid egg the one thing she can digest in the way of solid food. So I turned her on as movingly as I could not long since and was at last sold some eggs that were no better than common shop eggs, if that. So when I went there a fortnight or so ago I said my poor wife had been made very ill with them; it was no good trying to deceive her: she knew a new-laid egg from a bad one as well as any woman in London and she had so high a temper that it was very unpleasant for me when she found herself disappointed.

'Ah! sir', said the landlady, 'but you would not like to lose her.'

'I must not allow my thoughts ma'am', I answered, 'to wander in that direction, but it's no use bringing her stale eggs, anyhow.'

### LETHE

The river of death is the river of forgetfulness — the stream of life is memory.

### THE DEAD ARE OFTEN

just as living to us as the living are, only we cannot get them to believe it. They can come to us, but till we die we cannot go to them.  To be dead is to be unable to understand that one is alive.


## MYSELF AND NAUSICAA

I am elderly, grey-bearded and, according to Alfred, disgustingly fat.  I wear spectacles, and get more and more bronchitic as I grow older.  Still no young prince in a fairy story ever found an invisible princess more effectually hidden behind a hedge of dullness, nor more fast asleep than Nausicaa was when I woke her and hailed her as authoress of the *Odyssey*.  And there was no difficulty about it either.  All one had to do was to go up to the front door and ring the bell.


## THE WAGES OF VIRTUE

If the wages of sin are death, what else, I should like to know, is the wages of virtue?


## MYSELF, HOMER AND THE BASINS

When I came over from Calais last December after spending a few days at Boulogne according to my custom, it was rough, and I had a cold upon me, so I went down into the second-class cabin.  Several people of all ages and sexes were on the sofas, and they soon began to be sea-sick.  There was no steward, so I got them each a basin and placed it for them as well as I could; then I sat down at a table in the middle and went on with my translation, or rather analysis, of the *Iliad*, while they were sick all round me.  I had to get the *Iliad* well in my head before I began my lecture on *The Humour of Homer*, and I could not afford to throw away a couple of hours, but I doubt whether Homer was ever before translated under such circumstances.  (Feb. 4 1892.)

In his latest article (Feb. 1892) Prof. Garner says that the chatter of monkeys is not meaningless but that they are conveying ideas to one another. This seems to me hazardous. The monkeys might with equal justice conclude that in our magazine articles or literary and artistic criticisms, we are not chattering idly but are conveying ideas to one another.

## ANIMOSITY AND RIVALRY

To take away all animosity from a rivalry is like playing whist for love.

## MRS. BOVILL

She wrote to me for a rule of life, and to know how she could excel in this, that and the other, while attending to her household and children at the same time. How can she? And what could I say that would be of the smallest use to her beyond what she already knew better than myself? So I wrote as best I could and said, *inter alia*: 'Get as many nice people about you as you can, more particularly Jones and myself. Snub snobs. Stick to the Ten Commandments — they never forbid swearing — and really I do not know what else there is.' She said she did not find my letter as comforting as she hoped it would be.

## BOOKS

are like imprisoned souls till someone takes them down from a shelf and frees them.

Never have anything to do with the near surviving representatives of anyone whose name appears in the death column of the *Times* as having 'passed away.'

## INSPIRATION

is never genuine if it is known as inspiration at the time. True inspiration always steals on a person; its importance not being fully recognized for some time. So men of genius always escape their own immediate belongings, and indeed generally their own age.

## ACADEMIC AND ARISTOCRATIC

people live in such an uncommon atmosphere that common sense can rarely reach them.

## FOR COUNSELS OF IMPERFECTION

God will sit and sponge on a man, while buffeting and insulting him all the time, till he has got the last penny out of his purse and the shirt off his back; he is like man towards money — no matter how much we have we always want more.

## CONTRADICTION IN TERMS

(or perhaps extremes meeting). So we pay higher and higher in proportion to the service rendered till we get to the highest services, such as becoming a Member of Parliament, and this must not be paid at all. If a man would go yet higher and found a new and permanent system, or create some new idea or work of art which remains to give delight to ages — he must not only not be paid, but he will have to pay very heavily out of his own pocket into the bargain.

### THE DESTRUCTION

of great works of literature and art is as necessary for the continued development of either one or the other as death is for that of organic life. We fight against it as long as we can and often stave it off successfully both for ourselves and others but there is nothing so great — not Homer, Shakespeare, Handel, Rembrandt, de Hooghe, and the goodly company of other great men for whose lives we would gladly give our own — but it has got to go sooner or later, and leave no visible traces, though the invisible ones endure from everlasting to everlasting. It is idle to regret this for ourselves or others. Our effort should tend towards enjoying and being enjoyed as highly and for as long time as we can, and then chancing the rest.

### CONSCIENCE

is thoroughly well-bred and soon leaves off talking to those who do not wish to hear it.

### THE DAYS

run through me as water through a sieve.

### FOR COUNSELS OF IMPERFECTION

From a wordly point of view, there is no mistake so great as that of being always right.

If the writer of these words meant exactly what he said, he had so little wisdom that he might well seek more. He should have known that wisdom spends most of her time crying in the streets and public-houses, and he should have gone thither to look for her. If however he meant rather, 'Where shall wisdom be regarded?' this again is not a very sensible question. People have had wisdom before them for some time, and they may be presumed to be the best judges of their own affairs, yet they do not generally show much regard for wisdom. We may conclude, therefore, that they have found her less profitable than by her own estimate she would appear to be. This indeed is what one of the wisest men who ever lived — the author of the book of *Ecclesiastes* — definitely concludes to be the case, when he tells his readers that they had better not overdo either their virtue or their wisdom (*Ecc.* VII, 16). They must not, on the other hand, overdo their wickedness, nor presumably their ignorance. Still the writer evidently thinks that error is safer on the side of too little than of too much.

Reflection will show that this must always have been true, and must always remain so, for this is the side on which error is both least disastrous, and offers most place for repentance. He who finds himself inconvenienced by knowing too little can go to the British Museum, or to the Working Men's College, and learn more; but when a thing is once well learnt it is even harder to unlearn than it was to learn. Would it be possible to unlearn the art of speech or those of reading and writing even if we wished to do so? Wisdom and knowledge are, like a bad reputation, more easily won than lost; we got on fairly well without knowing that the earth went round the sun; we thought the sun went round the earth until we found it makes us uncomfortable to think so any longer — then we altered our opinion; it was not very easy to alter it, but it was easier than it would be to alter it back again. *Vestigia nulla retrorsum.* The earth itself does not pursue its course more steadily than mind does when it has once committed itself, and if we could see the movements of the stars in slow time we should probably find that there was much more throb and tremor in detail than we can take note of.

How, I wonder, will it be if in our pursuit of knowledge we stumble upon some awkward fact as disturbing for the human race as an enquiry into the state of his own finances may sometimes prove to the individual? The pursuit of knowledge can never be anything but a leap in the dark, and a leap in the dark is a very uncomfortable thing. I have sometimes thought that if the human race ever loses its ascendancy it will not be through plague, famine or cataclysm, but by getting to know some little microbe, as it were, of knowledge which shall get into its system and breed there till it makes an end of us. It is well, therefore, that there should be a substratum of mankind who cannot by any inducement be persuaded to know anything whatever at all, and who are resolutely determined to know nothing among us but what the parson tells them, and not to be too sure even about that.

### CONTRADICTION IN TERMS, SERIOUSNESS

Everything should be taken seriously, and nothing should be taken seriously.

### ON THE ART OF 'COVERY'

This is as important and interesting as 'dis-covery'. Surely the glory of finally getting rid of and burying a long and troublesome matter should be as great as that of making a great discovery — the trouble is that the coverer is like Samson who perished in the wreck of what he had destroyed. If he gets rid of a thing effectually he gets rid of himself too.

## MILK

is a kind of prescription which a cow makes up for her calf, inside her own body, and like all other chemists she never makes it up quite the same twice together.

F AND THE LITERARY AND SCIENTIFIC BIGWIGS

he *enfant terrible* of literature and science. If I
I know I cannot, get them to give me a shilling,
I know I can, heave bricks into the middle

S OF OXFORD AND CAMBRIDGE

cating the young men to be able to teach

## TRUTH

solutely lost sight of but it should not

UPREME MEN

me moments. Commonly they are
m the rest of us in the fact that,
or rising they can do so at once

CISM

whether he knows when and
vidence.

I know we should never get on together. I should have
had to cut him off with a shilling either for laughing at
Homer, or for refusing to laugh at him, or both, or neither
but still cut him off. So I settled the matter by tur[ning a]
deaf ear to his importunities and sticking to it that [I would]
not get him at all. Yet his thin ghost visits me at t[imes]
though he knows that it is no use pestering me f[or he]
looks at me so wistfully and reproachfully that [I am]
inclined to turn tail, and ask him to let me get h[im.]
But I should show a clean pair of heels if h[e did.]

Besides, he would probably be a girl.

### BUSINESS AND OLD MONUME[NTS]

Business makes wounds in old histori[c places like]
those of railway accidents which doctor[s say are the most]
frightful of all for their recklessness.

### TENNYSON'S FUNE[RAL]

I see they packed the volume of S[hakespeare]
near him when he died in a little ti[n box beside]
him. If they had to bury it they [should not have]
packed it at all, or, at the least, in[ ]
his friends should have taken it [out when they]
saw the end was near. It was n[ ]
the fact that the ruling passion [was strong with]
him in death. If I am reading, s[ay Shakespeare,]
up to the last of my conscious[ ]
take it out and put it in the [ ]
see that I have no further us[e ]
on burying it with me, say in[ ]
it at their own risk, and may[ ]
in that day.

I am t
cannot, an
I can, and
of them.

are too busy edu
them anything.

It should not be ab
be talked about.

s
are only supreme at supr
common. They differ fr
when the moment comes
and instinctively.

The test of a good critic is
how to believe on insufficient e

r,
...ning a
...I would
...mes and,
...urther, he
...I am half-
...im after all.
...e said 'Yes.'

...cal buildings like
...s say are the most

...hakespeare that he had
...box and buried it with
...should have either not
...a box of silver-gilt. But
...out of the bed when they
...ot necessary to emphasize
...for posing was strong with
...ay, *Ally Sloper's Half Holiday*
...hours, I trust my friends will
...waste-paper basket when they
...e for it. If, however, they insist
...an old sardine-box, let them do
...God remember it against them

is but to leave off dying and do the thing once for all.


## GOING AWAY

I can generally stand this, but I don't like leave-taking.


## THE GRAPE-FILTER

When the water of a place is bad it is safest to drink none that has not been filtered through either the berry of a grape, or else a tub of malt. These are the most reliable filters yet invented.


## GOD

There is little hope of his improving. He was satisfied with his own work, and that is fatal. Hence the same old 'As it was in the beginning, is now and ever shall be, world without end, amen' from everlasting to everlasting, without a sign of any effort at amendment of life on God's part.


## BORE

There is no bore like a clever bore.


## THE ART OF FEELING[1]

If there is truth in my lecture on the genesis of feeling, people cannot feel unless they know how to feel — i.e. what to feel under what circumstances. When, then, a position becomes too horribly novel for us to have had any experience that can guide us in knowing how to feel about it, the probability is that we cannot feel at all. Hence we may hope that the most horrible apparent suffering is not felt beyond a certain point, but is performed under a natural automatic anaesthetic.

[1] This note is an amalgamation of several which appear in the MS Notebooks under the title 'Scraps cut out of *Luck or Cunning*'.

It is generally held that animals feel; it will soon be generally held that plants feel; after that it will be held that stones also can feel. For, as no matter is so organic that there is not some of the inorganic in it, so, also, no matter is so inorganic that there is not some of the organic in it. We know that we have nerves and that we feel, it does not follow that other things do not feel because they have no nerves — it only follows that they do not feel as we do. The difference between the organic and the inorganic kingdoms will some day be seen to lie in the greater power of discriminating its feelings which is possessed by the former. Both are made of the same universal substance, but, in the case of the organic world, this substance is able to feel more fully and discreetly and to show us that it feels.

Animals and plants, as they advance in the scale of life, differentiate their feelings more and more highly; they record them better and recognize them more readily. They get to know what they are doing and feeling, not step by step only, nor sentence by sentence, but in long flights, forming chapters and whole books of action and sensation. The difference as regards feeling between man and the lower animals is one of degree and not of kind. The inorganic is less expert in differentiating its feelings, therefore its memory of them must be less enduring; it cannot recognize what it could scarcely cognize. One might as well for some purposes, perhaps, say at once, as indeed people generally do for most purposes, that the inorganic does not feel; nevertheless the somewhat periphrastic way of putting it, by saying that the inorganic feels but does not know, or knows only very slightly, how to differentiate its feelings, has the advantage of expressing the fact that feeling depends upon differentiation and sense of relation *inter se* of the things differentiated — a fact which, if never expressed, is apt to be lost sight of.

As human discrimination is to that of the lower animals, so the discrimination of the lower animals and plants is to that of inorganic things. In each case it is greater discriminating power (and this is mental power) that underlies the differentiation, but in no case can there be a denial of mental power altogether.

## AMERICA

America will have her geniuses, as every other country has. In fact she has had one in Walt Whitman, but I do not think America is a good place in which to be a genius. A genius can never expect to have a good time anywhere, if he is a genuine article, but America is about the last place in which life will be endurable at all for an inspired writer of any kind.

## THE LATE LORD TENNYSON

It seems that it was not the copy actually in bed with Tennyson when he died that was buried with him, but another copy, let us hope of the same edition, and equally well bound, was substituted for it, and it was buried 'in a metal case.' In the earlier accounts we were told it was buried in a tin case. Well, tin is a metal, is it not? and metal has a less kettley kind of feeling about it, and sounds better than tin, so we will not insist on the particular kind of metal; but surely the people who would keep the actual volume and bury another copy in a 'metal' case — well, they would have been very likely to fail in duty more than twice in the matter of Excalibur.

After all, suppose Bedivere[1] had not flung away Excalibur, but had kept it to put in the Museum, we cannot be sure that the consequences would have been so serious as we are given to understand they would have been.

[1] Butler names Lancelot as the Knight deputed to return Excalibur to the Lady of the Lake — perhaps a deliberate error to show his dislike of Tennyson.

If you choose to insist on the analogies and points of resemblance between men and women, they are so great that the differences seem indeed small; if on the other hand you are in a mood for emphasizing their points of difference, you can show that *au fond* men and women have hardly anything in common. And so with anything: if a man wants to make a case he can generally find a way of doing so.

## DEATH IS

only a loss of fortune greater than we can endure.

## COUNSELS OF IMPERFECTION

To kill self by too much mortification of the flesh is but another, more cruel, and more despicable kind of suicide.

## LOVE AND EATING

I have often said that there is no true love short of eating and consequent assimilation; the embryonic processes are but a long course of eating and assimilation — the sperm and germ cells, or the two elements that go to form the new animal, whatever they should be called, eat one another up, and then the mother assimilates them to more or less extent, through mutual inter-feeding and inter-breeding between her and them. But the curious point is that the more profound our love is the less we are conscious of it as love. True, a nurse tells her child that she should like to eat it, but this is only an expression that shows an instinctive recognition of the fact that eating is a mode of, or rather the acme of, love: no nurse really loves her child half well enough to want to eat it; put to such proof as this the love of which she is so profoundly, as she imagines, sentient proves to be but skin deep. So with our horses and dogs; we think we dote upon them, but we do not really love them.

What on the other hand can awaken less consciousness of warm affection than an oyster? Who would press an oyster to his heart, or pat it and want to kiss it? Yet nothing short of its complete absorption into our own being can in the least satisfy us. No merely superficial temporary contact of exterior form to exterior form will serve us. The embrace must be consummate, not achieved by a mocking environment of draped and muffled arms, that leaves no lasting trace on organization or consciousness, but by an enfolding within the bare and warm bosom of an open mouth — a grinding out of all differences of opinion by the sweet persuasion of the jaws, and the eloquence of a tongue that now convinces all the more powerfully because it is inarticulate and deals but with the one universal language of agglutination. Then we become made one with what we love — not heart to heart, but protoplasm to protoplasm, and this is far more to the want of purpose.

The proof of love, then, like that of any other pleasant pudding, is in the eating, and tested by this proof we see that consciousness of love like all other consciousness vanishes on becoming intense. While we are yet fully aware of it we do not love as well as we think we do. When we really mean business and are hungry with affection, we do not know that we are in love, but simply go into the love-shop — for so any eating-house should be more fitly called — ask the price, pay our money down, and love till we can either love or pay no longer.

And so with hate. When we really hate a thing it makes us sick, and we use this expression to symbolize the utmost hatred of which our nature is capable — but when we know we hate, our hatred is in reality mild and inoffensive. I, for example, think I hate all those people whose photographs I see in the shop windows, but I am so conscious of this that I am convinced in reality nothing would please me better than to be in the shop windows too. So when I see the universities conferring degrees on any one, or the learned

Societies moulting the yearly medals as peacocks moult their tails — (to be continued some other time).

## GOD AND THE DEVIL

are about as 12 to 9. There is enough preponderance on God's side to make it far safer to be on his side than the Devil's, but the excess is not so great as his professional *claqueurs* pretend it is. It is like playing at Monte Carlo. If you play long enough you are sure to lose, but now and again you may win a great deal of excellent money if you will only cease playing the moment you have won it.

## CAPITAL AND GENIUS

Capital is like genius, alike hated and coveted by those who are without it, or have but little of it, for no man is wholly destitute of either genius or money.

## 'WOE UNTO YOU WHEN ALL MEN SPEAK WELL OF YOU'

Yes, and 'Woe unto you when you speak well of all men.'

## EREWHON REVISITED

They have professors of all the languages of the principal beasts and birds. I staid with the Professor of feline languages who had invented a kind of Ollendorffian system for teaching the arts of polite conversation among cats.

## SQUARING THE CIRCLE

In old times people used to try and square the circle; now they try and devise schemes for satisfying the Irish nation.

Two or three people have asked me to return to this and explain it more fully from my own point of view. I have had the subject on my notes for some time and it has bored me so much that it has had a good deal to do with my not having kept my Note-Books posted for some time.

Briefly, in order to scotch that snake, my failure has not been so great as people say it has. I believe my reputation stands well with the best people. Granted it makes no noise, but I have not been willing to take the pains necessary to achieve what may be called guinea-pig review success, because I did not seriously need it from a money point of view, and because I hated the kind of people I should have had to court and kow-tow to if I went in for this sort of thing. I should never have carried it through, even if I had tried, and instinctively declined to try. A man cannot be said to have failed, because he did not get what he did not try for. What I did try for I believe I have got as fully as any reasonable man can expect, and I have every hope that I shall get it still more both so long as I live and after I am dead.

If, however, people mean that I am to explain how it is I have not made more noise in spite of my own indolence in the matter, the answer is that those who do not either push themselves into noise, or give some one else a substantial interest in pushing them, never do get made a noise about. How can they? I was too lazy to go about from publisher to publisher and decline to publish a book myself if I could not find some one to take it up. I could take any amount of trouble about writing a book but, so long as I could lay my hand on the money to bring it out with, I found publishers' ante-chambers so little to my taste that I soon tired and fell back on the short and easy method of publishing my book myself. Of course, therefore, it failed to sell. I know more about these things now, and will never publish a book at my own risk again, or at any rate I will send somebody else round the ante-chambers with it for a good while before I pay for publishing it.

However — I should have liked notoriety and financial success well enough if they could have been had for the asking, but I was not going to take any trouble about them and, as a natural consequence, I did not get them. If I had wanted them with the same passionate longing that has led me to pursue every inquiry that I ever have pursued, I should have got it fast enough. It is very rarely that I have failed to get what I have really tried for and, as a matter of fact, I believe I have been a great deal happier for not trying than I should have been if I had had notoriety thrust upon me.

I confess I should like my books to pay their expenses and put me a little in pocket besides — because I want to do more for Alfred than I see my way to doing. As a natural consequence of beginning to care I have begun to take pains, and am advising with the Society of Authors as to what will be my best course. Very likely they can do nothing for me, but at any rate I shall have tried.

One reason, and that the chief, why I have made no noise is now explained. It remains to add that from first to last I have been unorthodox and militant in every book that I have written. I made enemies of the parsons with my first two books once for all. The Evolution books made the Darwinians and, through them, the scientific world in general even more angry than *The Fair Haven* had made the clergy.

I have chosen the fighting road rather than the hang-on-to-a-great-man road, and what can a man who does this expect except that people should try and silence him in whatever way they think will be most effectual? In my case they have thought it best to pretend that I am non-existent. It is no part of my business to complain of my opponents for choosing their own line; my business is to defeat them as best I can upon their own line, and I imagine I shall do most towards this by not allowing myself to be made unhappy merely because I am not fussed about, and by going on adding to my pile.

That pile stands thus at present. 1 *Erewhon*; 2 *The Fair Haven* than which I do not think there is any simpler and more complete explanation of the case of Christianity; 3 *Life and Habit* which I see frequently adopted but never yet once seriously grappled with. 4 The complete exposure and discomfiture of Charles Darwin and Wallace in my three later books. 5 The resuscitation of Buffon, Erasmus Darwin and Lamarck. 6 The rediscovery of the portraits of Giovanni and Gentile Bellini, both side by side in four Venetian pictures of 1498 (?)-1514 (see *Athenaeum* about 9 years ago and subsequent notes). 7 The unearthing of Tabachetti, not to say of Paracca and of Gaudenzio Ferrari as far as the British public was concerned. 8 The proof that the *Danse des Paysans* at Basle is an original (though no doubt retouched) drawing of Holbein and finally 9 The discovery that the *Odyssey* was written at Trapani and the seeing what, however, I admit anyone but a fool must see — that the poem is written by a woman not a man . . . saying nothing about my poor old grandfather.

I submit that this list is more than any reasonable man could expect to claim. Supposing therefore that my good fortune now fails me and that I find out no more, I consider that I need not be disquieted. Nor am I disquieted, nevertheless if I can get more I will. Roughly, however, to return to my original subject, if I am asked to lay my hand on the theme which more than any other has prevented my making way in my own generation I should say it was my quarrel with Charles Darwin and the dirty tricks which he and his have never failed to play me when they got a chance.

Why should the botanist, geologist or other-ist give himself such airs over the draper's assistant? Is it because he names his plants or specimens with Latin names, and divides them into genera and species whereas the draper does not formulate his classifications — or at any rate only uses his mother tongue when he does? Yet how like the subdivisions of textile life are to those of the animal and vegetable kingdoms. A few great families — cotton, linen, hempen, woollen, silk and mohair and alpaca — into what infinite variety of genera and species do not these great families subdivide themselves? And does it take less labour, with less intelligence, to master all these and to acquire familiarity with their various habits, habitats and prices than it does to master the details of any other great branch of science? I do not know, but when I think of Shoolbred's on the one hand and, say, the ornithological collections of the British Museum upon the other, I feel as though it would take me less trouble to master the second than the first.

## UNCONSCIOUS LYING

So with lying: it is the unconscious liar that is the greatest liar.

## THE SIN AGAINST THE HOLY GHOST

Jones once asked me if I thought allowing oneself to be bored might be the sin against the Holy Ghost.

## CLERGYMEN AND BARRISTERS

Clergymen ought to be like barristers, and allowed to plead on a side which they know to be a wrong one without its being expected of them to pretend that they believe it true.

## FOLLOWERS

We are all followers more or less, just as we are all both prigs and blackguards more or less; but some know how to follow freely and gracefully, while others do so at once slavishly and so far as they can surreptitiously.

## HATING

with a hatred passing the hate of women.

## MORE OR LESS MAD

As every sane man has his percentage of madness, so all madmen have their percentage of sanity. So with priggishness, knavery and folly — everyone is in some respects both knave and fool, and yet in the main he may be honest, like the 'very honest woman, but somewhat given to lying' in *Antony and Cleopatra*.

## LOGIC

No mistake is more common and more fatuous than appealing to logic in cases which are beyond her jurisdiction; and all things, as for example art, religion, science, business, etc., have their limitations beyond which the writs of the rules do not run.

## ODYSSEAN NOTE

If a person would understand either the *Odyssey* or any other ancient work, he must never look at the dead without seeing the living in them, nor at the living without thinking of the dead. We are too fond of seeing the ancients as one thing and the moderns as another.

## NATURE AND OFFENCES

There are offences that nature cannot officially tolerate, and indeed flogs for with a grave face, but which, nevertheless, she will overlook if she can.

## WOMEN CAN STAND A BEATING

except when it is with their own weapons.

## THE OLDEST BOOKS

are still only just out to those who have not read them.

## I HAVE HAD TO STEAL MY OWN BIRTHRIGHT

I stole it and was bitterly punished. But I saved my soul alive.

## THE TIGHT BOOTS OF CHRISTIANITY

Our souls have worn the tight boots of Christianity for so many generations that they are becoming cramped hereditarily.

## CHAINED LIONS

I was reading *Pilgrim's Progress* the other day and was thinking how Odyssean it was in its sincerity and downrightness, as well as in the marvellous beauty of its language, its freedom from all taint of the schools and, not least, in complete victory of genuine internal zeal over a scheme so initially faulty as to appear hopeless.

I read that part where Christian passes the lions which he thought were free but which were really chained and it occurred to me that all lions are chained until they actually eat you and that, the moment they do this, they chain themselves up again automatically, as far as we are concerned. If one dissects this passage it fares as many a passage in the *Odyssey* does when we dissect it. Christian did not, after all, venture to pass the lions till he was assured that they were chained. And really it is more excusable to refuse point-blank to pass a couple of lions till one knows whether they are chained or not — and the poor wicked people seem to have done nothing more than this — than it would be to pass them. Besides, by being told, Christian fights, as it were, with loaded dice.

### LIFE AND DEATH

The whole life of some people is a kind of partial death — a long, lingering death-bed, so to speak, of stagnation and nonentity on which death is but the seal, or solemn signing, as the abnegation of all further act and deed on the part of the signer. Death robs these people of even that little strength which they appeared to have and it gives them nothing but repose. On others, again, death confers a more living kind of life than they can ever possibly have enjoyed while to others they seemed to be alive. Look at Shakespeare for example; can he be properly said to have lived in anything like his real life till a hundred years or so after his death? His physical life was but as a dawn before the sun-rise of that life of the world to come which he was to enjoy hereafter. True, there was a little life and movement — a little abiding of shepherds in the fields, keeping watch over their flocks by night — and men buzzing in knots waiting to be hired before daybreak — not to say a burglar or two here and there — an inchoation of life; but the true life of the man was after death and not before it.

Death is not more the end of some people than it is the beginning of others. So he that loses his soul may find it, and he that finds, lose it.

## DEATH

God seems to have fully made up his mind that come what may no one shall know when either he or anyone else is going to die. Even the condemned criminal on the scaffold cannot know this, for he may die of heart disease and thus cheat the gallows yet. Still, if he is to do this he must look sharp. Death, instead of being certain, as Justice Shallow said (?), is the most uncertain of all things.

## SOCIALISM

Cousens said to me last night that all good men were socialists. I thought to myself, 'No doubt, but no good man will so dub himself; he will let all that go without saying.'

## SCYLLA AND CHARYBDIS COUNSELS OF IMPERFECTION

They are everywhere. Just now coming up Great Russell Street I loitered outside a print shop. There they were as usual — Hogarth's Idle and Virtuous Apprentices. The idle apprentice is certainly Scylla, but is the virtuous apprentice so greatly preferable? Is not the right thing somewhere between the two? And does not the art of good living consist mainly in a fine perception of when to edge towards the idle and when towards the virtuous apprentice?

When John Bunyan (or Richard Baxter, or whoever it was) said, 'There went John Bunyan, but for the grace of God', had he a right to be so cock-sure that the criminal on whom he was looking was not saying much the same thing as he looked upon John Bunyan? Does any one who knows me doubt that if I were offered my choice between a bishopric and a halter, I should choose the halter? I believe half the bishops would choose the halter themselves if they had to do it over again.

is a kind of fire that spreads and blazes and consumes.

## AN OPEN MIND

is all very well in its way, but it ought not to be so open that there is no keeping anything in or out of it. It should be capable of shutting its doors sometimes, or it may be found a little draughty.

### LORD LET ME KNOW MINE END

[*Lord, let me know mine end, and the number of my days: that I may be certified how long I have to live* (Ps. xxxix. 5).]

Of all prayers this is the insanest. That the one who uttered it should have made and retained a reputation is a strong argument in favour of his having been surrounded with courtiers. 'Lord, let me not know mine end' would be better, only it would be praying for what God has already granted us. 'Lord, let me know A.B.'s end' would be bad enough. Even though A.B. were Mr Gladstone — we might hear he was not to die yet. 'Lord, stop A.B. from knowing my end' would be reasonable, if there were any use in praying that A.B. might not be able to do what he never can do. Or can the prayer refer to the other end of life and mean 'Lord, let me know my beginning?' This again would not be always prudent.

The prayer is a silly piece of petulance and it would have served the maker of it right to have had it granted. 'Cancer in about three months after great suffering' or 'Ninety, a burden to yourself and every one else' — there is not so much to pick and choose between them. Surely, 'I thank thee, O Lord, that thou hast hidden mine end from me' would be better.

If again he had prayed that he might be able to make his psalms a little more lively, and be saved from becoming the bore which he has been to so many generations of sick persons and young children — or that he might find a publisher for them with greater facility — but there is no end to it. The prayer he did pray was about the worst he could have prayed and the psalmist, being the psalmist, naturally prayed it — unless I have misquoted him.

### THE LIFE AFTER DEATH

That there is such a life is as palpable as that there is a life before death. See the influence that the dead have over us. But this life is no more eternal than our present life. Shakespeare and Homer may live long, but they will die, that is to say, become unknown as direct and efficient causes — some day.

Even so God himself dies, for to die is to change and to change is to die to what has gone before. If the units change the total must do so also.

As no one can say which egg or seed shall come to visible life and in its turn leave issue, so no one can say which of the millions of now visible lives shall enter into the after-life on death, and which have but so little life as practically not to count. For most seeds end as seeds or as food for some alien being, and so with lives, by far the greater number are sterile, except in so far as they can be devoured as the food of some stronger life. The Handels and Shakespeares are the few seeds that grow — and even these die.

And the same uncertainty attaches to posthumous life as to pre-lethal. As no one can say how long another shall live, so no one can say how long or how short a time a reputation shall live. The most unpromising weakly-looking creatures sometimes live to ninety while strong robust men are carried off in their prime. And no one can say what a man shall enter into life for having done. Roughly, there is a sort of moral government whereby those who have done the best work live most enduringly, but it is subject to such exceptions that no one can say whether or no there shall not be an exception in his own case either in his favour or against him.

### MORAL TRY-YOUR-STRENGTHS

There are people who, if they only had a slot, might turn a pretty penny as moral try-your-strengths, like those we see on stations for telling people their physical strength when they have dropped a penny in the slot. In a way they have a slot, which is their mouths, and people drop pennies in by asking them to dinner, and then we try our strength against them and get snubbed; but this way is roundabout and expensive. We want a good automatic asinometer by which we can tell at a moderate cost how great or how little of a fool we are.

### FASHION

is like God. Man cannot see it in its holy of holies and live, and it is, like God, increate, springing out of nothing, yet the maker of all things — ever changing yet the same yesterday, to-day and for ever.

### PRIESTS

are not men of the world; it is not intended that they should be; and a University training is the one best adapted to prevent their becoming so.

### MATRIMONY AND BACHELORHOOD

are both of them at once equally wise and equally foolish.

### 'HOME, SWEET HOME'

must surely have been written by a bachelor.

I was saying to Jones that I did not like bees; they were socialists, and too much off my beat. 'Oh, yes,' said Jones, 'and then they go and write books about Sir John Lubbock.'

## EREWHON REVISITED
### THE GREATEST HAPPINESS OF THE GREATEST NUMBER

It has long been held that those constitutions are best that promote most effectually the greatest happiness of the greatest number. Now the greatest number are none too wise nor too honest, and to arrange our systems with a view to the greater happiness of sensible straightforward people — indeed to give these people a chance at all if it can be managed — is to interfere with the greatest happiness of the greatest number. Dull, slovenly and arrogant people do not like those who are quick, painstaking and unassuming; how can we then consistently with the first principles either of morality or political economy encourage such people when we can bring sincerity and modesty fairly home to them?

Much we have to tolerate, partly because we cannot always discover in time who are really insincere and who are only masking sincerity under a garb of flippancy, and partly also because we wish to err on the side of letting the guilty escape rather than of punishing the innocent. Thus many people who are perfectly well known to belong to the straight-forward class are allowed to remain at large and may even be seen hobnobbing and on the best of possible terms with the guardians of public immorality. We all feel, as indeed has been said in other nations, that the poor abuses of the time want countenancing, and this moreover in the interests of the uses themselves, for the presence of a small modicum of sincerity acts as a wholesome stimulant and irritant to the prevailing spirit of academicism; moreover, we hold it useful to have a certain number of melancholy examples whose notorious failure shall serve as a warning to those who do not cultivate a power of immoral self-control which shall prevent them from saying, or indeed even thinking, anything that shall not be to their immediate and palpable advantage with the greatest number.

### MISTAKES

I am not sure that I do not begin to like the correction of a mistake, even when it involves my having shown much ignorance and stupidity, as well as I like hitting on a new idea. It does comfort one so to be able to feel sure that one knows how to tumble and how to retreat promptly and without chagrin.

### THE DICTIONARY OF NATIONAL BIOGRAPHY

When I look at the articles on Handel, on Dr. Arnold, or indeed on almost any one whom I know anything about, I feel that such a work as the *Dictionary of National Biography* adds more terror to death than death of itself could inspire. That is one reason why I let myself go so unreservedly in these notes. If the colours in which I paint myself fail to please, at any rate I shall have had the laying them on myself.

### LITERARY OFFSPRING AND PHYSICAL

If the literary offspring is not to die very young, almost as much trouble must have been taken with it as with the bringing up of a physical child. Still, the physical child is the harder work of the two.

### THE SPADE AND THE PIECE OF STRING

All things are either for separating and keeping apart, or for uniting and bringing together; but all contain a little of their opposite, and some, as the railway train, combine many examples of both. Thus the train is in the main used for bringing things together, but it is also used for sending them apart, and its divisions into classes are alike for separating and for keeping together. A hedge again is alike for separating and bringing together, whereas a piece of string is a thing that, on the whole, makes for togetheriness. The spade is on the whole a thing that makes for splitty-uppiness; still, there is an odour of togetheriness hanging about it, for it tends to bring potatoes into a man's stomach.

In high philosophy one should never look at a spade without considering it also as a piece of string, or at a piece of string without considering it also as a spade.

### EREWHON REVISITED

They live their life backwards, beginning as old men and women, with little more knowledge of the past than we have of the future, and foreseeing the future about as clearly as we do the past, winding up by entering into the womb as though it were being buried. But delicacy forbids me to pursue this subject further: the upshot being that it comes to much the same thing, provided one is used to it.

Let a criminal make a speech to a judge much as the judge's speech to the criminal in *Erewhon*.

### FORGIVE US OUR CHRISTMASSES

The little Strangs say the 'good words,' as they call them, before going to bed, aloud and at their father's knee, or rather in the pit of his stomach. One of them was lately heard to say 'Forgive us our christmasses as we forgive them that christmas against us.'

### TRANSLATING THE *ODYSSEY*

If you wish to preserve the spirit of a dead author, you must not skin him, stuff him, and set him up in a case. You must eat him, digest him and let him live in you, with such life as you have, for better or worse.

are like wine: if they are sound they ripen with keeping. A man should lay down letters as he does a cellar of wine.

## THOUGHT AND ACTION

Thought is not thought till it has also a little germ of action; in the purest thought there is still some action. So in the purest action there is still a little thought. We cannot have action without some thought, nor thought without some action.

## THE YOUTH OF AN ART

is, like the youth of anything else, its most interesting period. When it has come to the knowledge of good and evil it is stronger, but we care less about it.

## LORD ORFORD

In 1824 Lord Orford was invited to become president of the Norwich Bible Society. His reply was as follows:

'Sir — I am surprised and annoyed by the contents of your letter — surprised, because my well-known character should have exempted me from such an application; and annoyed, because it compels me to have even this communication with you.

'I have long been addicted to the gaming table; I have lately taken to the turf; I fear I frequently blaspheme; but I have never distributed religious tracts. All this was known to you and your society, notwithstanding which you think me a fit person to be your president. God forgive your hypocrisy.

'I would rather live in the land of sinners than with such saints.'

## COOKING AND DIGESTION

Cooking is half digesting; we do half our digestion, therefore, outside our own bodies.

. . . For God is not so white as he is painted, and he gets on better with the Devil than people think. The devil is too useful for him to wish him ill and, in like manner, half the devil's trade would be at an end should any great mishap bring God well down in the world. For all the mouths they make at one another they play into each other's hand and have got on so well as partners (playing Spenlow and Jorkins to one another) for so many years that there seems no reason why they should cease to do so. The conception of them as the one absolutely void of evil and the other of good is a vulgar notion taken from science whose priests have ever sought to get every idea and every substance pure of all alloy.

## COUNSELS OF IMPERFECTION

It is all very well to say mischievous writers like Thomas à Kempis and Père Grou maintain that we cannot serve God and Mammon. Granted that it is not easy, but nothing that is worth doing ever is easy. Easy or not easy, not only have we got to do it, but it is exactly in this that the whole duty of man consists.

If there are two worlds at all (and about this I have no doubt) it stands to reason that we ought to make the best of both of them, and more particularly of the one with which we are most immediately concerned.

There was a painter once who divided his time into two halves; in the one half he painted pot boilers with no other thought than the market; who would give most, most quickly, for what could be produced most cheaply. He was great at floods and never looked at Nature during this half of his time except in order to see what would make most show with least expense. On the whole he found nothing so effective as veiled heads.

The other half of his time he studied with the sincerity of Gio. Bellini, Rembrandt, Hogarth or de Hooghe. He avoided the temptation of letting either half absorb the other.

### GOD

Let man be true and every god a liar.

### IT IS BAD ENOUGH

to see one's own good things fathered on other people, but it is worse to have other people's rubbish fathered upon oneself.

### TIME AND MONEY

It is only very fortunate people whose time is money. My time is not money. I wish it was. It is not even somebody else's money. If it was he would give me some of it. I am a miserable, unmarketable sinner, and there is no money in me.

### A SICILIAN OATH

Santo Diavolo!

### PUBLIC EAR, THE — LIKE A COMMON

There is not much to be got off it, but that little is for the most part grazed down by geese and donkeys.

### EREWHON REVISITED

They consider 'wilful procreation,' as they call it, much as we do murder and will not allow it to be a moral ailment at all. Sometimes a jury will recommend to mercy and sometimes they bring in a verdict of 'justifiable baby-getting,' but they treat these cases as a rule with great severity.

### COUNSELS OF IMPERFECTION. VICE AND VIRTUE

Virtue is, as it were, the repose of sleep or death. Vice is the awakening to the knowledge of good and evil — without which there is no life worthy of the name. Sleep is a happier, more peaceful state than waking and, in a way, death is

277

better than life, but it is in a very small way. We feel such talk to be an insincere blasphemy against good life and, whatever we may say in death's favour, so long as we do not blow our brains out we show that we do not mean to be taken seriously. To know good, other than as a heavy sleeper we must know vice also. There cannot, as Bacon said, be a 'Hold fast that which is good' without a 'Prove all things' going before it. There is no knowledge of good without a knowledge of evil also, and this is why all nations have devils as well as gods, and regard them with sneaking kindness. God without the devil is dead, being alone.

### FRIENDSHIP

is like money, easier made than kept.

### WOMEN PECK

at some men's brains and hearts as daws steal spoons, not because they want them or know what they are, but because the glitter attracts them, and because they are naturally and instinctively fond of stealing.

### ABANDONED UNDERTAKINGS

The bodies of many of them lie rotting unburied up and down the country and their ghosts haunt the law courts.

### MYSELF

People sometimes give me to understand that it is a piece of ridiculous conceit on my part to jot down so many notes about myself, inasmuch as it implies a confidence that I shall one day be regarded as an interesting person. I answer that neither I nor they can form any idea as to whether I shall be wanted when I am gone or no. The chances are that I shall not. I am quite aware of it. So the chances are that I shall not live to be 85; but I have no right to settle it so. If I do as Captain Don did [*Life of Dr. Butler*, I, opening of Chapter VIII], and invest every penny I have in the world in an annuity that shall terminate when I am eighty-nine, who knows but that like him I may live on to ninety-six, and have seven years without any income at all? I prefer the modest insurance of keeping up my notes which others may burn or no as they please.

### IN THE MIDST OF VICE

we are in virtue, and *vice versa*.

### ON LIVING IN OTHERS

We had better do this as much as we can for many reasons and among others because we thus live more in the race, which God really does seem to care about a good deal, and less in the individual, to whom, so far as I can see, he is indifferent.

### 'GIVE PEACE IN OUR TIME, O LORD'

Is this indifference to what may befall the next generation, or does it proceed from a feeling that peace for a longer period is past praying for?

### FADDISTS

are generally also fastidious, at least I think so.

### POETRY IN RHYME AND RHYTHM

I have been trying to read *Venus and Adonis* and the *Rape of Lucrece* but find I cannot do so. They teem with fine things, but they are got-up fine things. I do not know whether this is quite what I mean but, come what may, I find the poems bore me. Were I a schoolmaster I should think I was setting a boy a very severe punishment if I told him to read *Venus and Adonis* through in three sittings. If, then, the magic of Shakespeare's name, let alone the great beauty of occasional passages, cannot reconcile us (for I find most people of the same mind) to verse, and especially rhymed verse as a medium of sustained expression, what chance has any one else? It seems to me that a sonnet is the utmost length to which a rhymed poem should extend.

### CANON AINGER
Jones said that Ainger was capable of bringing out an expurgated edition of Wordsworth.

### MR. WALTER PATER'S STYLE
To me it is like the face of some old woman who has been to Madame Rachel and had herself enamelled. The bloom is nothing but powder and paint and the odour is cherry-blossom.

### TO DIE COMPLETELY
a person must not only forget but be forgotten, and he who is not forgotten is not dead. This is as old as *non omnis moriar* and a great deal older, but very few people realize it.

### GOD
To lament that we cannot be more conscious of him and understand him better is much like lamenting that we are not more conscious of our circulation and digestion. Provided we live according to familiar laws of health, the less we think about circulation and digestion the better; and so with the ordinary rules of good conduct, the less we think of God the better.

### THOSE WHO WISH FOR POPULARITY
should bear in mind that people do not want generally to be made less foolish or less wicked. What they want is to be told that they are not foolish and not wicked. Now it is only a fool or a liar or both who can tell them this; the masses therefore cannot be expected to like any but fools or liars or both. So when a lady gets photographed, what she wants is not to be made beautiful but to be told that she is beautiful.

will be one day recognized as not less essential for national well-being than breeding is.

### LIFE AFTER DEATH

I refer of course to the life we live in others by reason of work that we have left behind us.

An immortal like Shakespeare knows nothing of his own immortality about which we are so keenly conscious. As he knows nothing of it when it is in its highest vitality, centuries, it may be, after his apparent death, so it is best and happiest if during his bodily life he should think little or nothing about it and perhaps hardly suspect that he will live after his death at all.

And yet I do not know — I could not keep myself going at all if I did not believe that I was going to have a good average three-score years and ten of immortality. There are very few workers who are not sustained by this belief, or at least hope, but it may well be doubted whether this is not a sign that they are not going to be immortal — and I am content (or try to be) to fare as my neighbours.

### GOD

In the eternal pendulum swing of thought we make God in our own image, and then make him make us, and then find it out and cry because we have no God and so on over and over again, as a child has new toys given to it, tires of them, breaks them and is disconsolate till it gets new ones which it will again tire of and break. If the man who first made God in his own image had been a good model, all might have been well; but he was impressed with an undue sense of his own importance and, as a natural consequence, he had no sense of humour. Both these imperfections he has fully and faithfully reproduced in the God of the Old and New Testaments.

## GOD BLACKING HIMSELF ALL OVER

God when he made the rain fall also upon the sea, was like the man who, when he was to play Othello, must needs black himself all over.

## THERE IS SUCH A THING

as doing good that evil may come.

## PHILOSOPHY

So far as I can see it is invariably an attempt to deny, circumvent or otherwise escape from the way in which the roots of things interlace with one another.

## MYSELF

I have known those things that I ought not to have known and I have not known those things that I ought to have known.

## VACCINATION

is the medical sacrament corresponding to baptism. Whether it is or is not more efficacious I do not know.

## GOD

He is like the sun; we come from him and we shall go to him; we owe him all things, but there is no use in praying to him.

## EXAMINATIONS AND PROFESSORSHIPS

We can only examine in respect of the more superficial qualities or acquisitions. We cannot examine for temper, patience, sagacity, daring or any of the more vital and deeper characteristics. And so with professorships. Fancy a professorship of any one of these things. If one wanted to encourage vice one should found a professorship of virtue.

## X-RAYS

Their moral is this — that a right way of looking at things will see through almost anything.

## A LANDLORD AND HIS PIG

I often walk from Rickmansworth across Moor Park to Pinner. On getting out of Moor Park there is a public-house just to the left where Alfred and I generally have some shandy-gaff and I buy some eggs. The landlord had a noble sow which I photographed for him; some months afterwards I asked how the sow was. She had been sold. The landlord knew she ought to be killed and made into bacon, but he had been intimate with her for three years and someone else must eat her, not he.

'And what,' said I, 'became of her daughter?'

'Oh, we killed her and ate her. You see we had only known her eighteen months.'

I wonder how he settled the exact line beyond which intimacy with a pig must not go if the pig is to be eaten.

## GENIUS AND PROVIDENCE

Among all the evidences for the existence of an over-ruling Providence that I can discover, I see none more convincing than the elaborate and for the most part effectual provision that has been made for the suppression of genius.

## LIFE AND LOVE

To live is like to love — all reason is against it, and all healthy instinct for it.

## A WELL-BALANCED MIND

is one which a little additional weight in either scale will unsettle; it is, therefore, being continually disturbed and unequilibrated, unless it can secure itself from new in-fluences of any kind.

The best kind, the most stable kind, of mind is one that is set down plump on the ground on a good broad base and without any approach to balance, so that nothing short of an earthquake can disturb it.

We ought to say that a man has a well balancing mind, if we mean that his judgment is generally good.

### VIRTUE
If you wish to understand virtue you must be subvicious; for the really virtuous man, who is fully under grace, will be virtuous unconsciously and will know nothing about it. Unless a man is out-and-out virtuous he is subvicious.

### LORD, I DO NOT BELIEVE,
help thou mine unbelief.

### BUNYAN'S PILGRIM'S PROGRESS
I have been reading this again — the third part and all — and wish that someone would tell me what to think about it.

The English is racy, vigorous and often very beautiful; but the language of any book is nothing except in so far as it reveals the writer. The language in which a man clothes his thought is like all other clothes — its cut raises presumptions about the thoughts, which generally turn out to be just, but it is no more the thought than a man's coat is himself. I am not however sure that in Bunyan's case the dress in which he has clothed his ideas does not reveal him more justly than the ideas do.

*Pilgrim's Progress* consists mainly of a series of infamous libels upon life and things; it is a blasphemy against certain fundamental ideas of right and wrong which our consciences most instinctively approve; its notion of heaven is hardly higher than a transformation scene at Drury Lane; it is essentially infidel. 'Hold out to me the chance of a golden crown and harp, freedom from all further worries, with angels to flatter me and fetch and carry for me, and I shall think the game worth playing, notwithstanding the great and horrible risk of failure; but no crown, no cross for me. Pay me richly and certainly and I will wait for payment, but if I have to give credit I shall expect to be paid better in the end.'

There is no conception of the faith that a man should do his duty cheerfully with all his might though, as far as he can see, he will never be paid directly or indirectly neither here or hereafter. Still less is there any conception that unless a man has this faith he is not worth thinking about. There is no sense that as we have received freely so we should give freely and be only too thankful that we have anything that we can give at all. Furthermore there does not appear to be even the remotest conception that all this honourable, comfortable and sustaining faith is, like all other high faiths, to be brushed aside very peremptorily at the bidding of common-sense.

What a pity it is that Christian never met Mr Common-Sense with his daughter, Good-Humour, and her affianced husband, Mr Hate-Cant; but if he ever saw them in the distance he steered clear of them, probably as feeling that they would be more dangerous than Giant Despair, Vanity Fair and Apollyon all together — for they would have stuck to him if he had let them get in with him.

Among other things they would have told him that, if there was any truth in his opinions, neither man nor woman ought to become a father or mother at all, inasmuch as their doing so would probably entail eternity of torture on the wretched creature whom they were launching into the world. Life in this world is risk enough to inflict on another person without his or her being consulted in the matter, but come what may death will give quittance in full. To weaken our faith in this full and certain hope of peace eternal (except so far as we have so lived as to win life in others after we are gone) would be a cruel thing, even though the evidence against it were overwhelming, but to rob us of it on no evidence worth a moment's consideration and, apparently, from no other motive than the pecuniary advantage of the robbers themselves is infamy. For the Churches exist but as an institution for the saving of men's souls from hell.

This is true enough, but it is also untrue that in practice

any Christian minister, knowing what he preaches to be both very false and very cruel, yet insists on it because it is to the advantage of his own order. In a way the preachers believe what they teach, but it is as men who have taken a bad £10 note and refuse to look at the evidence that makes against it, though, if the note were not theirs, they would see at a glance that it was a bad one. For the man in the street it is enough that what the churches teach in respect of a future state is palpably both cruel and absurd while, at the same time, they make their living by teaching it and thus preying upon men's fears of the unknown. If the churches do not wish to be misunderstood they should not allow themselves to remain in such an equivocal position.

But let this pass. Bunyan, we may be sure, took all that he preached in its most literal interpretation; he could never have made his book so interesting had not he done so. The interest of the book depends almost entirely on the unquestionable good faith of the writer and the strength of the impulse that compelled him to speak that which was within him. He was not writing a book which he might sell, he was speaking what was borne in upon him from heaven. The message he uttered was, to my thinking, both low and false, but it was truth of truths to Bunyan.

This will not do. The *Epistles of St. Paul* were truth of truths to Paul, but they do not attract us to the man who wrote them, and, except here and there, they are very uninteresting. Mere strength of conviction on a writer's part is not enough to make his work take permanent rank. Yet I know that I could read the whole of *The Pilgrim's Progress* (except occasional episodical sermons), without being at all bored by it, whereas, having spent a penny upon Mr Stead's abridgement of Fielding's *Joseph Andrews*, I had to give it up as putting me out of all patience. I then spent a penny on an abridgement of *Gulliver's Travels*, and was delighted with it. What is it that makes one book so readable and another so unreadable? Swift, from all I can make out, was a far more human and genuine person than he is generally represented, but I do not think I should have liked him, whereas Fielding, I am sure, must have been delightful. Why do the faults of his work overweigh its many great excellences, while the less great excellences of *Gulliver's Travels* outweigh its more serious defects? I suppose it is the prolixity of the former that fatigues me. Swift is terse, he gets through what he has to say on any matter as quickly as he can and takes the reader on to the next, whereas Fielding is not only long, but his length is made still longer by the disconnectedness of the episodes that appear to have been padded into the books — episodes that do not help you forward, and are generally so exaggerated and often so full of horse-play as to put one out of conceit with the parts that are really excellent.

Whatever else Bunyan is, he is never long; he takes you quickly on from incident to incident and, however little his incidents may appeal to us, we feel that he never gives us one that is not *bona fide* so far as he is concerned. His episodes and incidents are introduced not because he wants to make his book longer but because he cannot be satisfied without these particular ones, even though he may feel that his book is getting longer than he likes.

And here for the present at any rate I must break away from Bunyan. (1897.)

### WOMEN SOMETIMES SAY

that they have had no offers, and only wish that some one had ever proposed to them. This is not the right way to put it. What they should say is that though, like all women, they have been proposing to men all their lives, yet they grieve to remember that they have been invariably refused.

### THE WORLD

is like those men who look back with displeasure and dislike on themselves some three years back all through their lives, but like stories about their childhood.

### THERE WAS A WRITER

who left little or nothing about himself and the world complained that it was puzzled. Another, mindful of this, left copious details about himself, whereon the world said that it was more puzzled about him even than about the man who had left nothing, till presently it found out that it was also bored, and troubled itself no more about him.

### TRUTH

is that which seems true to the best and most competent men of any given age and place where truth is sought. It is what these men can acquiesce in with the least discomfort.

### CHRISTIANITY

As an instrument of warfare against vice, or as a tool for making morality, it is a mere flint implement.

### THE STORK THAT HATCHED A GOSLING

I was told not long since, but do not know where the story comes from, that someone from mischief or curiosity took a stork's egg out of the nest in which it lay, and substituted a gosling's egg. In due time a gosling was hatched, but the male stork as soon as it saw the young bird, ran his beak right through the mother and killed her.

### MY LIFE HAS BEEN SQUANDERED

as a half-crown given to a schoolboy. But then half, or more than half the fun a schoolboy finds in a half-crown is in the mere fact of having something to squander. Squandering is in itself delightful, and so I found it with my life in my younger days. I do not squander it now, but I am not sorry that I have squandered a good deal of it. What a heap of rubbish there would have been if I had not! Had I not better set about squandering it again now?

You can do very little with it, but you can do nothing without it.

The inference which Arthur Platt (*Journal of Philology*, Vol. 24, No. 47) wishes to draw from Eumaeus's being told to bring Ulysses' bow ἀνὰ δώματα (*Od.* XXI. 234) suggests to me the difference which some people in future ages may wish to draw between the character of Lord Burleigh's steps in Tennyson's poem, according as he was walking up or pacing down. Wherefrom also the critic will argue that the scene of Lord Burleigh's weeping *must* have been on an inclined plane.

is an attempt to get an irrefragably safe investment, and this cannot be got, no matter how low the interest, which in the case of religion is about as low as it can be.

asked her mother once whether riding or driving was the more difficult.

'Well, my dear,' answered her mother, 'if you don't take pains, everything is difficult.'

'Now, you know,' said Lil, 'that is the kind of answer that makes one hate people.'

that any very large number of people in this world should be positively wise, good, and well-to-do. If it had been, he would have taken measures to ensure that such should be the case.

is but a pair of pincers set over a bellows and a stewpan and the whole fixed upon stilts.

Obvious convenience often takes a long time before it is fully recognized and acted upon, but there will be a *nisus* towards it as long and as widely spread as the desire of men to be saved trouble. If truth is not trouble-saving in the long run it is not truth: truth is only that which is most largely and permanently trouble-saving. The ultimate triumph, therefore, of truth rests on a very tangible basis — much more so than when made to depend upon the will of an unseen and unknowable agency. If my views about the *Odyssey*, for example, will, in the long run, save students from perplexity, the students will be sure to adopt them, and I have no wish that they should adopt them otherwise.

## STYLE

In this day's silly *Sunday Times* (p. 2) there is an article on Mrs Browning's letters which begins with some remarks about style. 'It is recorded,' says the writer, 'of Plato, that in a rough draft of one of his Dialogues, found after his death, the first paragraph was written in seventy different forms. Wordsworth spared no pains to sharpen and polish to the utmost the gifts with which nature had endowed him; and Cardinal Newman, one of the greatest masters of English style, has related in an amusing essay the pains he took to acquire his style.'

I never knew a writer yet who took the smallest pains with his style and was at the same time readable. Plato's having had seventy shies at one sentence is quite enough to explain to me why I hate him. A man may, and ought to take a great deal of pains to write clearly, tersely and euphemistically: he will write many a sentence three or four times over — to do much more than this is worse than not re-writing at all: he will be at great pains to see that he does not repeat himself, to arrange his matter in the way that shall best enable the reader to master it, to cut out superfluous words and, even more, to eschew irrelevant matter: but in each case he will be thinking not of his own style but of his reader's convenience.

Men like Newman and R. L. Stevenson seem to have taken pains to acquire what they called a style as a preliminary measure — as something that they had to form before their writings could be of any value. I should like to put it on record that I never took the smallest pains with my style, have never thought about it, do not know nor want to know whether it is a style at all or whether it is not, as I believe and hope, just common, simple, straightforwardness. I cannot conceive how any man can take thought for his style without loss to himself and his readers.

I have, however, taken all the pains that I had patience to endure in the improvement of my handwriting (which, by the way, has a constant tendency to resume feral characteristics) and also with my MS. generally to keep it clean and legible. Alfred and I are having a great tidying just now, in the course of which the MS. of *Erewhon* turned up, and I was struck with the great difference between it and the MS. of *The Authoress of the Odyssey*. I have also taken much pains, with what success I know not, to correct impatience, irritability and other like faults in my own character — and this not because I care two straws about my own character, but because I find the correction of such faults as I have been able to correct makes life easier and saves me from getting into scrapes, and attaches nice people to me more readily. But I suppose this really is attending to style after all. (1897.)

### AUTHORESS OF THE ODYSSEY

The amount of pains which my reviewers have taken to understand my book is not so great as to encourage the belief that they would understand the *Odyssey*, however much they studied it. Again, the people who could read the *Odyssey* without coming to much the same conclusions that I have done are not likely to admit that they ought to have done so.

If a man tells me that a house in which I have long lived

is inconvenient, not to say unwholesome, and that I have been very stupid in not finding this out for myself, I should be apt in the first instance to tell him that he knew nothing about it, and that I was quite comfortable; by and by, I should begin to be aware that I was not so comfortable as I thought I was, and in the end I should probably make the suggested alterations in my house if, on reflection, I found them sensibly conceived. But I should kick hard at first.

This is what the reviewers are doing to me about the *Odyssey*. Thank heaven they can do no worse. Two small slips have been pointed out in the *Academy* which I will verify, but there has been nothing else. I believe, but have not sufficient evidence, that the articles in the *Times*, *Saturday Review*, *Academy* and *Morning Chronicle*, not to say perhaps others, are all by one man. What most surprises me is that no-one has fallen foul of me for having used the Latin names for Greek gods and heroes.

### ART AND USEFULNESS

Tedder, the Librarian of the Athenaeum, said to me when I told him (I have only seen him twice), what poor success my books had met with:

'Yes, but you have made the great mistake of being useful.'

This, for the moment, displeased me, for I know that I have always tried to make my work useful and should not care about doing it at all unless I believed it to subserve use more or less directly. Yet when I look at those works which we all hold to be the crowning glories of the world as, for example, the *Iliad*, the *Odyssey*, *Hamlet*, the *Messiah*, Rembrandt's portraits, or Holbein's, or Giovanni Bellini's, the connection between them and use is, to say the least of it, far from obvious. Music, indeed, can hardly be tortured into being useful at all, unless to drown the cries of the wounded in battle, or to enable people to talk more freely at evening parties. The uses, again, of painting in its highest forms are very doubtful — I mean in any material sense; in its lower forms, when it becomes more diagrammatic (if there is such a word), it is materially useful. Literature may be useful from its lowest forms to nearly its highest, but the highest cannot be put in harness to any but spiritual uses; and the fact remains that the 'Hallelujah Chorus', the speech of Hamlet to the players, Bellini's 'Doge' have their only uses in a spiritual world whereto the word 'uses' is as alien as bodily flesh is to a choir of angels. As it is fatal to the highest art that it should have been done for money, so it seems hardly less fatal that it should be done with a view to those uses that tend towards money.

And yet, was not the *Iliad* written mainly with a view to money? Did not Shakespeare make money by his plays, Handel by his music, and the noblest painters by their art? True; but in all these cases, I take it, love of fame and that most potent and, at the same time, unpractical form of it, the lust after fame beyond the grave, was the mainspring of the action, the money being but a concomitant accident. Money is like the wind that bloweth whithersoever it listeth, sometimes it chooses to attach itself to high feats of literature and art and music, but more commonly it prefers lower company. . . .

I can continue this note no further, for there is no end to it. Briefly, the world resolves itself into two great classes — those who hold that honour after death is better worth having than any honour a man can get and know anything about, and those who doubt this; to my mind, those who hold it, and hold it firmly, are the only people worth thinking about. They will also hold that, important as the physical world obviously is, the spiritual world, of which we know little beyond its bare existence, is more important still.

### THE LIFE AFTER DEATH

Why should we be so avid of honourable and affectionate remembrance after death? Why should we hold this the one thing worth living or dying for? Why should all that we can know or feel seem but a very little thing as compared with that which we never either feel or know? What a reversal of all the canons of action which commonly guide mankind is there not here. But however this may be, if we have faith in the life after death we can have little in that which is before it, and if we have faith in this life we can have small faith in any other.

Nevertheless there is a deeply rooted conviction, even in many of those in whom its existence is least apparent, that honourable and affectionate remembrance after death, and with a full and certain hope that it will be ours, is the highest prize which the highest calling can aspire to. Few pass through this world without feeling the vanity of all human ambitions; their faith may fail them here, but it will not fail them — not for a moment, never — if they possess it as regards posthumous respect and affection. The world may prove hollow but a well-earned good fame in death will never do so. And all men feel this whether they admit it to themselves or no.

Faith in this is easy enough. We are born with it. What is less easy is to possess one's soul in peace and not be shaken in faith and broken in spirit on seeing the way in which men crowd themselves, or are crowded, into honourable remembrance when, if the truth concerning them were known, no pit of oblivion should be deep enough for them. See, again, how many who have richly earned esteem never get it neither before death nor after it. It is here that faith comes in. To see that the infinite corruptions of this life penetrate into and infect that which is to come, and yet to hold that even infamy after death, with obscure and penurious life before it, is a prize which will bring a man more peace at the last than all the good things of this life put together and joined with an immortality as lasting as Virgil's, provided the infamy and failure of the one be unmerited, as also the success and immortality of the other. Here is the test of faith — will you do your duty with all your might at any cost of goods or reputation either in this world or beyond the grave? If you will — well, the chances are 100 to 1 that you will become a faddist, a vegetarian and a teetotaller.

And suppose you escape this pit-fall too. Why should you try to be so much better than your neighbours? Who are you that you think you may be worthy of so much good fortune? If you do, you may be sure that you do not deserve it. . . .

And so on *ad infinitum*. Let us eat and drink neither forgetting death unduly nor remembering it. The Lord hath mercy on whom he will have mercy, etc., and the less we think about it the better.

### PURGATORY
Time is the only true purgatory.

### GOD AND THE DEVIL
are an effort after specialization and division of labour.

### ALFRED AND THE CRUMB OF TOBACCO
The first time that Dr. Creighton asked me to come down to Peterborough before he became Bishop of London, I was a little doubtful whether or not to go. As usual, I consulted Alfred, who said:

'Let me have a look at his letter, sir.'

I gave him the letter, and he said:

'I see, sir, there is a crumb of tobacco in it; I think you may go.' I went and enjoyed myself very much.

### FORTUNE LIKE WISDOM
crieth in the streets, and no man regardeth. There is not an advertisement supplement to the *Times* — nay, hardly a half sheet of newspaper that comes into a house wrapping up this or that, but it gives information which would make a man's

fortune, if he could only spot it and detect the one paragraph that would do this among the 99 which would wreck him if he had anything to do with them.

### FASCINATING

Mrs. Skinner told Jones that Mrs. N. was a very fascinating woman, and that Mr. W. was very fond of fascinating with her.

### CHRIST AND THE L. AND N. W. RAILWAY

Admitting for the moment that Christ can be said to have died for me in any sense, it is only pretended that he did so in the same sort of way as the London and North Western Railway was made for me. Granted that I am very glad the railway was made and use it when I find it convenient, I do not suppose that those who projected and made the line allowed me to enter into their thoughts; the debt of my gratitude is divided among so many that the amount due from each one is practically nil.

### MYSELF, JONES AND THE BISHOP OF TRURO AT SIENA AND ST. GIMIGNANO

When we were prowling round the outside of the Cathedral of Siena in April (I think) last, we saw an English ecclesiastic with stringed sub-shovel hat whom from evidence collected at the Hotel Continental where we were staying we concluded to be the Bishop of Truro. He had a younger lady with him, presumably a daughter or niece; he eyed Jones and me much with the same incurious curiosity as that with which we had eyed him, and on having passed him we went inside the duomo. After a few minutes my Lord and the lady came in too. It was Sunday and mass was being celebrated. The pair passed us and, when they reached the fringe of the kneeling folk, the bishop knelt down too on the bare floor, kneeling bolt upright from the knees, a few feet in front of Jones and me. We saw him and

I am sure he knew we were looking at him. The lady seemed to hesitate but, after a minute or so, she knuckled down by his side and we left them kneeling bolt upright from the knees on the hard floor. We were sorry for them but it was their own doing.

We then went into the Biblioteca (I think it is called), to see the frescoes by Pinturicchio — which we did not like — and spent some little time in attending to them. On leaving we were told to sign our names in a book and did so. As we were going out we met the bishop and his lady coming in; whether they had been kneeling all the time, or whether they had got up as soon as we were gone and had spent the time in looking round I cannot say, but, when they had seen the frescoes, they would be told to sign their names and, when they signed, they would see ours and, I flatter myself, know who we were.

The next day or next but one, I forget which, Jones and I went to S. Gimignano and as we were coming down the main street, from the Piazza on which the Municipio stands to the hotel (the Leone Bianco) who should be mounting the incline but our bishop and his lady. The moment he saw us, he looked cross, stood still and began inspecting the tops of the houses on the other side of the street; so also did the lady. There was nothing of the smallest interest in these and neither Jones or I had the smallest doubt that he was embarrassed at meeting us and was pretending not to see us. I have seldom seen any like attempt more clumsily and fatuously done. Whether he was saying to himself, 'Oh my God! that wretch will be putting my kneeling down in another *Alps and Sanctuaries* or *Ex Voto*'; or whether it was only that I was a blackguard atheist who contaminated the air all round me, I cannot tell; but on venturing to look round a second or two after we had passed the pair, the bishop and the lady had got a good way onward.

At the Academy we found a portrait of the Bishop of

Truro — which though not good was quite good enough to assure us that it was the Bishop of Truro whom we had met.

### FUSELI AND 'LET ME GET OUT'

I have been told lately that Fuseli was travelling by coach and a gentleman opposite him said:

'I understand, Mr. Fuseli, that you are a painter; it may interest you to know that I have a daughter who paints on velvet.'

Fuseli rose instantly and said in a strong foreign accent, 'Let me get out.'

### THE ULTIMATE EFFECT OF MY BOOKS

Who can soberly foretell, what, if any, it will be? But setting sobriety on one side, I have sometimes thought that it may be more considerable than I suppose. Certainly nothing can be less considerable than the effect at present. (1899.)

### BALLARD'S STORY ABOUT MISSOLONGHI

An old governess, some twenty years since, was teaching some girls modern geography. One of them did not know the name of Missolonghi. The old lady wrung her hands:

'Why, my dear,' she exclaimed, 'when I was your age I could never hear the name mentioned without bursting into tears.'

I should perhaps explain that Byron died there.

### SCHOOLS AND COLLEGES

are not intended to foster genius and to bring it out. Genius is a nuisance, and it is the duty of schools and colleges to abate it by setting genius-traps in its way. They are as the hurdles and artificial obstructions in a hurdle race — tests of skill and endurance, but in themselves useless. Still, so necessary is it that genius and originality should be abated that, did not academies exist, we should have had to invent them.

A law student (in a *viva voce* examination) was asked what was necessary to render a marriage valid in Scotland. He replied: 'For a marriage to be valid in Scotland it is absolutely necessary that it should be consummated in the presence of two policemen.'

## ANSWERS TO CORRESPONDENTS

'W.C. No, you are mistaken. Leonardo da Vinci did not invent them.'

## FURNITURE AT FORDWICH

The meagrest I ever saw was at Fordwich, near Canterbury. The room in which the jury are locked up while finding their verdict is absolutely bare of all furniture whatever. It has neither table nor chair; not so much as a hook to hang a coat on; nothing in fact, but a round hole in the floor, some six inches in diameter, in case of some necessity on the part of a juror. Now this hole, which, in so far as it is subtracted from the floor is the very negation of furniture, is yet, I take it, in virtue of its design and purposiveness, actually furniture.

## PIORA, RAWLINSON FORD AND MYSELF AT

I am confident that I have written the following note in one or other of the earlier volumes of this series, but I have searched my precious indexes in vain to find it. No doubt as soon as I have retold the story I shall stumble upon it.

One day in the autumn of 1886 I walked up to Piora from Airolo, returning the same day. At Piora I met a very nice quiet man whose name I presently discovered to be Rawlinson Ford and who, I have since learned, is a well-known and most liberal employer of labour somewhere in the north of England. He told me that he had been induced to visit Piora by a book which had made a great impression upon him. He could not recollect its title, but it had made a great impression upon him; nor yet could he recollect the author's name, but the book had made a great impression upon him; he could not remember even what else there was in the book; the only thing he knew was that it had made a great impression upon him.

This is a good example of what is called a residuary impression. Whether I told him or no that the book which had so much impressed him was called *Alps and Sanctuaries*, and that it had been written by the person he was addressing, I cannot tell. It would be very like me to have blurted it all out and given him to understand how fortunate he had been in meeting me; this would be so fatally like me that the chances are ten to one that I did it; but I have, thank Heaven, no recollection of sin in this respect, and I am rather under the impression that, for once in my life, I smiled to myself and said nothing.

### PAST, PRESENT AND FUTURE

Perfect present has no existence in our consciousness. As I said years ago in *Erewhon*, it lives but upon the sufferance of past and future. We are like men standing on a narrow footbridge over a railway. We can watch the future hurrying like an express train towards us, and then hurrying into the past, but in the narrow strip of present we cannot see it. Strange that that which is the most essential to our consciousness should be exactly that of which we are least definitely conscious.

### LIES

I seem to see them crowding and crushing at a narrow gate and working their way in along with truths into the domain of history.

### THE HOLY GHOST

I begin to understand now what the man meant (whoever he may have been), who said that sin against the Holy Ghost was unforgiveable, while denial (verify) of the Father and the

Son might be forgiven.  I suppose he meant that a man might be pardoned for being unable to believe in the Christian mythology, but that if he made light of that spirit which the common conscience of all men, whatever their particular creed, recognizes as divine, there was no hope for him.  No more there is.

### MOUTHS

When I see a number of people at a dinner table, I see their mouths as the ends of the roots of a lot of plants sucking up their sustenance out of the earth.

### EMERY WALKER ON MYSELF

I met him in the court of Clifford's Inn and he asked how my *Sonnets* book had been received.  I said it had fallen just as flat as the others, and that he knew as well as I did that the reviewers would crab whatever I did.  He agreed, but we also agreed that it was probably much better for me that they should crab it, and that I might possess my soul in peace as regards the future.

### H. F. JONES AND MYSELF

We had been lunching at, I think, Chiusi, and had had some particularly good wine.  I said, 'I love my love with an A because she's alcoholic.'  Jones went on with some much better ones, and I said he was always doing that:

'I start some silly trifle and you immediately develop it; then I adopt your embellishments, developments and general improvements, and often even give you the credit of them.  Why don't you sometimes start the subject and leave me to develop it?'

Jones looked demure and said softly, 'Because you can't.'

I had said I hoped the weather would not be too fine inasmuch as if it was I should have no excuse for not doing better with my drawing.  He smiled and said, 'I dare say you may be trusted to discover one.'

His mother had put him to bed and, as he was supposed to have a cold, he was to say his prayers in bed. He said them, yawned and said, 'The real question is whether there is a God or no,' on which he instantly fell into a sweet and profound sleep which forbade all further discussion.

## ILLUMINATED MANUSCRIPTS

My neighbour, Cockerell, showed me a wonderful 13th or 14th century MS. very beautifully written and so profusely illustrated with such a monotonous variety or varied monotony of arabesques, let alone illustrated initial letters and full page illuminations, that it fatigued me to look at more than a few of its many hundred pages. It would take months to look at it, and one would forget the beginning long before one came to the end. Such books ought never to be made.

Cockerell said it would relieve the tedium of divine service. I said it might do so by accelerating slumber, but that if it failed to do this it would make matters worse, not better.

In any long work we want breaks, like chapters, so that we can at any rate flatter ourselves that we are making a fresh start and that all will go right in future.

That is why Jones and I stick to the old Handelian fashion of chopping our oratorio into set pieces, as against the Wagnerian continuity of music and action.

## AS FOR THE TEDIUM OF CHURCH

give me rather a robin, or a peripatetic cat, like the one whose loss the parishioners of St. Clement Danes are still deploring. When I was at school at Allesley the boy who knelt opposite me at morning prayers, with his face not more than a yard away from mine, used to blow pretty little bubbles with his saliva which he would send sailing off the tip of his tongue like miniature soap bubbles; they very soon broke, but they had a career of a foot or two,

I never saw anyone else able to get saliva bubbles right away from him, and though I have endeavoured for some five and fifty years to acquire the art, I never yet could start the bubble off my tongue without its bursting. Now things like this really do relieve the tedium of church, but no missal that I have ever seen will do anything but increase it.

### A DYING WISH

There was a man dying of a painless, gradual decay, whose friends asked him if there was anything he had a fancy for which they could get him. He said he had all his life thought he should like to have a cuckoo-clock, and the present would, he thought, be a proper occasion for acquiring one. A cuckoo-clock was bought and placed where he could see it as well as hear it. He said the last few days of his life were much cheered by it.

### A VERY SMALL FRAGMENT OF DISCOURSE
### FROM MY DEAR GOOD LAUNDRESS, MRS. CATHIE

It was the stairs done it, and yet them houses in York Street have got some good rooms in them — or else, he being a doctor you'ld have thought he'd have had the water laid on, but no, and he must have his shower bath, and all the time I kept dressing her finger, but that was before I come there. It was the very first money that ever I earned, and I had finished the dress, but while I was doing the trimmings I ran a needle into my thumb and then I got a bit of paint into the wound, and you can see, sir, I had three pieces of bone took out, and the doctor, he says, 'You must have that thumb cut off.' 'Oh dear me no, sir,' says I, 'no such thing.' 'But you must,' says he. 'The idea of the thing,' says I, 'and I with my living to get.' Anyway them stairs brought on the dyspepsia and the indigestion, and he says to me, 'Now who is it that has been dressing your thumb?' 'Why,' says I, 'I dressed it myself,' for I always washed it three or four times a day in loo warm water and he says, 'I will give it another week but if you don't get that thumb better by then, you will very likely lose your hand.' Well, her finger got worse and worse and worse from the moment I left off dressing it. 'Why don't you keep your finger cleaner?' says he, 'who is dressing it for you now?' 'Why, I dress it myself,' says she. I never see her for a good many years, but she went somewhere Norwich way and when I did see her I see she had lost her finger after all — and all because she did not keep it clean enough. So then he took to bringing up the water himself. 'It will do me good,' says he, and he used to bring canful after canful up them stairs for some days and then he had the water laid on. But no more nursing says I for me, 'I'd rather live by my needle.'

### TRUTH

does not consist in never lying but in knowing when to lie and when not to do so.

### HIGH ANGLICAN INTOLERANCE

When I had nearly finished *Erewhon Revisited* I took it to Charles Longman and asked him if he would publish it at my expense, as he had done all my recent books. He kept it three weeks, and then declined to publish it, on the ground that he had a large High Anglican connection, and that *Erewhon Revisited* would bring a hornet's nest about his ears. He used these words when he spoke to me about it.

This rather set my back up, and I wrote to him that I was very sorry, but as I had no High Anglican connection myself and had no present intention of trying to form one, I must write for the public whom I did wish to please rather than with a view to those whose power, as it seems to me, has increased, is increasing, and ought to be diminished.

### JESUS CHRIST

Whatever else he was, he was not a Jesuit.

## CONTRADICTION IN TERMS

EVERYTHING MATTERS MORE THAN WE THINK IT DOES and, at the same time, nothing matters so much as we think it does. The merest spark may set all Europe in a blaze, but though all Europe be set in a blaze twenty times over, the world will wag itself right again.

## A MENTAL WASTE-PAPER BASKET

Every one should keep one and the older he grows the more things will he the more promptly consign to it — torn up to irrecoverable tatters.

## MYSELF AT WILDERHOPE

When I was down there a fortnight ago, Harrie mumbled grace before meat as usual. I was a hundred miles away, and quite unconsciously, without the smallest guile or malice, instead of 'Amen' mumbled 'Thank you.' I hope she did not hear me but I am afraid she did.

## MYSELF AT WILDERHOPE

I am in disgrace at Wilderhope just now. I went there on the 8th of last month, and in the evening unfortunately took up the *Life of Archbishop Benson*, with which I was immediately fascinated, much as I had been with the present Lord Tennyson's *Life of Tennyson*, only more so; for bad as the *Life of Tennyson* was, the *Life of Archbishop Benson* is worse.

Still, both books are fascinating; they maintain such a high level of smug conceit; they give their subjects so delightfully and so unconsciously away — at least the *Life of Tennyson* does — for I think that Mr. A. C. Benson must have known that his father was a beast, and must have determined to give his readers a chance of seeing this also — but there is no knowing.

In both books the letters, whether sent or received, are so uniformly dull, and they are by people with such great reputations; even Edward FitzGerald's letters to Lord Tennyson have the Tennyson blight upon them. One is so comforted to find that there is no human touch of unaffected playfulness in either volume . . . However, let this be. I was devouring the *Life of Archbishop Benson*, and made no secret of the amusement it afforded me.

This gave great offence — 'But I assure you, Sam, the book has been *very* highly spoken of. Quite a number of people, really good judges, who know when a book is good as well as anybody, have enjoyed it extremely.'

'I assure you, my dear Harrie, they cannot have enjoyed it more heartily than I am doing.'

On this there was a severely abrupt change in the conversation.

Next morning at breakfast there was no tea. It was a year since I stayed with them before, and I concluded that they had forgotten that I always took tea, not coffee, when staying with them. But this was not so. May said, 'Oh, Sam, I think you like tea for breakfast, do you not? We can have some made in a moment.'

I assured her that I liked coffee very much, which I do; it is not coffee, but Wilderhope coffee that I do not like; I was not going, however, to explain this, and declared that when I was abroad, I always took coffee for breakfast — which is quite true. But I could see I was in disgrace.

In the course of the morning I went up into the town to look at the papers, and found, to my surprise, the excellent review of *Erewhon*, and *Erewhon Revisited*, in the *Times*, October 9th (on which day the books were published), and also the hardly less excellent review in the *Daily Chronicle*.

I knew that I ought not to say anything about these reviews to my sisters, but there are few so holy as to be able at all times to resist the temptation to rub a success in, although it be known that it will irritate, so I showed them to my sisters. Harrie made some short, slight remark indicating disapproval; May said not a word. They will probably have their revenge when the book is reviewed by the *Spectator* and *Guardian*.

In the evening I again took up the *Life of Archbishop Benson* and came upon the passage wherein he describes his meeting with Mr. Gladstone. It runs:

'14th July, 1871. Last Sunday I had a singular and interesting change. I went to Windsor to preach to the Queen, and saw something of, and *much admired*, Mr. Gladstone. His eyes alone afford sufficient reason for his being Prime Minister.'

At this I tittered, and read the passage aloud. 'It must have been his nose,' said I. 'The Bishop must have written "nose," and young Mr. Benson changed it into "eyes".'

Harrie fired up and desired me not to read anything more to her. On the following morning the *Life of Archbishop Benson* had disappeared.

Harrie was very cross at breakfast. 'You still continue to like coffee?' said she; 'we can have tea made for you if you like.' I still continued to like coffee, but when it proved that there was not enough to give me a second cup, I was firm, and she had to send for more. May was breakfasting in bed, so it rested with Harrie, who ate up all the four little pieces of toast without offering me a single one.

The next day I was leaving, and I think it was felt that I had been sufficiently punished, for she insisted on my having two of the usual four pieces of toast. What a beast I am for laughing at her, but I cannot help it, it was too comic! (November, 1901.)

# EXTRACTS FROM BUTLER'S PUBLISHED WORKS AND LETTERS

### MAETERLINCK

I believe, or strongly suspect that people will not think as highly of him in ten years as they do now. He has sat at the feet of Plato, Marcus Aurelius, Carlyle, and Emerson — I say nothing about Plotinus and Novalis for I do not know them. The others I have tried and at no such feet can I sit. They have no message for me. Plato is the best, his *Apology* is splendid; his descriptions of scenery and his episodial (if there is such a word) chats with friends on a fresh summer morning are delightful; but, take him all round, my feeling towards him is much what I gather Aristophanes to have entertained, and he is not for me.

Carlyle, again, is for me too much like Wagner, of whom Rossini said that he has 'des beaux moments mais des mauvais quarts d'heure' — my French is not to be trusted. I have never read a line of Marcus Aurelius that leaves me wiser than I was before. These men are not the teachers towards whose pupils I instinctively turn; on the contrary, I look on their devoted adherents with suspicion.

Again, Maeterlinck, it seems, is only 35 years old. Now, true genius cannot so soon be recognized. If a man of 35 can get such admiration he is probably a very good man, but he is not one of those who will redeem Israel; and at my age I turn to these alone or, at any rate, to such as I believe to be these alone. (1897.)

GRACE

And grace is best; for where grace is, love is not distant. Grace! the old Pagan ideal whose charm even unlovely Paul could not withstand; but, as the legend tells us, his soul fainted within him, his heart misgave him, and, standing alone on the seashore at dusk, he troubled deaf heaven with his bootless cries, his thin voice pleading for grace after the flesh. The waves came in one after another, the seagulls cried together after their kind, the wind rustled among the dried canes upon the sandbanks, and there came a voice from heaven saying, 'Let My grace be sufficient for thee.' Whereon, failing of the thing itself, he stole the word and strove to crush its meaning to the measure of his own limitations. But the true grace, with her groves and high places, and troops of young men and maidens crowned with flowers, and singing of love and youth and wine — the true grace he drove out into the wilderness — high up, it may be, into Piora, and into such-like places. Happy they who harboured her in her ill report.

### THE BEST SPENT LIFE

He has spent his life best who has enjoyed it most. God will take care that we do not enjoy it any more than is good for us.

### BELIEVING

Above all things, let no unwary reader do me the injustice of believing in *me*. In that I write at all I am among the damned. If he must believe in anything, let him believe in the music of Handel, the painting of Giovanni Bellini, and in the thirteenth chapter of St. Paul's *First Epistle to the Corinthians*.

### THE ESSENCE OF CHRISTIANITY

After all, what is the essence of Christianity? What is the kernel of the nut? Surely common sense and cheerfulness, with unflinching opposition to the charlatanisms and Pharisaisms of a man's own times. The essence of Christianity lies neither in dogma, nor yet in abnormally holy life, but in faith in an unseen world, in doing one's duty, in speaking the truth, in finding the true life rather in others than in oneself, and in the certain hope that he who loses his life on these behalfs finds more than he has lost.

### MONEY AND CULTURE

People oppose money to culture, and imply that if a man has spent his time in making money he will not be cultivated. Fallacy of fallacies! As though there could be a greater aid to culture than the having earned an honourable independence, and as though any amount of culture will do much for the man who is penniless, except make him feel his position more deeply. The young man who was told to sell all his goods and give to the poor, must have been an entirely exceptional person if the advice was given wisely, either for him or for the poor. How much more often does it happen that we perceive a man to have all sorts of good qualities except money, and feel that his real duty lies in getting every halfpenny that he can persuade others to pay him for his services, and becoming rich. It has been said that the love of money is the root of all evil. The want of money is so quite as truly.

### GOD

Resist God and he will fly from you.

### GOOD COMPANY

People are always good company when they are doing what they really enjoy.

### CHRISTIAN RELIGION

People in general are equally horrified at hearing the Christian religion doubted, and at seeing it practised.

### LIFE

Life is like playing a violin solo in public and learning the instrument as one goes on.

### BEING IN A PLACE, SEEING AND HEARING

What is being in a place? If I see the moon, so far I am in the moon. Which is most true — for a man who has spent hours and hours nightly looking into the moon through the most powerful known telescope, to say that he has been in the moon — or for one who passed through Rome at night fast asleep in a Pullman car to say that he has been in Rome? — or for an ascetic Catholic priest to say that he has ever been in this world at all?

Which again has heard the C Minor Symphony best? — Beethoven who was stone deaf when he wrote it, or some listener whose ears were perfect, but had no knowledge whatever of music?

Which sees a picture best? — An old painter gone blind to whom another painter explains it, or an unfortunate schoolboy who has been dragged to see it as a show, and whose heart is all the while in the cricket field?

### THE TRINITY

I think I am a Unitarian now, but don't know and won't say; as for the Trinity I cannot make head or tail of it, and feel inclined to agree with a negro who was heard in church here the other day repeating the Athanasian Creed: 'The Father impossible, the Son impossible, and the Holy Ghost impossible. And yet there are not three impossibles, but one impossible.'

Professor Sale, when I read him this in MS., told me it was not quite accurate; he was present in church and heard the nigger say 'uncomfortable,' not 'impossible.' He was reading from his prayer-book and 'uncomfortable' was as near as he could get to 'incomprehensible,' which was the word under his eyes.

### WHEN A THING

is old, broken, and useless, we throw it on the dust-heap, but when it is sufficiently old, sufficiently broken, and sufficiently useless, we give money for it, put it into a museum, and read papers over it which people come long distances to hear.

### 'THE WAY OF ALL FLESH'

Mr. Heatherley said I had taken all the tenderest feelings of our nature and, having spread them carefully over the floor, stamped upon them till I had reduced them to an indistinguishable mass of filth, and then handed them round for inspection. I do not take this view of the matter myself. (1883.)

He may be, and I dare say is, a very wonderful man, but what little I know of him repels me and, what is worse, bores me.

### AN HONEST GOD

An honest God's the noblest work of man.

### CATS

I must have a cat whom I find homeless, wandering about the court, and to whom, therefore, I am under no obligation. There is a Clifford's Inn euphemism about cats which the laundresses use quite gravely: they say people come to this place 'to lose their cats'. They mean that, when they have a cat they don't want to kill, and don't know how to get rid of, they bring it here, drop it inside the railings of our grass-plot, and go away under the impression that they have been 'losing' their cat. This happens very frequently and I have already selected a dirty little drunken wretch of a kitten to be successor to my poor old cat. I don't suppose it drinks anything stronger than milk and water but so much milk and water must be bad for a kitten that age — at any rate it looks as if it drank; but it gives me the impression of being affectionate, intelligent and fond of mice, and I believe, if it had a home, it would become more respectable; at any rate I will see how it works.

### THE ARTS

I find that those who are devoted to music and the arts of painting and sculpture are unwilling to turn to the art of literary poetry. On the other hand, those who are devoted to the art of literary poetry are less interested in music and in the fine arts.

I am firmly persuaded that our Shakespeare did not like music and knew nothing at all about the fine arts. Milton certainly loved music, and I admit that a man may successfully cultivate two of the three great provinces of poetry, namely (1) music; (2) the arts that are strictly imitative (even when they are also creative); and (3) literature; but to cultivate all three — this is too much.

Human sympathy is not capable of embracing simultaneously three wives so exacting and so jealous of one another. For me there exist two poets, Homer and Shakespeare; the others are doubtless very good sort of people but I have not, and never shall have, the honour of their acquaintance.

This is, I know, a brutal confession, but a man had better not pretend to have something which he has not. When I want poetry to set to music I write the words myself; but for the rest I prefer prose — prose as terse, as lucid, as sincere as I can make it. Those who go down into the Inferno for the purpose of seeing all their enemies in that place and then write their adventures in poetry — well, to speak the truth, I have no sympathy with this sort of thing. . . .

### HEAVEN AND HELL
The Heaven of men's loving thoughts; the Hell of men's hatred and contempt.

I FALL ASLEEP
IN THE FULL AND CERTAIN HOPE
THAT MY SLUMBER SHALL NOT BE BROKEN
AND THAT
THOUGH I BE ALL-FORGETTING
YET SHALL I NOT BE ALL-FORGOTTEN
BUT CONTINUE THAT LIFE
IN THE THOUGHTS AND DEEDS OF THOSE I LOVED
INTO WHICH
WHILE THE POWER TO STRIVE WAS YET VOUCHSAFED ME
I FONDLY STROVE TO ENTER

# UNTRACED NOTES

I do not mind lying, but I hate inaccuracy.

### THE CHANNEL PASSAGE

How holy people look when they are sea-sick! There was a patient Parsee near me who seemed purified once and for ever from all taint of the flesh. Buddha was a low, worldly minded, music-hall comic singer in comparison. He sat like this for a long time until . . . and he made a noise like cows coming home to be milked on an April evening.

### DOGS

The great pleasure of a dog is that you may make a fool of yourself with him and not only will he not scold you, but he will make a fool of himself too.

### SUPREME OCCASIONS

Men are seldom more commonplace than on supreme occasions. I knew of an old gentleman who insisted on having the original polka played to him as he lay upon his death-bed.

### SAINT COSIMO AND SAINT DAMIANO AT SIENA

Sano di Pietro shows us a heartless practical joke played by these two very naughty saints, both medical men, who should be uncanonized immediately. It seems they laid their heads together and for some reason, best known to themselves, resolved to cut a leg off a dead negro and put it on to a white man. In the one compartment they are seen in high glee cutting the negro's leg off. In the next they have gone to the white man who is in bed, obviously asleep, and are substituting the black leg for his own. Then, no doubt, they will stand behind the door and see what he does when he wakes. They must be saints because they have glories on, but it looks as though a glory is not much more to be relied on than a gig as a test of respectability. (1889.)

The entrance to this hotel at Chiavenna is through a covered courtyard; steps lead up to the roof of the court-yard, which is a terrace where one dines in fine weather. A great tree grows in the courtyard below, its trunk pierces the floor of the terrace, and its branches shade the open-air dining-room. The walls of the house are painted in fresco, with a check pattern like the late Lord Brougham's trousers, and there are also pictures. One represents Mendelssohn. He is not called Mendelssohn, but I knew him by his legs. He is in the costume of a dandy of some five-and-forty years ago, is smoking a cigar and appears to be making an offer of marriage to his cook. Down below is a fresco of a man sitting on a barrel with a glass in his hand. A more absolutely worldly minded, uncultured individual it would be impossible to conceive. When I saw these frescoes I knew I should get along all right and not be over-charged.

### NOT TO BE OMITTED

I must get in about the people one meets. The man who did not like parrots because they were too intelligent. And the man who told me that Handel's *Messiah* was 'très chic,' and the smell of the cyclamens 'stupendous.' And the man who said it was hard to think the world was not more than 6000 years old, and we encouraged him by telling him we thought it must be even more than 7000. And the English lady who said of some one that 'being an artist, you know, of course he had a great deal of poetical feeling.' And the man who was sketching and said he had a very good eye for colour in the light, but would I be good enough to tell him what colour was best for the shadows.

'An amateur,' he said, 'might do very decent things in water-colour, but oils require genius.'

So I said: 'What is genius?'

'Millet's picture of the *Angelus* sold for 700,000 francs. Now that,' he said, 'is genius.'

After which I was very civil to him.

At Bellinzona a man told me that one of the two towers was built by the Visconti and the other by Julius Caesar, a hundred years earlier. So, poor old Mrs Barratt at Langar could conceive no longer time than a hundred years. The Trojan war did not last ten years, but ten years was as big a lie as Homer knew.

We went over the Albula Pass to St. Moritz in two diligences and could not settle which was tonic and which was dominant; but the carriage behind us was the relative minor.

There was a picture in the dining-room but we could not get near enough to see it; we thought it must be either Christ disputing with the Doctors or Louis XVI saying farewell to his family — or something of that sort.

### 'THE LOST CHORD'

It should be 'The Lost Progression,' for the young lady was mistaken in supposing she had ever heard any single chord 'like the sound of a great Amen.' Unless we are to suppose that she had already found the chord of C Major for the final syllable of the word and was seeking the chord for the first syllable; and there she is on the walls of a Milanese restaurant arpeggioing experimental harmonies in a transport of delight to advertise Somebody and Someone's pianos and holding the loud pedal solidly down all the time. Her family had always been unsympathetic about her music. They said it was like a loose bundle of fire-wood which you never can get across the room without dropping sticks; they said she would have been so much better employed doing anything else.

### SUNDAY MORNING AT SOGLIO

The quarantine men sat on the wall, dangling their legs over the parapet and singing the same old tune over and over again and the same old words over and over again. 'Fu tradito, fu tradito da una donna.' To them it was a holiday.

Two gnomes came along and looked at me. I asked the first how old it was; it said fourteen. They both looked about eight. I said that the flies and the fowls ought to be put into quarantine, and the gnomes grinned and showed their teeth till the corners of their mouths met at the backs of their heads.

The skeleton of a bird was nailed up against a barn, and I said to a man: 'Aquila?'

He replied: 'Aquila,' and I passed on.

The village boys came round me and sighed while they watched me sketching. And the women came and exclaimed: 'Oh che testa, che testa!'

And the bells in the windows of the campanile began, and I turned and looked up at their beautiful lolling and watched their fitful tumble-aboutiness. They swung open-mouthed like elephants with uplifted trunks, and I wished I could have fed them with buns. They were not like English bells, and yet they rang more all' Inglese than bells mostly do in Italy — they had got it, but they had not got it right.

There used to be two crows, and when one disappeared the other came to the house where it had not been for a month. While I was sketching it played with a woman who was weeding; it got on her back and tried to bite her hat; then it got down and pecked at the nails in her boots and tried to steal them. It let her catch it, and then made a little fuss, but it did not fly away when she let it go, it continued playing with her. Then it came to exploit me but would not come close up. Signor Scartazzini says it will play with all the women of the place but not with men or boys, except with him.

Then there came a monk and passed by me, and I knew I had seen him before but could not think where till, of a sudden, it flashed across me that he was Valoroso XXIV, King of Paphlagonia, no doubt expiating his offences.

And I watched the ants that were busy near my feet, and

listened to them as they talked about me and discussed whether man has instinct.

'What is he doing here?' they said; 'he wasn't here yesterday. Certainly they have no instinct. They may have a low kind of reason, but nothing approaching to instinct. Some of the London houses show signs of instinct — Gower Street, for example, does really seem to suggest instinct; but it is all delusive. It is curious that these cities of theirs should always exist in places where there are no ants. They certainly anthropomorphise too freely. Or is it perhaps that we formicomorphise more than we should?'

And Silvio came by on his way to church. It was he who taught all the boys in Soglio to make a noise. Before he came up there was no sound to be heard in the streets, except the fountains and the bells. I asked him whether the curate was good to him.

'Si,' he replied, 'e àbbastanza buono.'

I should think Auld Robin Gray was 'abbastanza buono' to Mrs. Gray.

One of the little girls told me that Silvio had so many centesimi and she had none. I said at once:

'You don't want any centesimi.'

As soon as these words fell from my lips, I knew I must be getting old.

And presently the Devil came up to me. He was a nice, clean old man, but he dropped his h's, and that was where he spoiled himself — or perhaps it was just this that threw me off my guard, for I had always heard that the Prince of Darkness was a perfect gentleman. He whispered to me that in the winter the monks of St. Bernard sometimes say matins over-night.

The blue of the mountains looks bluer through the chestnuts than through the pines. The river is snowy against the 'Verdi prati e selve amene.' The great fat tobacco plant agrees with itself if not with us; I never saw any plant look in better health. The briar knows perfectly well what it wants to do and that it does not want to be disturbed; it knows, in fact, all that it cares to know. The question is how and why it got to care to know just these things and no others.

Two cheeky goats came tumbling down upon me and demanded salt, and the man came from the saw-mill and, with his great brown hands, scooped the mud from the dams of the rills that watered his meadow, for the hour had come when it was his turn to use the stream.

There were cow-bells, mountain elder-berries and lots of flowers in the grass. There was the glacier, the roar of the river and a plaintive little chapel on a green knoll under the great cliff of ice which cut the sky. There was a fat, crumby woman making hay. She said:

'Buon giorno.'

And the 'i o r' of the 'giorno' came out like oil and honey. I saw she wanted a gossip. She and her husband turned their scythes in two-part, note-against-note counterpoint; but I could hear that it was she who was the canto fermo and he who was the counterpoint. I peered down over the edge of the steep slippery slope which all had to be mown from top to bottom; if hay grew on the dome of St. Paul's these dreadful traders would gather it in, and presently the autumn crocuses would begin to push up their delicate, naked snouts through the closely shaven surface. I expressed my wonder.

'Siamo esatti,' said the fat, crumby woman.

For what little thing will not people risk their lives? So Smith and I crossed the Rangitata. So Esau sold his birthright.

It was noon, and I was so sheer above the floor of the valley and the sun was so sheer above me that the chestnuts in the meadow of Bondo squatted upon their own shadows and the gardens were as though the valley had been paved with bricks of various colours. The old grass-grown road ran below, nearer the river, where many a good man had gone up and down on his journey to that larger road where the reader and the writer shall alike join him.


### AMBER

In one piece of amber there was a whole willow-leaf, and in another a little snail-shell . . . The odds against the preservation of that willow-leaf were heaven knows how many million to one, still it was preserved. On the other hand, the odds against no willow-leaf having been preserved, if there was any amber exuding in the neighbourhood, were also heaven knows how many millions to one. So that squares it, and prevents our being compelled to accept the Christian miracles.


### THE THREE MOST IMPORTANT THINGS

a man has are briefly, his private parts, his money, and his religious opinions.


### PAULI

was having an argument with a man whom he could not shut up and who showed himself an ass generally. He says he said, 'I wish I knew you well enough to tell you you are a bloody fool.'


### LOVE

The pleasure of love is that it is the one place where you may let yourself go and feel as strongly as you like.


### SEA-SICKNESS

is the moral pain at seeing our converts escape us.

# INDEX

Butler, Samuel—*contd.*
  and his country, 150
  and his failure, 261-3
  and his humour, 200-1
  and his obscurity, 95, 141
  and his notes, 5-7, 222, 226, 238, 273,
    278-9
  and his thoughts, 52
  and the General Confession, 138
  and 'unconscious humour', 245
  attacks Mr. Darwin, 167
  disappointing people, 159
  *enfant terrible* of literature, the, 253
  his shortcomings, 282
  not to be believed in, 309
  squanders his life, 288
  steals his birthright, 266

CANARIES, water, 16
Cathie, Alfred Emery, 8, 34, 35, 36,
  39-44, 201, 295
Cathie, Mrs., 39-40, 180, 193, 303-4
Cat-ideas and mouse-ideas, 127
Cats, 124, 137, 140, 312
Cells, rows with one's, 117
Certainty, 195, 238
Change, 119, 127, 198
Chichester, the Bishop of, 177-8
Chickens, 118, 133-5
Children, 18, 125, 168, 170, 273, 302
Children, unborn, 19, 238
Chord, the Lost, 316
Christ, 58, 87, 88, 100, 296, 304
Christianity, 54, 56, 91, 120, 139, 186,
  199, 266, 288, 309, 310
Christmasses, Forgive us our, 274
Church, 58, 120, 139, 302
Circe, 26
Circle, squaring the, 260
Clergymen, 34, 133, 196, 264, 271
Clothes, 201
Clothes, on a clothes line, 109, 227, 228
Colonists, 135
Colour, 111, 194
Company, good, 310
Conceit, 60, 141
Conduct, moral and immoral, 82
Conscience, 63, 140, 250

Conscientiousness, 83, 140
Consciousness, 153, 193
Conservatories, 53
Contradiction in terms, 157, 202, 238,
  241, 249, 252, 305
Contralto voice, 13
Controversy, 112, 198
Cooking, 59, 275
Correspondents, answers to, 299
Covery, the art of, 252
Cow, eyes like a, 132
Creighton, Dr., 295
Critics, 111, 253
Croesus's kitchen-maid, 75-7
Crossing oneself, 192
Crystals, 176
Culture, 88, 309-10

DANTE, 77
Darwin, Charles, 84, 88, 90, 93, 167,
  233, 263
Dead, the, 120, 221, 223, 246-7
Death, 53, 54, 57, 72, 102, 111, 117,
  119, 127, 138, 139, 144, 145, 147-9,
  150, 168-9, 174, 190, 194, 241-4, 246,
  255, 258, 267, 268, 269, 278, 280
Dentists, 89
Destruction of works of art, 250
Detective with Prince of Wales, 86
Devil, the, 154, 191, 260, 276, 278, 295,
  318
Dickens, Charles, 73
*Dictionary of National Biography*, 273
'Die, I want to', 51
Digestion, 275, 280
Direction, a, 170
Divorce Novelette, The, 56-7
Dogs, 92, 314
Dons, 253
Dragons, 61, 114
Drunkard, a, 107
Dumb-bells, 113
Duty, 121
Dyer, Mrs. Thistleton, 120
Dying wish, a, 303

EAR, the public, 277
Eating, 53, 80, 96, 98, 99, 116, 198,
  258-60